W9-CLH-203

HIDING IN PLAIN SIGHT

Hiding in Plain Sight

THE SECRET LIFE OF

Raymond Burr

Michael Seth Starr

APPLAUSE
THEATRE & CINEMA BOOKS

An Imprint of Hal Leonard Corporation ▪ New York

Copyright © 2008 by Michael Seth Starr

All rights reserved. No part of this book may be reproduced in any form,
without written permission, except by a newspaper or magazine reviewer who
wishes to quote brief passages in connection with a review.

Published in 2008 by Applause Theatre & Cinema Books
An Imprint of Hal Leonard Corporation
19 West 21st Street, New York, NY 10010

Printed in the United States of America

Book design by Mark Lerner

Library of Congress Cataloging-in-Publication Data is available upon request.

ISBN 978-1-4234-7371-8

www.applausepub.com

To Gail and Rachel

Your love, encouragement, and support never cease to amaze me.

CONTENTS

ACKNOWLEDGMENTS

I would like to thank the following people for their help in research-ing this book: Cathy Cherbosque, curator, Historical Prints and Ephemera, the Huntington Library; Kelly Stewart, assistant archi-vist, New Westminster Museum and Archives; Laura Harris and the *New York Post* library staff; and Patricia Bergamaschi, transcription-ist. I also appreciate Angela Buckley's hard work in copyediting the manuscript.

And a special thank-you goes to Michael Messina at Applause Books for his enthusiasm and belief in this project.

HIDING IN PLAIN SIGHT

CHAPTER ONE

A Burr in the Saddle

On June 1, 1943, England awoke to the grim news that Leslie Howard was dead. The suave London-born actor, who delighted audiences on both sides of the Atlantic in screen classics including *Pygmalion* and *Gone with the Wind,* was just fifty years old. Only recently had Howard retreated from Hollywood to devote himself to the war effort. Now he'd paid for his commitment with his life.

The newspaper reports were short on detail, saying only that Howard was flying back to England from Lisbon when his KLM plane was shot down by Nazi fighters over the Bay of Biscay. There were no survivors.

Across the ocean the news reverberated in Hollywood, where the filmmaking industry mourned the death of a favorite son. Howard embodied everything the image makers sought to cultivate: heroism, good looks, idealism. There were even whispers he was on a secret mission for British intelligence when he died. He seemed straight out of central casting, a publicist's delight.

One young actor in particular took special notice of Howard's death. It would come in handy later on.

Raymond Burr had failed to make a dent in Hollywood. He had the good looks—dark wavy hair, moonish, piercing blue eyes, a baritone voice rich in dramatic import—but his weight was a problem. It had always been a struggle, ever since he was a kid in New Westminster, the city in British Columbia where several branches of the Irish Burr clan had settled decades before.

Photos of a young Raymond, posing in his Sunday-best sailor suit with his cousins Errol Wintemute and Mary Phelan, show a chubby, serious-looking child. His white sailor hat seems barely able to contain his thick mop of black hair, styled in a Prince Valiant cut and combed straight down over his forehead. His white knee-length socks cover chubby legs and peek through shiny black shoes.

Raymond's roundish physique wasn't unusual in the Burr family. The Burrs were a hardy lot, weathered by years of Irish winters and the country's tough climate. The family, divided into five clans, traced its ancestry all the way back to General Burr, one of King William's leading military men in the 1690 Battle of the Boyne. Family lore has it that, after that battle, King William deeded the Burr clan acres of land and the requisite castle in County Carlow, which is where the family settled.

Raymond's grandfather, Joseph Burr, was born in County Carlow to Benjamin Burr, a government official, and his wife, Eliza. In 1859, when he was in his late twenties, Joseph, along with his brothers Benjamin Jr. and Hugh, emigrated to Canada during the country's feverish gold-rush days. They were joined by other members of the Burr clan, who fanned out far and wide across Canada's expanse.

Joseph was the first Burr family member to settle in New Westminster. Just prior to his arrival there, the city had been named the first capital of British Columbia, the colony newly established by Queen Victoria, who named the city after her favorite part of London. That designation earned New Westminster its moniker "the Royal City."

Situated twelve miles southeast of Vancouver on the banks of the Fraser River, New Westminster quickly became the hub for the Cariboo gold rush, allowing prospectors and businessmen like Joseph Burr to travel by steamboat or by canoe to ports including Yale and Port Douglas.

By 1876, Joseph found himself in love with Mary Jane Johnston. Born in Maryborough, Ontario, in 1854, Mary Jane had moved with her parents in the late 1870s to nearby Surrey, where her father operated a well-known farm that supplied the surrounding area with milk, meat, and other necessities.

Joseph and Mary Jane married after a whirlwind courtship, and in the late 1870s Joseph became a guard at the newly opened British Columbia Penitentiary. The locals called the prison the "skookum house," borrowing a term from the English-Chinook dialect. Joseph's brother Ben took a similar job at the federal penitentiary about a mile away.

The many years Joseph Burr spent guarding prisoners at the skookum house were anything but dull. Some of the area's more colorful outlaws stood trial in New Westminster and were imprisoned in the skookum house.

According to local lore, it was Joseph who personally escorted the Indian outlaw Slumach to the scaffold to hang for killing a man near the Pitt River. Joseph also came into contact with nefarious types confined to the skookum like Stroebel, also known as "the Huntington Mouth-Organ Killer," and Hugh Lynn, "the Savary Island Murderer." They were the types of B-movie killers and hoodlums Joseph's grandson Raymond would later play in Hollywood.

Joseph and Mary Jane were eager to start a family of their own, and they bought a plot of land at 624 Royal Avenue in New Westminster, settling into a spacious three-story Victorian house. It was there, in 1889, that Mary Jane gave birth to William Johnston Burr, Raymond's father. The family eventually expanded to include four girls and William's brother, James.

The Burrs weren't yet local celebrities—that would come much later—but the family forever ingrained themselves into local lore during the Great New Westminster Fire of 1898. The blaze ravaged New Westminster for two days in September that year and was on a direct course for the Burr house. That was bad enough, but there was worse news: the dry weather had sapped most of the city's water supply.

Joseph and his family, along with a group of friends, put up a fierce fight as the blaze tore its way through the city and toward the Burr house. Using well water from their own supply, they formed what came to be known as "the Burr Bucket Brigade." They covered the house's walls and roof with blankets, mattresses, and whatever else they could find and climbed to the roof, which had a deck. From there, they poured their buckets of water onto the fire, refilling each bucket as soon as it was emptied with assembly-line precision. Their hard work saved the house from the roaring fire. Their next-door neighbor, St. Paul's Reformed Episcopal Church, wasn't so lucky. It was completely destroyed, as were buildings on over twenty square blocks of the city.

Joseph Burr provided well for his family, and his son William, whom everyone called Bill, had a relatively happy childhood. Joseph wanted Bill to go to college, but his son "was anxious to get out and work," and when he was twelve he got his first job, delivering parcels for a local dry goods company. At fourteen he began what would be a lifelong affiliation with the hardware business when he started work at Anderson-Lusby, a wholesale hardware store in New Westminster. "I was the youngest salesman, only three years later, when I was sent out on the roads of B.C. [British Columbia] to sell wholesale hardware," Bill would recall later in life to a local newspaper. "I continued with the company another five years until I started up with T. J. Trapp, who offered me a few more dollars a month."

In the meantime, Bill had met and fallen in love with an attractive young woman he encountered near Boundary Bay. Minerva Smith was four years younger than Bill, and she was from the "lower 48." She was born in Chicago in 1893, and shortly thereafter her parents, Anna and William Smith, moved the family. They relocated to Michigan for a few years and, when Minerva was five, moved to Canada.

It was after the move to Canada that Minerva, who had always been musically inclined, began to shine. She learned to play the piano and proved quite talented at tickling the ivories; she also excelled at the pipe organ. After her first encounter with Bill Burr near Boundary Bay, the couple began dating, and after a quick courtship they were married in 1914. World War I broke out that same year in Europe, and the rest of the Smith family moved back to the States, where William Smith enlisted in the navy. He was stationed at the Mare Island Naval Shipyard in Solano County, California, about twenty-five miles northeast of San Francisco.

Bill Burr, however, couldn't do much for the war effort. At twenty-five he was too old for active service duty. So, while the war raged in Europe, Bill continued with his everyday sales work at T. J. Trapp while he and Minerva moved into a house on Queens Avenue, one of New Westminster's main thorough-fares. Minerva Burr occupied herself with her homemaker duties and, every Sunday, played the organ at church. To earn some extra income, she would occasionally play the piano at the Edison Theater on Columbia Street, accompanying the silent-movie shows. In the late summer of 1916 she announced that she was pregnant, and on May 21, 1917, she gave birth to a boy. They named him Raymond William Stacy Burr.

Baby Raymond weighed in at a hefty twelve pounds, exhibiting from the very beginning of his life the girth that would both help and haunt him the rest of his days. He developed into a chubby baby and then into a fat child, and the odds of achieving a healthier weight were stacked against him. His diet was extremely starchy, thanks in part to a nationwide famine that made potatoes a highly valued commodity. And his weight gain was exacerbated by his frequent visits to Grandpa Joe and Grandma Mary Jane's house, which was just a few blocks away on Royal Avenue.

"My grandparents pulled out the rose garden in order to plant potatoes and all kinds of vegetables," he would tell a newspaper reporter years later by way of explaining his substantial girth. "Everyone grew their own food. This was one of the reasons I grew up as a chubby boy, overweight for my age. I was what they call a 'potato baby.' I was born during a famine in Canada right after World War I. And I weighed twelve-and-three-quarter pounds when I was born. And I didn't lose weight."

Raymond's lack of physical activity didn't help the situation. He wasn't particularly athletic, and because of his large size, he winded easily. "The weather used to be a lot colder [in New Westminster], and we had colder winters," Raymond's cousin Errol Wintemute, a year older, recalled. "So, when we were kids, we would go sleigh riding together. He was quite a bit heavier than me. I was the operator of the sleigh, with Raymond on top of me. He was twice the size of me. He was a big guy. He wasn't too mobile for sports or things like that."

The extended Burr family was very close-knit, and Raymond wasn't lacking for love or attention. The arrival of a sister, Geraldine, in 1920, and a brother, James Edmond (whom everyone called Edmond), a year later, gave him two more built-in playmates.

"In the summers we enjoyed going down to the beach at Boundary Bay, where the family used to camp," cousin Errol remembered. "In the early days, we'd go down in the horse-and-buggy. We'd have picnics and generally chase each other around on the sand barge. It was a good time."

Raymond's large size, however, took its toll on his emotional demeanor. He was warmly embraced by his family, but to outsiders he was a sensitive young boy who was extremely shy and had few friends. He was extremely attached to his mother, Minerva, and spent a lot of time alone in the garden, admiring the flowers and daydreaming. "He never smiled much," his mother recalled. "Everything was a serious matter to him. He was very well-mannered and obedient."

But even at that young age Raymond was conflicted. He was a quiet, retiring boy who, behind the thoughtful facade,

dreamed of a career in the spotlight. It was a strange dual-
ity. "When Raymond was a young boy he told his mother he
would choose one of three careers," his father recalled. "He
would be either a lawyer, a preacher or an actor. And he said
he wanted to be an actor."

He'd been exposed to the theater as a young boy in elemen-
tary school. "And I decided I wanted to be an actor," he said.
"I never wanted to be anything else. At that time our church,
where my mother played the organ, was doing a lot of theat-
ricals and I was in every single one of them."

But there was trouble on the horizon. With three children
and a wife to clothe and feed, Bill was finding it difficult to
support his family. They weren't going hungry, but the constant scrambling to make ends meet began to take its toll
on Bill and Minerva's relationship. "The family was poor," a
friend recalled. "They were never hungry, but there was the
possibility that they might not find the next meal. Raymond
knew how it felt to be poor."

It was a feeling Minerva didn't like, and in 1923 the issue
came to a head. She was intent on making a better life for
herself and the children, so she took six-year-old Raymond,
along with Geraldine and Edmond, south to her parents in
California. Bill stayed behind at the house on Queens Avenue, promising to join his family when the time was right.

Raymond's grandfather, William Smith, had bought a small
hotel after retiring from the navy. The Empress, as it was
called, was in Vallejo, about an hour outside of San Francisco. So it was there that Minerva and the children landed
after leaving New Westminster for the last time. "When I
got down there, I was sick for several weeks and, during that

time, I kept turning things over in my mind," Minerva said. "Mr. Burr was making such a small salary back in Canada that I felt sure he could do better in Vallejo. I wrote him my feelings and he came down."

True to his word, Bill joined his family a short time later, and they moved into a rented house. Bill Burr, though, never would have much use for California, even later in life, and now he longed to return to New Westminster. He got his wish eight months later, returning to Canada—alone. "He just wasn't happy away from familiar surroundings, so he returned to Canada . . . I kept hoping Mr. Burr would change his mind, but he didn't," Minerva recalled. She was simplifying the situation, but it was a life-altering decision with far-reaching ramifications for the Burr family, especially for Raymond.

After Bill returned to New Westminster, Minerva and the children remained in Vallejo, moving back into the Empress with her parents. Her marriage to Bill was over.

Life in Vallejo wasn't any easier for Raymond than it had been during his first few years in New Westminster. Not having his father there didn't help, and his weight continued to be an issue, perhaps even a symptom of his parents' breakup.

Raymond was taunted at school with chants of "fatso," and he made few friends. What little fun he did have was at the Empress, where he interacted with guests and explored the grounds with Edmond. According to Raymond's first biographer, Ona Hill, Grandpa Will schooled Raymond and Edmond in electronic wiring, the painting of rooms, mixing cement, glazing windows, and working with bricks and mortar.

"I'm grateful for all the training," Raymond said about his grandfather. "He trained me so well I have put the knowledge to work many times in my daily life. He was an excellent disciplinarian too, and I idolized him."

Raymond was having enough trouble in public school, but the situation grew worse when he turned eleven and Minerva packed him off to the San Rafael Military Academy, located in the San Francisco Bay area. She hoped that he "would learn the importance of following strict routines" at the academy, which was originally founded in 1890 as the Mount Tamalpais Academy, changing its name to San Rafael only three years before Raymond's arrival.

San Rafael required its students to wear uniforms and to adhere to a strict code of discipline. Minerva hoped Raymond would benefit from the academy's structured environment.

But it wasn't to be. Raymond spent only one year at San Rafael and was miserable the entire time. His weight became an issue again, and though he was growing taller, he had trouble keeping off the pounds and was teased mercilessly by his classmates. "When you're a little fat boy in a public school, or any kind of school, you're just persecuted something awful," he later said.

Though he had been riding horses for years, school officials now barred Raymond from riding in the school's cavalry parades because of his weight. He looked ridiculous in his too-snug uniform. His class photo shows an unsmiling, grim-faced young boy glaring at the camera during a time he would later refer to as "purgatory."

Ostracized by his classmates—a schoolmate killed Raymond's goldfish—and unable to strike up a meaningful friendship, he turned inward. He spent long hours walking alone and brooding in a garden he had discovered on the edge of the San Rafael campus. "I would sneak very quietly into that garden and just look at the flowers," he recalled. "One day, this woman came out of the house, spotted me, and said, 'You don't have to be afraid. I left the gate open for you. You can come down.'" The boy who dreamed of performing in front of an audience had only himself to entertain.

Raymond also began taking cello lessons that year, riding the ferry over to Berkeley once a week, which put him within spitting distance of his mother. The temptation was too much, and one week he used his cello lesson as an excuse to rush home to Minerva in Vallejo, vowing never to return to San Rafael. The ruse didn't work, and upon his return to school, Raymond was punished by having his military stripes stripped off. It was yet another humiliation. "It was so hard [for him] to put that uniform on every day and see a bare spot where the ribbons had been," Minerva said. Raymond finished out the school year and Minerva finally relented, taking him out of the academy. The San Rafael experiment was over, much to his relief.

In the meantime, there were other changes in the Burr family. Minerva, who had been playing the piano and pipe organ for years, now decided she wanted to go back to school to earn a master's degree. She wanted to teach music professionally, and she signed up for night classes at the University of California, Berkeley. The family moved out of the Empress and into rented rooms near the Berkeley campus. This way, Minerva could shuttle the three kids to school before beginning her own studies. She used a four-carat diamond ring as the collateral for her tuition.

Raymond attended Willard Junior High School for a while and even snared a singing part in a production of *Naughty Marietta*. But the role's demands on his time were too great to balance with a regular school schedule. And without a dominant male figure around the house, he became a surrogate parent to Geraldine and Edmond. It didn't take him long to grow into his role as a de facto househusband, cooking and cleaning and watching over his brother and sister. He was only twelve. But he never complained.

In later years, when he was asked about this period in his life, Raymond always spoke in glowing terms about Minerva's decision to go back to school and was careful never to criticize his father for not being around. "While we were growing up without a father in the house, we never actually felt any insecurity because of it," he said. "At least I didn't."

"He knew how to handle us better than a father, I think," Geraldine said of her big brother. "All the love in the world was with him, taking care of us, doing things for us, always doing something for me. But he never complained one bit. There was always food on the table, always a little money he had made and shared with mother."

That October brought the collapse of the stock market in what became known as "Black Friday." The country was plunged into the Great Depression, and the Burrs, like everyone else, scraped to make ends meet. Raymond took odd jobs where he could find them while Minerva worked during the day and attended her classes at night. The tough times brought mother and son even closer than before. It was almost as if Raymond was a stand-in for Bill; he was someone Minerva could talk to and confide in. "They were very, very close," Geraldine recalled. "He once said to me, 'You know, sister, I'd rather take my mother out to lunch than anyone else I know because she's such a lady.' My eyes filled up with tears because he meant every bit of it."

Minerva and Raymond had another personality trait in common—their shared disgust for regimentation. It had driven Raymond away from San Rafael and now drove Minerva away from teaching. After finally earning her teaching degree, Minerva now discovered that she didn't want to be tied down to a regular teaching job. She solved the problem by becoming a traveling music teacher, leaving home several times a week to give piano lessons in Oakland and neighboring San Francisco.

Raymond, who was now back in school, finally graduated from Berkeley High, Minerva's alma mater, and got a job at the local JCPenney store. It was menial work, but when his manager was transferred to a branch store in San Jose, he offered Raymond the chance to join him there. Raymond accepted the offer and left home, enrolling in San Jose State while continuing to work at Penney's. He moved into a room at the local YMCA and also took his first serious stab at becoming an actor by forming a theatrical group at the Y. "Raymond suddenly became enamored of acting," Minerva recalled.

But a theatrical group at the Y, meeting informally several times a week, wasn't enough for Raymond. Whenever he had the chance, he would make the long drive down to the Pasadena Playhouse, where he took acting lessons from Gilmor Brown, who'd founded the playhouse nearly twenty years earlier. The playhouse was considered one of the finest acting schools in the country, and it was a known quantity in Hollywood. Showbiz insiders called it the "Star Factory" because of its famous alumni, who included Randolph Scott, Robert Young, and William Holden.

Raymond's dream of becoming a full-time actor just wasn't feasible. He couldn't afford Brown's lessons on anything more than a sporadic basis, and Berkeley didn't offer much for an aspiring actor—especially one as well-fed as Raymond. His weight tended to fluctuate, but he was never thin. By the time he was seventeen, Raymond was tipping the scales at well over two hundred pounds.

He had developed a strong bond with nature from his earliest days and was fascinated with flowers, especially orchids. He loved to garden, inheriting his green thumb from his absent father. So, at Minerva's urging, Raymond decided to join the Civilian Conservation Corps. The CCC, as it was called, had been put in place the previous year as part of newly elected president Franklin D. Roosevelt's New Deal. Like other New Deal agencies, it was designed to help stimulate the moribund economy by providing much-needed jobs to Americans still reeling from the Depression.

Raymond's CCC unit was stationed in Seiad Valley, California, near the Klamath River and the Oregon border. The work was outdoors—it was tough, but it was *work*. And that's all that counted.

"All of us learned the meaning of hard work, the joy of a job well done, while being paid for it," Raymond recalled in a quote sounding suspiciously like it was written by a press agent. "I was paid 30 dollars per month and 20 dollars went to my family." (Raymond was no hero—CCC regulations required *every* employee to send $25 to their families.) Raymond's work in the

CCC ran the gamut from digging trenches to building fences and pouring concrete. The physical exertion helped the chubby seventeen-year-old shed some weight from his massive frame. That could only be good news for his acting aspirations.

Raymond knew that character actors, even those weighing over two hundred pounds, weren't in especially big demand. Leading men of that heft were even rarer. One exception was movie actor Laird Cregar, whom Raymond admired from afar. Cregar had a successful Hollywood career despite weighing over three hundred pounds. He died in 1944, at the age of thirty-one, after shedding more than one hundred pounds on a crash diet and suffering a heart attack.

Unlike the other far-fetched tales about his life that would be would be spun through the years, including half-truths and outright lies perpetuated by Raymond himself, he really *did* spend about a year in the CCC. There's even visual proof, a black-and-white photograph showing Raymond in his CCC uniform, towering over his cohorts.

CHAPTER TWO

California Dreamin'

Over the next several years, Raymond chased his dream of becoming a full-time actor. He worked odd jobs to sustain himself and to pay the bills while he went on auditions and continued his acting lessons with Gilmor Brown at the Pasadena Playhouse. It's nearly impossible to pinpoint exactly what jobs Raymond held during this time, or for how long he held them, since too much of his early biography was fabricated by Raymond himself or by eager Hollywood press agents.

One account has him selling tinted photographs door-to-door; in another apocryphal version of his fabricated "Raymond Burr Story," he traveled to China (!) to manage some land owned by his grandfather and learned to speak one of the many Chinese dialects (falsely) attributed to his linguistic repertoire.

It is true, however, that Raymond was in and around Hollywood at this time auditioning for movie roles. The legwork finally paid off in June 1940, shortly after his twenty-third birthday, when he snared his first movie job in *Earl of Puddlestone* (1940). The movie was a forgettable entry in Republic Pictures' popular *Higgins Family* series starring James, Lucile, and Russell Gleason as Joe, Lil, and Sidney Higgins. If *Earl of Puddlestone* is remembered at all, it's for director Gus Meins, who killed himself shortly after filming wrapped (could it have been that bad?). Raymond's part in the movie was tiny and unbilled: he played the chauffeur of Mrs. Millicent Potter (Betty Blythe) and uttered the immortal line "Mrs. Potter's car for the Honorable Elizabeth Higgins." According to Raymond's first biographer, Ona Hill, he was paid the princely sum of $66 for his week of work. The movie opened that August and quickly disappeared.

Raymond was unable to parlay his *Earl of Puddlestone* appearance into other movie work, and his frustration mounted. His weight again was becoming a problem, and there just wasn't much call for someone of his size, despite his obvious good looks. His six-foot-two build was crowned by a head of wavy black hair that framed a ruggedly handsome face. His large, piercing blue eyes gave him a perpetual look of wounded sadness.

Raymond's first big break, it turned out, would come not on the sound stages of Hollywood but on the boards in New York, where he headed in late 1940. He rented a small apartment in Greenwich Village and began the audition process, winning a small part, in January 1941, in a troubled Broadway musical revue called *Crazy with the Heat*, which had encountered problems in its out-of-town tryouts in Boston.

The two-act revue opened at the 44th Street Theater in mid-January, on one of the coldest nights of the year, and was shuttered four days later—generating no interest except for a critical thrashing from *New York Times* critic Bosley Crowther. It was rescued, for a brief time, by *New York Daily News* columnist Ed Sullivan, who took over as producer and raised $20,000 to keep the production afloat. Sullivan reopened *Crazy with the Heat* on January 30, but despite a cast featuring comedian Willie Howard and tap dancer Betty Kean, the show closed after ninety-two performances.

("Good bits: the veteran Willie Howard, whose Jewish accent cannot be cut with a knife, as a ballet dancer; hot little Diosa Costello shaking everything shakeable in a scorching conga," *Time* magazine noted in its brief review.)

Raymond, who appeared in four sketches, blamed the show's failure on the fact that it opened the same week as *Lady in the Dark*, which featured the talents of Ira Gershwin, Kurt Weill, and Moss Hart and ran for nearly five hundred performances. In addition, "some of the material in the sketches in our show, banned in Boston, never was put back in the New York version," he said.

Raymond bounced around New York for a little while, but with no prospects and even less money, he headed back to California and to the Pasadena Playhouse. This time, he enrolled at the Playhouse on a full-time basis and paid for his tuition by working various odd jobs. He resumed his acting classes with Gilmor Brown, who also served as supervising producer for all student productions, and struck up what would become a lasting friendship with Playhouse director Lenore Shanewise. She directed Raymond in his first Playhouse production, *Quiet Wedding*, and years later Raymond returned the favor by casting her in several episodes of *Perry Mason*. With a Broadway credit under his belt, Raymond now had some cachet, and he began teaching his own acting classes at the Playhouse. With his dark good looks, formidable size, and booming baritone voice, he soon became one of the more recognizable figures around the Pasadena Playhouse campus.

The Playhouse staged about one play each month, with a rotating ensemble of actors. Throughout 1942 and 1943, Raymond's appearances in *Charley's Aunt, Arsenic and Old Lace, The Intimate Stranger,* and Booth Tarkington's *Colonel Satan* (featuring John Carradine) ran the gamut from star to supporting player. *Los Angeles Times* critic Katherine Von Blon, reviewing *Quiet Wedding,* described Raymond as "engaging as the young lover."

In reality, he was the exact opposite. Women didn't seem to hold much interest for the young actor, and besides his extremely close relationship with his mother, and now Lenore Shanewise, there were no girlfriends to write home about, no romance to speak of. Ona Hill repeated an apocryphal story about Raymond becoming "smitten with a young ballerina from the Ballet de Monte Carlo" whom he supposedly chased throughout Europe, while learning to speak several foreign languages, of course. It was all hogwash.

The constant theatrical work was a tonic for the melancholy actor. For all his time spent in and around the Playhouse, Raymond's circle of friends was extremely small, if it even existed at all. His relationships with Gilmor Brown and Lenore Shanewise were more of the student-mentor variety. Raymond could be convivial enough, often treating his fellow troupers to dinners he could barely afford, but lasting friendships weren't in the cards. He was still the fat boy who had grown up with few friends, forced to be a father figure at a young age while finding refuge in flowers and gardening.

"Although Ray is a very genial person, he is also quite private and disinclined to speak readily about his personal life and relationships," said Bobker Ben Ali, who directed Raymond in several Playhouse productions. "He is quite correctly described as a 'workaholic,' but one who leaves no room for personal chit-chat or trivia."

The pattern would continue, at least as it pertained to his Playhouse colleagues. After he became famous, Raymond shied away from attending Playhouse reunions. "His devotion to the Playhouse," said Ben Ali, "really was his devotion to Gilmor Brown and Lenore Shanewise, two people who he dearly loved."

Burr did forge one important alliance in Pasadena. With money scarce, he earned some extra dough working side jobs, including laying bricks at the Ivar House, a popular restaurant in Hollywood. He was working on the patio there one extremely hot day when he got into a testy exchange with a customer who wouldn't move her feet. The woman wearing the floppy hat was none other than powerhouse Hollywood gossip columnist Hedda Hopper. When tempers subsided, she asked Burr what he did for a living. He told her he was an actor. Her advice to him? "Stick to your profession and starve for it." They struck up a friendship that would pay handsome dividends in the years to come.

The onstage exposure at the Playhouse boosted Raymond's confidence, and he decided to give Broadway another shot. He left the Playhouse in late 1943 and headed for wintry New York City and another round of auditions. It didn't take him long to land a leading role as Voulain in novelist/playwright Patrick Hamilton's *The Duke in Darkness*, a historical allegory of Germany's occupation of France.

(One of Hamilton's plays, *Rope*, would become an Alfred Hitchcock classic. His 1941 novel *Hangover Square*, was later adapted into a movie starring Raymond's hero, burly Laird Cregar—whose death came after slimming down for this role.)

The Duke in Darkness opened at the Playhouse Theater on January 21, 1944, with Raymond, Edgar Stehli, Louis Hector, and Philip Merivale as the leads—and it closed twenty-four performances later, a victim of chilly reviews and frostier ticket sales.

"As melodrama of either character or action it is dull, and as literature it is quite often like a parody nationally circulated magazines pay real money to acquire," sniffed *New York Times* critic Lewis Nichols. "As serious theatre put away the thought . . . They [the characters] are all very pat." Raymond, who was billed third behind Stehli and Merivale, didn't merit a mention in Nichols's review.

It wasn't all doom and gloom, though. Those critics that did mention Raymond generally had good things to say about his performance. "Raymond Burr, a newcomer to the New York stage, is extremely effective as the patriot Voulain," John Chapman noted in the *New York Daily News.* "His performance is uneven and frequently rough but he has fire and intensity."

E. C. Sherburne, writing in the *Christian Science Monitor*, thought Raymond was "stirring as the soldierly leader of the rescuers."

If Raymond's brief Broadway run didn't pay off in instant acclaim, at least it opened up some other doors for him. His turn as Voulain caught the eye of Hollywood agent Edith Van Cleve, who had connections to RKO and promised to find Raymond movie work when he went back to Los Angeles.

Raymond returned to the Pasadena Playhouse in the spring, and that summer he landed at the Elitch Gardens Theater in Denver, Colorado. He costarred with Martha Sleeper in *Another Love Story* and spent the rest of that summer acting in several other Elitch Gardens plays. He closed the season with *Let Us Be Gay*.

Raymond's write-up in the Elitch Gardens playbill, which described him as "suggesting Victor Mature in profile and with the physique of an All-American fullback," is an early indication of the biographical fabrications he repeated until they snowballed into a Greek tragedy—starring Raymond Burr as its main character.

"In London, he was featured in 'Tonight [sic] Must Fall' and later toured Australia in an extended run of this successful hit," his bio breathlessly reported. "Burr had his own Shakespearean troupe in England, appearing at Stratford and he was the youngest actor cast in the role of Macbeth. His other London plays were a revival of 'Tonight at Eight-Thirty' and he was playing in 'Mandarin' when war was declared."

None of it was true.

Certainly with World War II still raging overseas, wouldn't there be some mention here of the military service to which Raymond would later lay claim—or of the Purple Heart, the very symbol of selfless bravery, that he was supposed to have earned from the navy after being shot in the stomach at Okinawa? Or was it the Purple Heart he won for being on a ship attacked by Japanese kamikaze pilots? The story was changed often, without any rhyme or reason.

It would be easy to blame an overeager press agent for these tall tales, but at this early stage of the game, Raymond had no press agent. Outside of the Pasadena Playhouse community, and maybe some hardcore Broadway fanatics, he had no name recognition. He'd obviously been repeating these stories for some time now, sometimes altering the "facts" just a bit to keep things interesting.

"He was in the London production of 'Night Must Fall' and also had his own Shakespearean Repertory Company in Toronto," *Los Angeles Times* critic Katherine Van Blon wrote a year-and-a-half earlier, shortly after Raymond joined the Pasadena Playhouse. England. Toronto. It didn't seem to make any difference.

Edith Van Cleve, meanwhile, had kept her promise of finding Raymond some movie work, landing him a $150-a-week contract at RKO, one of the "Big Five" studios in Hollywood. RKO's greatest days were long gone, and the studio's biggest star was Robert Mitchum. It was now churning out low-budget B movies, sprinkling in the occasional gritty noir.

The studio contract system, or "paid slavery" as most actors called it, was in its waning days when Raymond came upon the scene, but it would stagger on for another few years. Raymond also had the bad luck to join RKO just as flighty billionaire Howard Hughes was buying the studio from investor Floyd Odlum. Hughes eventually ran the studio into the ground through mismanagement (or, more accurately, *no* management).

In any event, Raymond at least had the promise of steady work, and he made his (uncredited) RKO debut in *Without Reservations* (1946) as Claudette Colbert's silent dance partner. He would later have another uncredited blink-and-you'll-miss-it role, in *Fighting Father Dunne* (1948), in which he was seen in a montage as the prosecutor who sends Dwayne Hickman's character to the electric chair.

Raymond finally earned his first credited part, and a bit of screen time, in *San Quentin* (1946), a cheesy, platitudinous prison yarn extolling the benefits of prison reform.

In *San Quentin*, Lawrence Tierney plays Jim Rowland, an ex-con turned war hero who founded the Inmates' Welfare League while in the slammer to help cons and ex-cons keep on the straight and narrow. Now he finds himself hunting down notorious bank robber Nick Taylor (Barton MacLane), who escapes from San Quentin while en route to help publicize the Welfare League—shooting and injuring the warden with a bullet meant for Rowland and embarking on a killing spree.

Raymond's role as Taylor's henchman, Jeff Torrance, is lateral (he received tenth billing) but is a key one: Rowland pays a surprise visit to Torrance's hideout and beats the living daylights out of him, forcing Torrance to give up Taylor's whereabouts (he's in Fresno). Torrance is seen a little later clandestinely delivering a bagful of groceries to Taylor, for which he demands $200, getting only $100 for his efforts and narrowly avoiding being gunned down. In his last scene, Torrance is led wordlessly to a waiting police car outside his hideout.

San Quentin opened to mediocre reviews. "There is nothing very startling in the film and a lot of it seems pretty far-fetched," wrote *Chicago Tribune* film critic Mae Tinee. "Mr. Tierney does all right in his role and others in the cast are as capable as need be."

But Raymond's part, however small, was a turning point in his career. With RKO steadily cranking out turgid thrillers, he had all the ingredients for the perfect supporting B-movie heavy: he was a brooding, hulking presence who could scowl with the best of them and project menace with his deep voice, which he would sometimes reduce to a rasp to heighten the suspense. Raymond was well aware of his leading-man limitations, at least on the big screen. But that didn't matter. Before long, he was on the short list of reliable heavies. He was a casting agent's dream and had found his niche.

If Raymond needed a jolt of leading-man adrenaline, there was always the adoring crowd at the Pasadena Playhouse. He hadn't abandoned them while trying to build his movie career, and he returned to the Playhouse to star in several productions that he sandwiched in between his movie work. But Hollywood, not Pasadena, now occupied more and more of his time.

In December 1946, a month before the premiere of *San Quentin,* he directed and costarred in a Playhouse production of *Murder Without Crime* under the watchful eye of Gilmor Brown. The following June found him playing Lieutenant Mulvaney in *While the Sun Shines.* ("Raymond Burr courtesy of RKO-Radio Pictures," the playbill proudly noted.) In May 1948, he starred as French artist Paul Gauguin in *Gauguin,* opposite Madge Blake, who would later find fame on television as Aunt Harriet on *Batman.*

Also in the *Gauguin* cast was a young actress named Isabella Ward. She was known to friends and intimates as Mrs. Raymond Burr.

CHAPTER THREE

An Old Wives' Tale

They first met in 1943, during Raymond's first season at the Playhouse. Isabella, or "Bella" as she preferred to be called, had traveled to Pasadena in 1940 from Delaware. Born in Elizabeth, New Jersey, the daughter of an oil refinery trouble-shooter, she was one of four very active sisters in a family that moved around often, eventually settling in Dover, Delaware, during the Depression.

Bella was a talented dancer and member of the girls' choir and always had the acting bug. She played the lead in all the school plays, including *Pride and Prejudice*. "She was an excellent student, very interested in sports, all sorts of extra-curricular activities," recalled her friend Minnie Short. "Bella was always very sure of herself. Her one and only dream was to become an actress."

After graduating from high school in 1937, Bella attended business school for two years at the insistence of her father, "in case we ever had to support ourselves." But acting was her real passion, and as soon as she earned her degree, Bella's parents bankrolled her trip to Pasadena. She landed at the Playhouse in 1940 with a fresh crop of recruits. Among her classmates was Eleanor Parker, who would later be featured on the big screen in *The Sound of Music*.

Raymond's arrival at the Playhouse coincided with Bella's swan song in Pasadena, but she immediately took notice of the strapping actor with the deep blue eyes and commanding voice. "I met him at the Pasadena Playhouse sometime during my third and last year at the school," she said. "He became a teacher there in 1942."

The two actors costarred in Raymond's first Playhouse production, *Quiet Wedding* (Isabella played a character named, like herself, Bella), but Bella left town shortly thereafter "because the war had started" and returned to Delaware, where she remained for the duration of the war.

She eventually dipped her toe back into the acting pool in New York and joined the National Repertory Theater, which had been founded by a couple of Playhouse colleagues. "They asked if I would like to join, I did, and since California was their headquarters we went back to the Coast in the summer of 1947," she said. The company put on several shows, including *The Duchess of Malfi* and *Tartuffe,* and Bella made her one and only (brief) movie appearance in *Reign of Terror* (1949), starring Richard Basehart, Arlene Dahl, and Bob Cummings.

She also reconnected with Raymond. They met accidentally one day while walking down the street and began dating shortly thereafter. This in itself was big news, since Raymond, as far as anyone could tell, had never seriously dated *anyone.* If he *had* dated anyone, he certainly never discussed it.

"Ona Munson, the Belle Watling of G.W.T.W., is flirting with San Franciscan Raymond Burr," gossip columnist Ed Sullivan noted in March 1940, around the time Raymond was trying to jump-start his acting career. It was a nice try, on Sullivan's part, to link the up-and-coming actor with an actress from *Gone with the Wind*. But there was one small problem: Ona Munson, a Burr family friend, was also a lesbian. She was thrice married and was later linked to Marlene Dietrich and Greta Garbo.

But Raymond and Bella seemed to hit it off, and after a whirlwind courtship, they were married on January 10, 1948. Raymond's sister Geraldine provided her house in Bakersfield for the occasion. The wedding was a small affair. In addition to Geraldine and her husband Jack, only Jack's boss and his wife, Raymond's friend Norman, and the minister and his wife were there to witness the marriage. "I had planned to wear a simple suit because it was such a small wedding," Bella said, "but the secretary of Ray's business manager insisted that I wear her daughter's long white satin wedding dress."

The couple didn't go on a honeymoon, and they moved into Raymond's bachelor pad near Hollywood and Vine—which in reality wasn't much of a bachelor pad. Raymond's friend Norman, who'd been at the wedding, also lived there, as did Raymond's mother Minerva and her parents, the Smiths. "There was a small apartment on the basement floor which opened out on a patio, which Ray and I used," Bella recalled. That was about as much description of the marriage as she would ever offer.

The marriage didn't last. Trouble seems to have set in from the get-go, although just what that trouble was, or how it manifested itself, neither Raymond nor Bella would ever say. Perhaps the presence of Norman, or of Raymond's mother and grandparents, struck a note of discord in the couple's married bliss. Raymond, for his part, never talked about the marriage, under the guise of fiercely protecting his private life. "She had deep-set personal problems and so did I," was all he ever said on the record. "The combination of the two made our life impossible."

The couple did manage to work together for one Playhouse production, costarring in *Gauguin*, but by the fall of 1948 the marriage was over.

"Our relationship was not a favorable one," Bella said years later. "If it had been [favorable], we never would have gotten divorced. Some people are just not marrying people and I think I'm one of them. I'm not a natural cook or housekeeper."

"She wasn't happy, I'm sure of that," said Bella's friend Minnie Short. "I don't know what happened and I've never asked. Perhaps the life she found out there just wasn't for her. She has never talked about Burr."

Bella moved back to Delaware, and then on to Baltimore to live with her sister. She and Raymond would stay married, on paper, for another four years, but they never saw each other again. Neither one would ever remarry.

———

If marriage wasn't in the cards, Raymond was being dealt a winning hand in Hollywood. Along with his ever-expanding waistline, his movie career was beginning to take off. Although his role in *San Quentin* was a minor one, his appearance in the movie jolted his career into overdrive. "As the heavy, literally and figuratively, a newcomer named Raymond Burr does a sinister and fascinating job," the *New York Times* wrote in 1948 about his role in *Pitfall*, in which he menaced Dick Powell and stalked Lizabeth Scott.

Directors of the moody, atmospheric "noir" dramas prevalent in Hollywood lumped Raymond in with actors like Mike Mazurki, Lawrence Tierney, Barton MacLane, and Laird Cregar, reliable supporting players who had the "look" of gangsters and underworld types yet could easily transfer that countenance to a western or even a comedy if needed (still playing the bad guy, of course). If Robert Mitchum, Dick Powell, and Humphrey Bogart were the undisputed kings of noir, then Raymond, Mazurki, et al. were their dark princes.

Raymond, in fact, was often confused with Cregar. Their physical resemblance was striking, not only in their burly bulks but also in their facial similarities. For years afterward, Raymond was often misidentified as Cregar's brother. It probably didn't displease him too much. Like Raymond, Cregar was a Pasadena Playhouse alumnus and hung around the playhouse between movie jobs. His charisma apparently rubbed off on Raymond.

Bobker Ben Ali, a Pasadena Playhouse compadre who later directed Raymond in several stage productions, was convinced the young actor assumed his hero's mantle after Cregar's untimely death. "When I saw Raymond Burr next, he had the size and shape of Laird Cregar. He could have passed for a handsome, slightly younger brother of Cregar's," Ben Ali told Ona Hill. "Indeed, I hardly recognized Burr for himself. It was apparent, moreover, that the new RB could easily have taken any of the film roles that Cregar might have played: *The Lodger*, *Hangover Square* . . . And, indeed, RB did play a number of such roles thereafter—whether by design or by happenstance."

Burr made nine movies in 1948 alone, including *Raw Deal*, which is generally considered the best of his early noir performances. *Raw Deal* was directed by Anthony Mann, who had already established himself with gritty noirs including *He Walked by Night, Railroaded!, T-Men,* and, the previous year, *Desperate*—in which Raymond played menacing mobster Walter Radak, who sets up innocent deliveryman Steve Randall (Steve Brodie) to take the fall for a deadly truck hijacking.

Raw Deal tells the tale of small-time hood Joe Sullivan (Dennis O'Keefe), who's serving time in the state pen after taking a bum rap to protect his boss, the dapper mobster Rick Coyle (Burr). Rick, who speaks in a sinister whisper, is a dandy of sorts, lolling around in a bathrobe and cravat while barking orders to his lackeys Fantail (John Ireland) and Spider (Curt Conway). Rick also has a strange fascination with fire that's coupled with a streak of sadism in a lethal combination (he thinks nothing of nonchalantly burning Spider's ear with his cigarette lighter).

Rick still owes Joe $50,000 from their previous heist, but he has no intention of parting with the dough. He arranges for Joe's dame, Pat Regan (Claire Trevor, who provides the cheesy voice-over narration), to help Joe escape from prison. Rick knows the odds are in his favor; Joe will be killed or be caught, either way ensuring his silence so that Rick can keep his loot.

Rick sums up his feelings about Joe rather succinctly: "He was screaming he wanted out. When a man screams, I don't like it. He might scream loud enough for the DA to hear. I don't wanna hurt the DA's ears. He's *sensitive.*"

Joe completely messes up Rick's plan by bucking the odds and escaping from the big house, with Pat driving the getaway car as they speed toward their new future in Panama. But when those plans go awry, Joe and Pat kidnap Joe's comely lawyer, Ann Martin (Marsha Hunt), who's in love with Joe but doesn't know it yet. Ann, too, was visiting Joe while he was behind bars. She visited frequently, she said, to discuss his case with him (but we know better).

With the cops in hot pursuit, Joe, Pat, and Ann hightail it to a mountain retreat. Joe and Ann wrestle with their growing feelings for each other while Pat builds up an unhealthy resentment of her new rival (which is relayed to us through her intrusive voice-overs). The trio is still one step ahead of the cops when they drive to Crescent City, where Joe expects to meet Rick and get his $50,000 payoff.

Rick, meanwhile, is stunned to learn that Joe has successfully escaped from the hoosegow, and he doesn't take kindly to Fantail's chiding. ("Someday I'm gonna figure out something for you. Something very special, something very funny," Rick sneers to his lackey.) Rick, of course has no intention of meeting Joe, but we know what's going to happen next. The entire movie has been setting us up for the inevitable showdown.

It finally arrives in the last seven minutes of *Raw Deal* when Rick kidnaps Ann in order to lure Joe to his hideout on "Corkscrew Alley" for their face-off. "Joe, you know I never carry a gun," says Rick—who promptly shoots Joe in the chest. Our hero, however, doesn't die just yet. He wrestles with Rick, and in their ensuing melee, a lit candelabra (there's that fire motif again) is knocked to the floor, igniting the drapes and setting the place ablaze. It's the perfect symbolic send-off for pyromaniac Rick as Joe pushes him through the fire-ringed window and he plunges (screaming) to his death.

Joe stumbles outside and dies in Ann's arms. Pat arrives at the scene with a cop and nods approvingly at the touching scene. She knows, deep in her heart, that Joe died in the arms of the woman he truly loved. We weep.

His portrayal of Rick earned Burr a slew of critical kudos. While *Raw Deal* itself generated only lukewarm praise, most of the criticism leveled at Raymond and/or director Anthony Mann was focused on Rick's level of brutality—particularly in the movie's most memorable scene, when Rick is told about Joe's successful prison escape.

Standing up to absorb the news, Rick is accidentally jostled by one of his flunkies, who's dancing with Rick's moll (on the boss's orders). As they bump into Rick, a drink is spilled on Rick's shoulder, soaking his expensive suit. Infuriated, Rick takes his birthday flambé, which was lit a minute earlier, and throws it at the moll, scalding her face (we only hear her painful shriek). "Take her away," Rick sneers. "She shoulda been more careful."

"Raymond Burr, as Rick, the heavy, is photographed as more menacing than he actually seems, if you know what I mean," Philip K. Scheuer wrote in the *Los Angeles Times*. "Anthony Mann deserves special praise for the tight-knit, no-nonsense economy of his direction . . . I did think he went overboard occasionally for the sake of sensationalism—as in the sadistic scalding by Rick of one of his dames."

Edward Barry, reviewing *Raw Deal* in the *Chicago Tribune*, also praised Raymond's performance. "Raymond Burr and John Ireland contribute two remarkable impersonations of criminals—one the sleek and polished type who dislikes to bloody his own hands, the other the sneering, trigger-happy variety."

Raymond continued to work at a breakneck speed, and his movie roles following *Raw Deal* were, more often than not, some sort of variation on Rick Coyle. It was artistically monotonous, and only the genres differed.

"How can one avoid calling him the archetypal heavy?" wrote film critic David Thomson of Burr. "His bulk was invested with every degree of villainy, from the robust to the perverted. To add to his size, his sad features were always ready to sink into grave jowls and puffy malice."

If Raymond's characters weren't being punched, stabbed, or shot in turgid movie dramas like *Sleep, My Love*, or *Walk a Crooked Mile*, they were the evil landowners or scheming, skulking pikers in westerns (*Stations West, Code of the West, New Mexico, A Man Alone*) or the back-stabbing, jealous second fiddles in costume dramas (*The Magic Carpet, Fort Algiers, Bandits of Corsica*).

He cheated Errol Flynn in *Mara Maru* (1952), and menaced Fred MacMurray and Claire Trevor (again!) in 1950's *Borderline* ("Raymond Burr, as a dope-smuggling chieftain . . . turns in a first-rate bit of acting," *Variety* noted). In *Pitfall* (1948), he played a jealous private eye stalking a model (Lizabeth Scott) whose one-night fling with a married insurance adjuster (Dick Powell) throws them both into a murderous plot. "Mr. Burr is appropriately cold and brutal," noted the *Christian Science Monitor*.

Noted film noir expert James Ursini, who's published several books on the subject with writing partner Alain Silver (*The Noir Style, Film Noir Reader*), considers Burr a major contributor to the genre—and points to movies like *Pitfall* as prime examples of Burr's ability to dig beneath the rough surface of his heavies. "He tried to make you see the psychosis below the surface, even when the parts weren't huge," Ursini says.

"If Burr was just a villain, we would never have had much interest in him and he wouldn't have become an icon of film noir. He was able to bring such complexity and different levels to those characters, and create sympathy for his characters even though they were doing reprehensible things. He was very much in the tradition of Laird Cregar, who was physically very similar to Burr and played villainous parts. Even their eyes were very similar.

"Burr always gave a performance as powerful as he could deliver considering the material," Ursini continues. "I think his sensitivity comes through in most of his performances. That's what makes him interesting, as opposed to Laird Cregar, whose performances are a little more effeminate than Burr's. If you see close-ups of Burr, there's something in those eyes beyond the hulking guy.

"He was able to convey all his characters' emotional baggage to the audience."

He was Lucille Ball's jealous suitor in *The Magic Carpet,* and in one of his few big-screen comedies, he still played a hood—only this time a heavy chasing Harpo Marx in *Love Happy* (which included a brief cameo from Marilyn Monroe).

"It was written for Harpo, no other Marx Brother was going to be in it, but the picture was so bad and it was so mixed-up that pretty soon Harpo begged Groucho to be in it and then they both begged Chico to be in it," Raymond said. "So what was going to be a picture with Harpo Marx turned out to be the last Marx Brothers picture." Harpo never bothered to mention the movie in his autobiography.

Frank Sinatra's singing career was in tatters, and he suffered a further (on-screen) indignity when Raymond beat him to a pulp in *Meet Danny Wilson* (1952). But Sinatra's Danny Wilson got his revenge, killing Raymond's controlling mobster, Nick Driscoll, in a nicely staged shootout in Chicago's Wrigley Field. All in a day's work.

"Raymond Burr is a standard, menacing villain," the *New York Times* noted in its review of *Meet Danny Wilson*, and Raymond missed out on another chance to torture Sinatra, and this time to kill him, in Sinatra's comeback movie, *From Here to Eternity* (1953). Raymond claimed he lost the role of Fatso Judson to Ernest Borgnine because he was traveling abroad and was unavailable when the studio called.

If Raymond did play a "good" character, which was a rarity in his oeuvre, there always seemed to be a caveat. His role in Joseph Losey's 1951 remake of Fritz Lang's *M*, for example, was a minor one. What *was* noteworthy was that Pottsy, the fedora-wearing mobster Raymond played in a croaking, hoarse whisper, helps nab a psychotic child molester.

———

Burr was now earning a healthy living as "one of Hollywood's most prominent bad men," as the *Christian Science Monitor* branded him. Radio also became a source of easy income between movie shoots. And Raymond, with his booming baritone voice, was a natural for the medium.

The steady radio work coincided with the successful arc of Raymond's movie career, peaking in the late 1940s. He acted in literally hundreds of radio dramas playing a variety of roles. Often, he went unbilled. His credits included parts in many

Armed Forces Radio productions, as well as roles in some of the better-known serials, including *Pat Novak for Hire, Dr. Kildare,* and *Mike Shayne.* He costarred opposite Jack Webb in several episodes of *Dragnet* in 1949, and when the show moved to television in 1951, he appeared in its inaugural broadcast on NBC.

The aural world of radio offered another bonus for Raymond: he couldn't be seen. With his gargantuan appetite for food, that was often a good thing. Raymond's lifelong battle with the bulge was a constant source of embarrassment, even if it did mean steady work and a steady stream of income. At his heaviest he was topping the scales at 340 pounds. And even when he made an effort to shed the weight—by chain-smoking and sticking to a spartan cottage-cheese-and-fruit diet (but doing no exercise)—he inevitably gained it right back. It was an ugly cycle.

By putting his face onto a movie screen or his voice onto the airwaves, Raymond was making himself available to millions of viewers and listeners. It was an exciting prospect for an actor seeking the spotlight, but it was a dangerous game for someone so private. The little boy who spent hours alone in the garden, but longed for the acclaim of an audience, was a grown man now—but he still wrestled with the contradiction.

Raymond's star was rising quickly in Hollywood, and if he wasn't ever going to be a leading man, he was at least becoming a recognizable supporting player often acting alongside the screen's biggest stars. Fans were beginning to ask questions about the dark-haired, handsome man who costarred opposite Clark Gable in *Key to the City* or opposite Robert Mitchum in *His Kind of Woman* (Raymond was reportedly cast

in that movie on orders from studio chief Howard Hughes).
The public was curious about the hood who threatened Fred
MacMurray in *Borderline* or the corrupt town official out to
get Ray Milland in *A Man Alone*.

But there was one problem: Raymond didn't want to tell
them about himself.

To sidestep the intricacies of his private life, fabrications
like those that appeared in his bios for the Pasadena Playhouse
became necessary. It wasn't an especially difficult accom-
plishment in the studio days of Hollywood, when overeager
publicists were charged with transforming low-level contract
players into ever-so-fascinating—sometimes even mythical—
figures. It was a tradition as old as the movies themselves in
an industry trafficking in illusion. Everyone loves a hero, or
at least is willing to play along. And what actor didn't shave
a few years off his age, or gild the lily a bit in relating his
up-by-the-bootstraps rise to the top? It wasn't uncommon to
read about so-and-so's distinguished war record or about his
fiancée—even if so-and-so never served a day in the military.
And was gay.

And now that Raymond was at RKO, he, too, was expected
to provide details about a colorful past (hopefully) awash in
lost loves, romantic conquests, and remarkable accomplish-
ments—with a dash of war heroics thrown in for good measure. And if none of that existed, well, not a problem. It could
easily be cobbled together out of thin air, and Raymond was
ready, willing, and able to supply the fiction.

The color Raymond chose for his story was a mournful
blue, a world barely afloat in a sea of heartbreak and un-
speakable tragedy, of hardship and harrowing self-sacrifice. It

would have made a lesser man crumble. It would have made *Raymond* crumble, if only it was true.

The lies and half-truths regarding Burr's past and present were there from the very beginning of his movie career, starting with his first studio biography, released in conjunction with *San Quentin*.

The biography is peppered with fabrications. Not only did it have Raymond living with his parents in China for five years "in Cheefee, Shanghai, Peiping and Hong Kong," but he'd also "traveled around the world five times" and was forced to leave San Rafael Military Academy when he was thirteen because "his parents lost their fortune." This must have been big news to Bill Burr, the small-town hardware salesman who wasn't even living with his family when Minerva enrolled Raymond in military school. And the closest the Burr family ever came to China was a whiff of fine porcelain.

It notes that Raymond "worked as a traveling salesman, taught school and was an explorer" and "managed to amass six years of college education at Stanford, the University of California and Columbia University." It's possible that Raymond could have been likening his "explorer" days to his time in the Civilian Conservation Corps (CCC), but that's a stretch. He did teach at the Pasadena Playhouse—"taught school" is just vague enough—and although he did take classes at San Jose State Junior College, there's no documentation of any of his other supposed educational pursuits.

In a later interview with *TV Radio Mirror*, Raymond attempted to lend some credence to these claims while inventing more typically fantastic tales. "I went to Yucatan with some archaeologically minded friends of mine. One day, I fell in a hole and accidentally discovered some ancient Mayan ruins," he said of his "explorer" days.

In that same interview, he talked about his "teaching" and rattled off a rather extensive list of credits. "I have a degree in psychology from the University of California and a degree in English Literature from McGill," he said, adding for good measure that he taught "at Amherst, Columbia, the Pasadena Playhouse." When another publication, *Inside TV*, checked with Amherst on the veracity of Raymond's claims, they received this response: "No record of Raymond Burr on Amherst College faculty."

The *San Quentin* biography also contained this whopper: "He is a widower, his wife, a non-professional, having died in a plane crash in England four years ago." The "wife" here isn't identified, but Raymond, and/or his subsequent studio biographers, would take care of that. Her name, they said, was Annette Sutherland, a Scottish actress Raymond ostensibly met while touring England in the early 1940s. Perhaps in Raymond's mind it was while he was touring with "his own Shakespearean troupe," that very same troupe so proudly trumpeted in his Elitch Gardens biography.

But it wasn't just any old plane crash that had claimed Annette's life. That would have been too pedestrian for the wife of Raymond Burr. And it lacked dramatic import. Annette did not die in vain, but selflessly sacrificed herself for the good of her country. According to Raymond's subsequent versions—and repeated in print as fact until the day he died—Annette had perished with Leslie Howard in that June 1943 plane crash, shot down by the Nazis over the Bay of Biscay. Raymond himself repeated the tale. "My first wife went down in the same plane as Leslie Howard," he told an interviewer before cutting him short and refusing to discuss it further.

It didn't seem to matter, of course, that there was no record of an Annette Sutherland on Leslie Howard's flight, which listed thirteen passengers and four crew members on its manifest. Newspaper reports at the time named three women as being on the flight, none of them named Annette Sutherland. All of this was easily verifiable, but who was going to bother checking the sob story of an unknown actor making his big-screen debut?

It's anyone's guess as to why Raymond and his handlers, or some wild-eyed studio publicist, chose this elaborate scenario to perpetuate a lie that would snowball out of control. It was probably a combination of reasons. One, to forge a sympathetic image for a big-screen heavy trying to soften his tough-guy facade. Two, to cover up and muddle the issue of his sexuality. And three, because it was Raymond himself who needed people to pity him.

"Ray had a pathetic nature about him. He wanted people to feel a certain way about him, like feeling sorry for him," said close friend and *Perry Mason* producer/director Art Marks. "When he told the story of a wife dying in an airplane crash, that a son died . . . he would almost get teary-eyed, and I would say, 'Ray, you're acting now.' He tried very hard to have a secret life . . . a lot of it was imaginative and made up, like 'I have suffered and I've done this and the whole world has put a big stamp on me like a thumbprint.'"

If Raymond *had* really been married to Annette Sutherland, who died such a tragic death, wouldn't he have told the harrowing tale to the woman he subsequently *did* marry? But this was all news to Isabella Ward. "I was Ray's first wife," she said. "If there had been a wife before me he would have told me."

He also would have shared the news of his marriage to Annette with members of the close-knit Burr family. None of them ever met Annette Sutherland or heard her name mentioned. "We didn't know it, let's put it that way," said Raymond's cousin Errol Wintemute. "We didn't know if it was true or not." Minerva, who was extremely close to Raymond, never spoke publicly on the subject of Annette.

Raymond was twenty-nine and unmarried at the time his *San Quentin* biography appeared. He had never been romantically linked to any woman, save for Ed Sullivan's gossipy two-line mention of his "flirting" with Ona Munson back in 1940. But that was six years earlier. And she was a lesbian.

Raymond needed a woman, *any* woman, even a dead one, to offset the whiff of homosexuality. If word got out about his sexuality it would sink his promising career, which at this point was built on playing hulking, macho thugs. Forgiving moviegoers could snicker knowingly at the fey mincing of a Franklin Pangborn and wink along with the joke. But a virile bruiser type like Raymond Burr? He wouldn't be so lucky if his secret was discovered.

Raymond's dead-wife story waffled a bit from time to time. Two years later, in his studio biography for *Bride of Vengeance*, there's no mention of a dead wife, only the very much alive Isabella Ward. The *Bride of Vengeance* bio also adds a few new wrinkles to the Burr mythology. We learn that Raymond read movie scripts "for a motion picture company in New York" and "has had a number of articles and fiction stories published by national magazines and is now engaged in writing a novel and screenplay." In a nod to his surly, hulking *Bride of Vengeance* character, Michelotto, Raymond, in this version of his life, was a "football and swimming star" in his school days.

A dead wife who never existed could be forgiven as the fantastic creation of a young actor looking to make his mark. The Annette Sutherland story would be repeated, time and again, in article after article written about Raymond once he became famous. He never corrected the error, choosing instead to brush aside the doubts and whispers by simply refusing to ever discuss his personal life. It was too painful, after all, to rehash the old history.

But that wouldn't stop him from embellishing his already heartbreaking mythology. He later upped the ante, adding a dead son and yet another dead wife to the tragic mix.

No one ever met Michael Evan Burr, the supposed product of Raymond's supposed union with the supposed Annette Sutherland. According to Raymond Burr mythology, the phantom child was born in 1943, conveniently just before Annette's fatal plane flight.

Michael Evan would have been around five years old when Raymond married Isabella Ward in 1948. He never materialized during their short marriage, nor was he ever seen by any member of the Burr family. Raymond never mentioned a son to Isabella. Perhaps Michael was living with his phantom grandparents back in Scotland. And if Raymond's parents were proud grandparents, they had a strange way of showing it. In their many interviews after Raymond became famous, they never spoke publicly about a grandchild.

Raymond himself never uttered a word about Michael Evan until the late 1950s; by that time, the imaginary boy had been dead and buried for several years.

Little Michael Evan, according to Raymond, died in 1953 after battling leukemia. He was ten years old. Raymond, of course, was too heartbroken to go into detail, and no one was going to press the anguished father any further. He would embellish the tale in later accounts. In one version, he took a year off to travel the country with Michael, a father and his dying son seeing the sights together for one last time. But that would have been a good trick, since Raymond appeared in eight movies from 1952 to 1953, leaving little time to cruise around the United States.

And Raymond's horrific dead-son nightmare had a suspiciously familiar ring to it. In 1958, comedian Red Skelton took his terminally ill nine-year-old son, Richard, on a trip to Europe so he could see the sights before he died—from leukemia. Richard Skelton's death was noted in *Time* magazine. Michael Evan Burr, the son of well-known actor Raymond Burr, had no obituary.

Isabella Ward was asked years later if she ever met Michael in her brief marriage to Raymond. "No, I never met him. Because there was no son," she said. "But I don't want to talk about that—it isn't my place to say anything about that."

CHAPTER FOUR

(Un)true Romance

In the meantime, there were more movies to make. Raymond appeared on the big screen a total of eight times in 1951 alone, capping the year with one of his best roles yet as the determined district attorney Frank Marlowe in *A Place in the Sun*.

The movie had all the earmarks of a winner. Directed by Hollywood veteran George Stevens, its cast boasted up-and-comers Elizabeth Taylor, Montgomery Clift, and Shelley Winters ("Three Flaming Young Stars!" trumpeted the movie's trailer). It was the second big-screen treatment of Theodore Dreiser's novel *An American Tragedy*, following Josef von Sternberg's 1931 interpretation (starring Sylvia Sidney, Phillips Holmes, and Frances Dee), which Dreiser detested.

Stevens, who also produced the movie, shifted its focus a bit. Dreiser had based his novel on the real-life murder trial of Chester Gillette, who was convicted in 1906 of killing his ex-girlfriend at a lake in the Adirondack Mountains in upstate New York. Michael Wilson and Harry Brown's screenplay for *A Place in the Sun* shifted the narrative to the present day, while retaining some similarities to Dreiser's novel.

Montgomery Clift played George Eastman, an itinerant drifter who takes a menial factory job with his wealthy uncle Charles and begins a secret love affair with coworker Alice

Tripp (Winters), whose low social standing would never be acceptable to the upper-crust Eastmans.

George's love for Alice is fleeting, because he soon sets eyes on Angela Vickers (Taylor), a stunning, sophisticated society gal he flirts with at one of his uncle's soirees. There's an instant attraction between the rough-hewn George and the delicate Angela. George, a social climber, falls for Angela's beauty and the breeding seemingly out of his reach; she, in turn, is taken with his rugged good looks and soulful vulnerability.

But there's trouble in paradise. George gets a big promotion and breaks it off with Alice, who wants only to marry, settle down, and start a family, even if she suspects George's love lies elsewhere. She announces that she's pregnant— ostensibly quashing George's dreams of a better life with Angela.

A panicky George concocts a scheme: He'll take the unwitting Alice out on a rowboat on a remote lake, wait until dark, then kill her and dump her body overboard. He'll never be suspected, since no one knows they were romantically involved. But once they're out on the water, a sweaty, distracted George waffles about committing the murder while Alice yammers on about trying to start a new life together. George's dilemma takes a deadly turn when Alice stands up and the rickety rowboat overturns, sending them both tumbling into the murky water. Only George emerges, getting into his car, driving away, and telling no one about the tragedy or how he did nothing to save the drowning Alice. His luck, it seems, has finally turned a corner as he returns to Angela—and to the privileged life he so intensely desires.

The drowning attracts the attention of the bespectacled, cane-carrying DA Frank Marlowe, who smells a rat after an eyewitness tells of a car leaving the crime scene. Marlowe's suspicions are confirmed when he discovers George's link to Alice. He charges George with murder, intent on proving that he killed Alice in cold blood by whacking her over the head with an oar. If George is convicted, he'll get the electric chair.

George's resulting trial constitutes the movie's penultimate scene, and Raymond, limping around the courtroom with his cane, shines as Marlowe takes center stage.

(Raymond weighed around three hundred pounds while making *A Place in the Sun,* and never explained why Marlowe needed a cane. It could have been to help support the actor's immense girth, although a friend claimed Raymond had hurt his leg skiing.)

While George sits timidly on the witness stand, seemingly resigned to his fate, Marlowe questions him with a rapid-fire intensity that borders on a soliloquy. The entire time he refers to George only as "Eastman."

"I'm referring to your heart, Eastman. Did you leave that behind you? Did you, Eastman? Out there on that terrace in the moonlight? You left behind . . . the girl you loved, and with her your hopes, your ambitions, your dreams? You left behind everything in the world you ever wanted, including the girl you loved. But you planned to return to it, didn't you Eastman?"

Marlowe, not content to simply badger George with accusations, then drags a rowboat into the middle of the courtroom and forces George to reenact that fateful night. Marlowe hammers and hectors until George is nearly catatonic, reeling from the verbal assault. Reaching the climax of his closing argument in the rapt courtroom, Marlowe climbs into the rowboat:

"I'll tell you one thing. You knew she was drowning and you just let her drown! She was sitting there defenseless in the back of the boat and you picked up this oar like this and you crashed it down on that poor girl's head like this!"

And with that, Marlowe grabs the oar, lifts it over his head, and brings it crashing down, splintering the wood in two.

"You pushed that poor girl into the lake and you watched her drown! Isn't that the truth?!"

It is only a half-truth, but it doesn't matter. The jury convicts George of murder, sending him to the electric chair. Marlowe has won his case.

It was important for Raymond to give a solid performance in *A Place in the Sun*. Marlowe, one of his few "good-guy" roles, gave him the chance to show his range. It was a rare on-screen opportunity to be on the right side of the law for a change, playing a somewhat sympathetic character.

A Place in the Sun opened in late August to mostly positive reviews, with critics predicting an Oscar windfall. (Clift and Winters were nominated for Academy Awards. Stevens won for Best Director, and other Oscars included a statuette for screenwriters Michael Wilson and Harry Brown.)

The *New York Times* called the movie "a work of beauty" and Clift's performance "full, rich, restrained and, above all, generally credible and poignant," reserving similar accolades for Taylor and Winters. It also made note of Raymond's important contribution: "Under Mr. Stevens' expert direction,

Raymond Burr, as the doggedly probing district attorney . . . as well as most of the supporting players, contribute fitting bits to an impressive mosaic."

Raymond, who said he made it a point to never watch his own movies, broke his own rule when it came to this particular project. "I've seen A *Place in the Sun* six times in its entirety and I'm sure I will see it six times more, because each time I see something else in it that Stevens had in those scenes," he said. "It is a marvelous motion picture."

George Stevens Jr., then a nineteen-year-old production assistant working on his father's movie, remembered Raymond's performance as "a wonderful combination of forcefulness, while at the same time being understated. It's very compelling. For me, I find this quite remarkable that, fifty years after its making, it has the kind of truth and compelling power and does not fall into the cliché of courtroom scenes."

Raymond reverted to villainous form in his next movie, *Mara Maru*, reuniting with Errol Flynn, with whom he'd costarred three years earlier in *The Adventures of Don Juan*. In *Mara Maru*, Flynn played Greg Mason, a luckless salvage diver hunting for a cache of sunken diamonds in the waters off Manila. Ruth Roman played his love interest; Raymond was Benedict, a shady promoter involved in the salvage operation ("Ruth Roman and Raymond Burr struggle in supporting roles," noted the *Chicago Tribune*).

Once again, Raymond's weight was a problem. He fluctuated wildly from enormous to simply overweight, often in a short time frame. Gossip columnist Hedda Hopper was visiting Raymond on the set of *Mara Maru* and noticed the difference. "I thought my eyes had gone bad when I walked on the *Mara Maru* set at Warners and spotted Raymond Burr," she wrote in November 1951. "In *A Place in the Sun* he weighed a strapping 300 pounds. But now, as a romantic leading man, he tips the scales at 185. We forgot movies for a spell and had a long chat about dieting."

The cast also featured Paul Picerni, who was five years younger than Raymond. He played Ranier, a detective who switches allegiances throughout *Mara Maru* between Benedict and Mason (depending on who looks like the winner). Picerni was a Warner Brothers contract player who'd tested with Raymond for several movies in years past.

On the *Mara Maru* set they became fast friends, drinking brandy, and getting the giggles one day while shooting a particularly wet scene (a typhoon that rocked Mason's boat). Raymond often invited Picerni back to his dressing room to play cribbage. He was "very subtle" in his approach, but it was soon apparent to Picerni, who was straight, why the burly actor had taken such an interest in him.

"He talked about his wife in England and his two sons [*sic*]. I guess that threw me off," Picerni said. "And then we're playing cribbage and suddenly I see the look in his eyes and I said to myself, 'My God, he's on the make!' Nothing ever happened. He was a great guy and very subtle in his homosexuality, I guess."

Picerni was more straightforward in his autobiography:

"When I took a look up from my cards . . . I saw him staring at me. With his big blue eyes. And with this strange expression on his face. For the first time in my life, I felt like a DAME. Then it hit me: He'd been giving me all this bullshit about his wife and his two kids in London, when in fact he was gay, and he was makin' a move on me!"

It wasn't the last time, either. Raymond hit on Picerni again (unsuccessfully) when Picerni guest starred on *Perry Mason,* trying to loosen him up with a few glasses of scotch. "But I loved Ray," Picerni said. "He was a delightful guy with a great sense of humor."

Raymond also had a big heart. He could be counted on by friends and colleagues to lend money in a pinch, and in the early 1950s he began what would become a lifelong devotion to entertaining servicemen by touring military bases and staging musical numbers and sketch-comedy acts. He started his own repertory company, "The Raymond Burr Troupe," consisting of a four-piece band; dancer, singer, and comedian Evelyn Russell; vocalist Ann McCormack; a tap dancer; and impersonators Don and Doni.

"Last but not least in the evening's entertainment was the scene of how movies are made, and the rendition of 'If You Were the Only Boy,'" wrote one reviewer. "The show was concluded by the entire troupe coming out on the stage and singing that beautiful song, 'May the Good Lord Bless and Keep You.'"

Raymond toured military bases up and down the West Coast and elsewhere, sometimes in the company of A-list celebrities like Martha Raye. He made his first trip to Korea during the conflict there (while he was supposedly spending his last days with son Michael) and somehow managed to jam all this in between movie, radio, and television appearances.

In December 1952, Raymond joined nine others for a two-week holiday tour of isolated bases in the Northeast Air Command covering Greenland, Baffinland, Newfoundland, and Labrador. Raymond's brother Edmond, who was now chief conductor for the Los Angeles Police Band, joined another troupe that worked with the USO in the Northeast Air Command. A third troupe, including Debbie Reynolds and Peter Lawford, traveled to Korea.

Raymond was accompanied on the tour by his old friends Marilyn and Flo-Ann Hedley, sisters he directed in summer stock at the Player's Ring Theater in Hollywood. Their father, Eli Hedley, was an iconic California millionaire nicknamed "the Beachcomber" for amassing a fortune through his catalog—which consisted of refuse collected on the beach.

"Ray heard about some men manning a weather station as far north as you go could go at that time. They'd been there for two years not seeing anybody, so we went," recalled Marilyn Hedley. "When we got there the men were astounded that Raymond Burr had come all that way to see them. They cried and we cried when we left."

The troupe performed four shows a day and was at a base in Labrador on Christmas Eve when Raymond called the group together at midnight. "We expected to hear that warm, vibrant voice, which has charmed thousands, deliver one of its usual pep talks," wrote Marilyn Hedley. "Instead, his voice sort of broke and Ray said, 'Kids, don't I remember that it says somewhere, 'Tis more blessed to give than to receive?' Now come on, let's sing some carols."

The group returned to Burbank in early January and Raymond was soon off again, this time for a six-month USO tour of Korea, Japan, and the Philippine Islands. His agent, Lester

Salkow, figured that the chunk of time overseas cost his client about $85,000 in lost acting jobs.

The USO show was called "You Asked for It," and the schedule was grueling, while the accommodations were often one step above deplorable. Marilyn Hedley was on the tour again, as were singer/dancer/comedian Evelyn Russell and singer Ann McCormack. "That 1953 trip was pretty memorable," Raymond said. "We did a show every afternoon and evening and then every night I was flown up to the front lines to stay in the bunkers with the fellows.

"The Army wanted to know whether it might mean a great deal to them to have visits from somebody who didn't have to be there. So I got acquainted with a lot of the boys that way." According to legendary gossip columnist Walter Winchell, Raymond was getting *very* acquainted with Evelyn Russell. "Roz Russell's kin, Evelyn Russell, will become Mrs. Raymond Burr," he wrote in his inimitable style. Winchell was feared for his accuracy, but even he screwed up sometimes. This was one of those "wrongos," as he called them.

Raymond was aware of how much the troops depended on entertainment and how much it meant to them to have someone from "home" showing an interest in them. And they weren't picky when it came to being amused and distracted from the horrors of the war.

"We once did *Charley's Aunt* in Korea. I rewrote it for a GI background," Raymond said. "The three boys were sergeants, the three girls were WACs, and the real aunt was a delegate from the U.N. We carried our own props, of course. We could expect anything from a tumbledown building to a service club or mess hall, and used what benches or chairs there were. We learned to do shows that were sixty or seventy percent visual, because oftentimes there were Belgians or Turks or Ethiopians invited to come and watch."

Raymond starred in the troupe's showstopper, the "Stand-in Sketch." "They get this real dumb character and they bring him in—the stand-in—every time something is going to happen to the leading man," he explained. "And all hell breaks loose: he gets hit with water and mops and pails, and slugged, and gets thrown down and stomped upon and finally gets hit with a pie—real slapstick."

Offstage, Raymond wasn't a shrinking violet, either. He exhibited an almost uncanny fascination with the rigors of soldiering and insisted on traveling to the front lines at most of the stops on the tour to meet and greet the men. On one occasion, less than half a mile from the Chinese line, Raymond surprised a group of men under the command of Major Stan McClellan of Company L, 7th Infantry Regiment, 3rd U.S. Infantry Division.

"Into our bunker walked the most God-awful sight we had ever seen. Here was Ray in a red-knit short-sleeved sport shirt, blue civilian slacks, yellow buckskin shoes, dragging a U.S.M.C. armored vest in one hand and a steel helmet in the other," McClellan said.

Raymond followed McClellan and his men "in and out of bunkers, weapons positions, half-destroyed trenches, ammo supply points," the major said. "I can't describe the open-mouthed amazement with which he was greeted by every soldier we met. He stopped and talked to each of them. It did more than anything else to convince the men of this fighting outfit that the 'folks at home' were really not so far away after all."

Later, on another USO tour, Raymond brought along Bungy Hedley, Marilyn and Flo-Ann Hedley's baby sister. Raymond knew Bungy well; several years earlier, as a favor to the family, he had escorted Bungy to her San Pedro High School prom (causing quite a stir at the school). Marilyn and Flo-Ann gave up touring after the 1953 Korean sojourn, so Raymond asked Bungy to join him on the USO circuit.

"I begged him when I became eighteen to let me go on the USO tour with him, but he said, 'No, you're too young,'" she recalled. "Marilyn and Flo had gone on with their lives and he said, 'Well, I guess I'm going to have to take you because I have to have a Hedley in there!' I had never been away from home . . . so before we left Ray invited me and two others out and took us to this club where Nat King Cole was singing, and [Cole] came over and sat at our table." Raymond and Cole knew each other after appearing together in *The Blue Gardenia* with headliners Anne Baxter, Richard Conte, and Ann Sothern.

Raymond didn't stop there. After hearing that Nike bases along the West Coast were not part of the USO itinerary, he formed his own troupe of twelve players and hit virtually "every Nike base and every gun site on the Pacific coast." Later, the show was changed—"all the uniforms and all the nomenclature"—and staged for the air force.

Raymond's devotion to the military was honorable, and he put himself in harm's way, time and again, in his zeal to entertain the troops. He worked just as hard, or harder, as that epitome of USO touring, Bob Hope. And he did it without anywhere near the attention paid to Hope's tours.

But there could have been another subconscious factor at play. Raymond's fabricated biography included not only a dead wife and son, but also a military past that didn't exist. The closest he came to any military service was a brief stint in the U.S. Coast Guard (and *that* was according to Minerva), although he claimed to have served in the navy. Some press accounts even went a step further; Raymond, they said with a flourish, was shot in the stomach on Okinawa and still had some leftover bullet fragments in his belly. In other claims, he had been awarded a Purple Heart for his heroism after surviving a Japanese kamikaze attack.

None of it was true.

Postwar Hollywood, like the rest of the country, was caught up in the nation's patriotic fervor and was a culpable partner in Raymond's deceit. A handsome young actor could burnish his reputation with a mention of military service; Raymond, as was his wont, took it a step further. The story, like all the others regarding the "facts" of his life, would prove to be false.

The National Personnel Records Center (NPRC) is an archival repository servicing all branches of the military. It shows no record of Raymond Burr's war service. "We have conducted extensive searches of every records source and alternate records source at this Center; however, we have been unable to locate any information that would help us verify the veteran's military service," the NPRC wrote to this author. Had Raymond served even one day in the military, his name would have surfaced.

Burr's name did continue to surface, though, in movie after movie as he kept up a steady pace in Hollywood. The work was financially rewarding—Raymond was earning around $100,000 a year as one of the industry's most sought-after character actors—but the roles, for the most part, rarely varied. If it was a brooding noir drama, he was the hulking villain; if it was a western, he was the corrupt town elder or the sleazy malcontent; if it was a costume epic, he was the sneering, malevolent sidekick.

If the roles were monotonous, at least on screen Raymond had the opportunity to threaten, harass, and cajole some of Hollywood's biggest stars. They included Jimmy Stewart, who played wheelchair-bound photographer L. B. Jefferies in Alfred Hitchcock's *Rear Window*. Raymond was cast as white-haired wife-killer Lars Thorwald in this Technicolor adaptation of Cornell Woolrich's 1942 short story "It Had to Be Murder."

Jefferies, or "Jeff" as his friends call him, is a globe-trotting photographer laid up in his Manhattan apartment after breaking his leg while on assignment. Bored and with his leg in a cast, he starts spying on his neighbors, using his binoculars and his wide-angle lens for his own voyeuristic enjoyment. Jeff's courtyard becomes his personal playground, much to the consternation of his "too-perfect" fiancée, fashion plate Lisa Fremont (Grace Kelly).

Jeff, though, can't help himself from spying on his neighbors, and he grows fascinated with the pedestrian world unfolding in the courtyard. With little else to do, he becomes obsessed with the stories being played out on stage left, right, and center, and he creates his own little soap opera. Over there is the character he dubs "Miss Lonelyhearts," who's unlucky in love and growing more depressed with each passing day. Over there is the young newlywed couple going about their newlywed business (the movie's comic relief). Across the way is the woman with the little dog she puts in a basket and lowers by winch, while her neighbor, a struggling musician, looks for inspiration and a dancer Jeff calls "Miss Torso" practices her (suggestive) moves.

Jeff also focuses in on Lars Thorwald, the burly traveling salesman who lives directly across the courtyard. Thorwald's bedridden wife nags her put-upon husband, and the couple argue frequently. One night, too late to be making a sales call, Thorwald leaves his apartment with his sample case in tow just as Jeff is drifting off to sleep. Shortly thereafter, Jeff makes his daily courtyard sweep with the binoculars and notices that Thorwald's wife is missing. The salesman then ships a trunk out of his apartment.

Jeff starts scrutinizing Thorwald's shifty behavior, using his binoculars and a powerful telephoto lens to figure out what's going on across the way. The salesman not only seems to chat on the phone with someone who's not his wife, but Jeff spies him examining his wife's jewelry in the quiet apartment. He's soon convinced something is amiss—that Thorwald killed his wife after an argument and disposed of her body in the trunk. This is all news to Lisa, who's more interested in getting some attention from her boyfriend than in his far-fetched murder scenario. Maybe the sexy lingerie she packs for a daring overnight stay will distract him.

Jeff doesn't have any better luck convincing his old army buddy, sardonic Detective Thomas Doyle (Wendell Corey), that Thorwald is a murderer. Doyle attributes his friend's suspicions to an overactive imagination and, to humor him, conducts his own cursory investigation—only to find that Mrs. Thorwald boarded a train out of town. Is that so unusual? No . . . but, as Lisa points out, "It's simply that women *don't* leave their jewelry behind when they go on a trip."

One of the many terrific components of *Rear Window* is the huge, expansive, multitiered courtyard set designed by Sam Comer and Ray Moyer, which allows the camera to float freely from one apartment to the next, picking up drifts of dialogue. Because the movie is told from Jeff's perspective, the set needed to be as lifelike as possible to avoid a feeling of claustrophobia and to keep the action interesting.

Nowhere is the set's dramatic impact more evident than when Lisa breaks into Thorwald's apartment searching for his wife's wedding ring (as evidence to prove that he killed her). Jeff and his feisty masseuse, Stella (Thelma Ritter), watching anxiously from across the way, see Thorwald returning to the apartment, but with Lisa still inside, they're powerless to help her. Thorwald catches Lisa red-handed and nearly strangles her; only her screams, and the ensuing commotion, save her life as the cops bust into Thorwald's apartment. Lisa, her hands behind her back, signals to Jeff that she has the wedding ring—a move that catches Thorwald's eye. He glances up from the wedding ring to Jeff's apartment window, aware now that he's been watched.

The movie's climactic scene unfolds in the darkness of Jefferies's apartment. Jeff answers his phone, thinking it's Doyle—but the quick click of a hang-up tells him that it's Thorwald, signaling to his wheelchair-bound prey that he's coming to seek his revenge.

As Jeff sweats it out, we hear Thorwald's plodding steps coming closer and closer. Thinking quickly, Jeff grabs his camera and a bunch of flashbulbs he'll use to ward off Thorwald—whose steps continue to close in until he's actually in the apartment. For the first time we see the hulking Thorwald up close. His blue eyes glint malevolently behind clear eyeglasses, his young face framed by a shock of snow-white hair. He speaks to Jeff slowly in a gravely, almost plaintive whisper.

Thorwald: "What do you want from me? Your friend, the girl, could've turned me in, why didn't she? What is it you want, a lot of money? I don't have any money. Say something. Say something! Tell me what you want! Can you get me that ring back?"

Jeff: "No."

Thorwald: "Tell her to bring it back."

Jeff: "I can't. The police have it by now."

Thorwald moves in for the kill, but he's temporarily blinded by the popping of Jeff's flashbulbs. Rubbing his eyes, Thorwald descends on his prey and grabs Jeff by the throat—but not before Jeff can scream out for Doyle, who's with Lisa outside Thorwald's apartment door across the courtyard. Thorwald and Jeff struggle, and Thorwald dangles Jefferies out the window—the photographer hanging on by his fingertips—until Doyle's men finally arrive and grab Thorwald as Jeff plunges to the courtyard below (breaking his other leg).

Jeff, of course, was right all along. Thorwald quickly confesses (off-camera) to murdering his wife and scattering her remains around the East River—and keeping a piece of her in a hatbox in his apartment.

Raymond, seen only from a distance for most of *Rear Window*, does a terrific job portraying Thorwald's inherent evil while imbuing the salesman with a pathetic streak bordering on sympathetic. "For the first part of the picture you don't see this man close up at all, but you have to know exactly what he is, from the way he walks," he said. "So I had to walk in a certain way, and I had to be kind of middle-aged and tired and beat."

Hitchcock reportedly crafted Thorwald in the image of his nemesis, studio chief David O. Selznick, down to the white hair and rimless glasses. The role apparently changed a bit from the time Raymond signed on to the project in November 1953. "Raymond Burr has been signed for a top role in Alfred Hitchcock's *Rear Window* at Paramount," reported feared gossip columnist Hedda Hopper. "Altho [sic] his voice will not be heard in the picture, he got the job when Hitch heard him on a radio program and sent for him."

Hopper followed this report with a column note two months later. "Raymond Burr, hired by Alfred Hitchcock for *Rear Window* because of his beautiful voice, is seen but not heard in the picture," she wrote. "When they got into the film, Hitch thought that wasn't fair, so he's written a scene at the finish for Burr and Jimmy Stewart."

Rear Window opened on August 1, 1954, to rave reviews and brisk business at the box office. Stewart and Hitchcock were widely praised, as was the movie's pulse-pounding finale. (The movie earned four Oscar nominations, including nods for Hitchcock and for screenwriter John Michael Hayes.)

For Raymond, *Rear Window* meant huge exposure in a mainstream, sophisticated project. For the first time, the movie going public sat up and *noticed* the burly character actor, who wasn't exactly a stranger to them but wasn't a household name, either. *Rear Window* changed all that, even though Raymond's role, save for Thorwald's final struggle with Jeff, was limited to distant camera shots and barely discernible dialogue.

"Since enacting his role of the perpetrator of the 'perfect crime' in *Rear Window*, Raymond Burr is due to become even more of a personality on the screen than heretofore," Edwin Schallert noted in the *Los Angeles Times* on August 27, a month after the movie's premiere. "That may be one reason why William Wyler has selected him for the top role of the police officer who is tracking down Humphrey Bogart in *Desperate Hours*, which is quite a switch. However, Wyler calls him 'one of the very best character actors.' Burr is still abroad for *Adventure in Rio* with Scott Brady, so the deal was settled over the transatlantic phone."

The *Desperate Hours* role never came to fruition, but Burr was fielding offers for his services left and right. There was talk that his agent, Lester Salkow, was shopping him for a television project called *International Story Theater*, a twenty-six-episode series to be filmed in the Philippine Islands, Japan, and India. Raymond would play a different character in each episode.

He also set up a company called Bursal Productions with Salkow, ostensibly to produce three independent movies, each written by Raymond, in which he would also star. The first movie, *Listen, World*, was to be shot in Korea ("familiar territory for Burr since he made seven tours to that area," the *Los Angeles Times* dutifully noted). It would be followed by *The Black Wind* and *The Day the Sky Went Out of Its Mind*. Raymond was supposed to visit Chicago and New York to arrange financing for the movies, but the projects never materialized.

What did materialize in 1956—at least in the headlines of the fan magazines and gossip columns—was a romance, or at least an undeniably strong friendship, between Raymond and young Natalie Wood, his costar in *A Cry in the Night*. Raymond's relationship with Wood, his only public flirtation with a woman, was the prototypical "Hollywood romance" straight out of the traditional playbook: two costars falling madly in love on the set, just in time to publicize their movie.

But since this was Raymond, there was a wrinkle—their age difference. Raymond was thirty-eight and Natalie only seventeen at the time they filmed *A Cry in the Night*. To the gossip columnists and movie magazines breathlessly reporting what appeared to be a fledgling romance, Raymond was the older, sophisticated man of the world and Natalie the naive waif being cultivated at the feet of the master.

Forget the fact that Natalie had already earned an Oscar nomination for *Rebel Without a Cause*, while Raymond, though clearly respected in Hollywood, was relegated to supporting roles. He was receiving equal billing opposite an Oscar nominee now. The movie needed publicity. Tongues needed to wag. What better way than to manufacture a studio romance?

The couple's off-screen relationship certainly didn't mirror their interaction in *A Cry in the Night*, which was written by David Dortort. Dortort and Raymond had worked together a few years earlier, when Dortort wrote a television adaptation of *The Ox-Bow Incident*, in which Raymond starred with Robert Wagner. Dortort would later create the long-running television series *Bonanza*, which put up a touch-and-go ratings fight against *Perry Mason*.

In *A Cry in the Night*, Raymond was cast as Harold Loftus, a thirty-two-year-old mentally challenged man-child living with his doting mother. Their weird relationship created in

Harold a psychological stew of misplaced sexual confusion. Simply put, this is a guy with issues. Desperate for the companionship of a woman *not* called Mother, Harold takes to spying on couples necking in a nearby lover's lane under the cover of darkness.

It's there that Harold finally loses control and attacks Liz Taggart (Wood) and her boyfriend, Owen Clark (Richard Anderson). He knocks Owen unconscious and drags Liz to his secret seedy lair in the bowels of a brickyard, where he plans to rape her. What Harold doesn't realize is that he's kidnapped the daughter of a veteran cop (Edmund O'Brien), who mobilizes the force under Capt. Ed Bates (Brian Donlevy) to find his little girl and bring her home safely.

Dortort, who was on the set of *A Cry in the Night* watching the filming, noted some interesting parallels between Harold and Raymond.

"There was a considerable amount of talk about the dual nature of the man," he said of Raymond. "In spite of his large size, he had certain feminine attributes that made for a very interesting actor, because he had to hold those [feminine attributes] back, in a sense, and push the image of a very strong, tough man—which he wasn't."

It was those "feminine attributes," Dortort said, that helped color Raymond's performance as the hulking man-child. "That's why he was so good in it," he said. "He was playing something very close to him. It was a tough role for him to play. What I wanted to do was to create some sympathy [for Harold], some understanding of him, and Raymond really appreciated that."

Wood, who lobbied strongly for the part of Liz, had been a fan of Raymond's since watching him in *A Place in the Sun* five years earlier. Once shooting began on *A Cry in the Night*, the two developed an intense, close friendship that played itself out as a sort of mentor—protégé relationship.

Raymond, a well-read gourmet who quoted poetry, would teach young Natalie, who'd just opened her first bank account, the ways of the world. He invited her to dinner one night, where they dined on snails and sipped fine wine. Shortly thereafter they became an item, stepping out to premieres and Hollywood parties together. So enamored of Natalie was Raymond, according to Hedda Hopper, that he made an effort to lose weight, shedding fifty pounds from his bulky frame. "As the pounds melted off, he progressed from heavy to hero, tho [*sic*] he made no headway with her," Hopper wrote in her autobiography.

"Burr was a very classy guy and he saw her talent and the potential in her, and he really wanted to cultivate her, the way Orson Welles cultivated Rita Hayworth—and it was done very lovingly," Wood's friend Maryann Marinkovich told Wood's biographer Suzanne Finstad.

"I knew that they were good friends and she enjoyed doing the movie with him very much," said Natalie's eventual husband, Robert Wagner. "I wouldn't tell you [about a romance] even if it was true. We just all liked Raymond very much and I never asked [Natalie] those questions."

Richard Anderson, who was working on the set with Raymond and Natalie, says he noticed an immediate chemistry between them. "He was just wild about her. I remember that," Anderson said. "There was something going on there with the two of them. Natalie probably adored him. She was very young and getting started . . . he could've been the 'older man' thing but I think he just adored her and she adored him and it was one of those things when you are making a movie.

"I think everybody knew about his sexual preferences," Anderson said, "but that was just something that was in the motion picture business."

The "sexual preferences" bugaboo was, of course, a roadblock in the relationship. The seventeen-year-old Natalie, entranced by the worldly older man with the rich baritone voice and smoldering blue eyes, didn't seem to be in the loop of Hollywood insiders who knew Raymond was gay.

"It was the most devastating thing when she found that Raymond Burr was gay and there was no way they were going to have an affair, because she tried her darnedest," Natalie's friend Jackie Eastes told Suzanne Finstad. "She thought with her charm she could make the difference."

Natalie's *Rebel Without a Cause* costar and close friend Dennis Hopper took it one step further. "She may have gone into a period where she was interested in gay men," he said, suggesting Raymond was using his "romance" with Natalie to "cover his gayness."

Whatever the true situation, once the Burr-Wood relationship became public, Warner Bros., the studio behind *A Cry in the Night,* moved quickly to break it up, not wanting its very young starlet associated with a man over twice her age. In January 1956, columnist Joan Curtis saw Natalie at a party hosted by Robert Wagner, "sulking . . . over the fact that the older man she was then tingling over had been declared off-limits by her studio . . . in fact, a studio man was present to see the edict was carried out."

Despite the Warner Bros. interference, Raymond's relationship with Natalie continued into the spring. They made plans to costar in a Pasadena Playhouse production of *Anne of the Thousand Days,* and talked about traveling to Korea together for a USO tour. Natalie went so far as to gush to columnist Sheila Graham about the couple's future together. "It's beginning to look like a marriage for young Natalie Wood and Raymond Burr," Graham wrote.

"To me he's exciting as an actor and as a person," Natalie said. "He's so kind, so intellectual." The movie magazines picked up on the relationship—through no help from Warner Bros., which continued to pressure the couple into breaking it off. The fan magazines coyly focused their attention on Raymond and Natalie's teacher-pupil angle rather than anything remotely hinting of a sexual nature in their relationship.

"[Raymond's] influence on her has been more of that of a casual date," *Movie Stars Parade* noted in December 1956. "He's opened new worlds of culture to her, encouraged her to seek even more for herself." The article featured two photos of Natalie and former costar Tab Hunter, at the time a closeted homosexual, wearing wide grins while taking turns spanking each other.

When Natalie announced that she would attend the upcoming Academy Awards with Raymond, the studio finally put its foot down. Fearful of even more publicity, the powers-that-be insisted that Natalie ditch Raymond and take Tab Hunter to the awards instead. And that was that. Natalie caved in to the pressure and moved on, while Raymond, whether or not he really meant it, mooned over his lost love to anyone who would listen. "Raymond Burr . . . makes no secret of the fact that he's carrying a torch for Natalie Wood, and will be devastated if she marries Robert Wagner," Dorothy Kilgallen reported a year after the breakup.

"I was very attracted to her and she was to me," Raymond said. "Maybe I was too old for her, but there was so much pressure upon us from the outside and the studio, it got awkward for us to go around together."

At least that was the safe explanation.

If Raymond couldn't tame the beauty, he had better luck with a beast named Godzilla. A deal he'd signed earlier that year sent him over to Visual Drama Studios in Los Angeles to spend the day filming his role in *Godzilla: King of the Monsters*.

The movie was originally shot two years earlier in Japan, where it was called *Gojira*. It told the story of a dinosaur-like, fire-breathing creature that terrorizes Japan after a wave of nuclear testing disturbs its undersea slumber. *Gojira's* antinuclear message was loud and clear from a country devastated by two nuclear attacks only nine years before. Filmed on the cheap, with cheesy special effects (wires and shadows from cameras are visible in several scenes), the movie nonetheless did brisk box-office business in Japan.

In a bid to appeal to a mainstream American audience enjoying the mid-1950s horror-movie renaissance, *Gojira* was imported to the United States by a company called Jewell Enterprises, which renamed it *Godzilla* and (badly) dubbed it into English. The Americanized version included a new character, Raymond's Steve Martin, a wire service reporter visiting an old friend in Japan. When Godzilla strikes Tokyo, Steve breathlessly reports on the creature's deadly rampage for his news agency back home.

Raymond shot all his scenes in one day at Visual Drama. Those scenes were then edited into the already existing *Gojira*, and several English-speaking Japanese actors were hired for scenes requiring Steve to interact verbally with other characters. When it premiered in late April 1956, *Godzilla* didn't exactly wow the critics—Bosley Crowther labeled it "an incredibly awful film" in the *New York Times*—but it spawned a movie franchise and a legion of fans, including Raymond. Nearly thirty years later, he appeared (as a much older Steve Martin) in *Godzilla 1985*.

These good-guy roles were few and far between, though, and Raymond, now nearing forty, was tiring of the bad-guy act. Typical of his screen roles was this description from a critic writing of his work in *Horizon's West* opposite Rock Hudson and Robert Ryan: "Raymond Burr is as cold-hearted a villain as we've had since Erich Von Stroheim." He began trolling for projects that would change his image.

The heavy wanted to lighten up a bit.

"Ray was always identified as one of the better actors in Hollywood," said friend Art Marks. "There was no question that people always looked upon him as a class actor. But he wanted to change his image . . . to become a leading man. And that was from the very beginning. He had a couple of chances early and didn't cut it."

The image change wouldn't be easy. Hollywood continued to see him as a villain and, despite his protestations, he continued to accept the roles. He flew to Havana to film *The Fever Tree* (eventually retitled *Affair in Havana*), in which he played a white-haired, wheelchair-bound sugar tycoon plotting to kill his wife (Sara Shane) and her lover (John Cassavetes)—the white hair and wheelchair not-so-subtle reminders of Lars Thorwald and L. B. Jefferies from *Rear Window*.

While he was in Cuba filming *Affair in Havana*, Raymond bought the rights to Cuban writer Juan Jimenez's book *Florida Key*, about a Prohibition-era rum runner who's also a lawyer and ends up defending himself in court. Raymond would star in the picture, which had a feel-good ending (the rum runner/lawyer keeps $5 million and lives it up in Florida), but it was never produced.

The one bright spot in all the "heavy" movie roles during this time was *Please Murder Me,* Raymond's first—and last—romantic leading role. The part was enough of a departure for Raymond to merit a mention in the *New York Times* ("Raymond Burr will play his first romantic lead in nine years of movie acting"), and it cast Raymond opposite Angela Lansbury, who was slowly working her way back into the Hollywood game after a lull in her career.

"I had left MGM and was freelancing for the first time in my career, and it was kind of lean times for me, because I was no longer under contract," Lansbury said. "I was a young married at that time, and my husband [Peter Shaw] hadn't yet established himself in the business, so doing a movie like *Please Murder Me* . . . I think we shot it literally in a supermarket on Hollywood Boulevard."

The movie's turgid title pretty much sums it all up. While Raymond hoped to display his leading-man qualities in *Please Murder Me,* the movie did little to help him in that department. He played attorney Craig Carlson, a firm believer in truth and justice (a precursor to Perry Mason) who defends beautiful socialite Myra Leeds (Lansbury) against a charge of murdering her husband.

Craig, who firmly believes in Myra's innocence, falls in love with her during the trial, which ends in her acquittal. He's done his job, and he's done it well. But it's soon apparent that the scheming siren really *did* kill her husband—who mailed a letter he wrote before his death blaming Myra for his murder.

Craig is horrified by the realization that he successfully defended a guilty woman, and he makes the decision to sacrifice his own life in order to bring Myra to justice. He sets up an elaborate scheme resulting in his own murder at Myra's hand—and records it all on a tape recorder (shades of Fred MacMurray's insurance salesman Walter Neff in *Double Indemnity*).

Please Murder Me opened and closed without much fanfare, and it did more for Lansbury's career than it helped Raymond polish his good-guy image. "That was the beginning of me establishing myself and playing a good heavy," Lansbury said. "And it took me years to live it down."

Lansbury didn't get to know Raymond very well. "He managed to maintain a kind of closed book on himself," she said, and she was unaware at the time of his sexual orientation. "It never occurred to me. Isn't that strange?" she said. "I knew a great many gay men in those days. Certainly I never thought of [Raymond] in that light." (Lansbury's first husband, actor Richard Cromwell, was gay, a fact unknown to her when they married. The union was dissolved a year later.)

"He actually was functioning in an era where he was pretty safe and people didn't necessarily question if you didn't marry, I don't think," Lansbury said. "There were bachelors. There were self-respecting men who were 'confirmed bachelors' . . . like Randolph Scott and Cary Grant, Tyrone Power, and all those people.

"We now know there were certain aspects of their lives that weren't necessarily one thing or another, but in those days they were such icons in the movies that nobody bothered— and certainly it never occurred to the public, I'm sure."

Raymond, though, was a tiger of a different stripe. He wasn't an "icon," and, for the public record, he'd been twice married and had fathered a (now deceased) son. "In those days it was understood among the press that they never re-ferred to the fact that they knew [about someone being gay]," Lansbury said. "Certainly the columnists [didn't] . . . I don't think Hedda [Hopper] or Louella [Parsons] would ever have inferred such a thing. It just wasn't done."

Raymond's ballooning waistline also continued to hold him back from better roles. He seesawed from a high of 340 pounds to the low two hundreds, and when he got disgusted, he'd go on a crash diet of cottage cheese and fruit (and plenty of cigarettes) to lose the lard. His reputation as a gourmand didn't help. Raymond's appetite for food was legendary in Hollywood circles, and he loved to eat in massive quanti-ties, downing it all with lots of wine. The unhealthy food he ate while he was on his many USO tours only exacerbated the problem. "When I was doing heavies, being a real-life heavy didn't bother me too much," he said. "In fact, it often helped get me the part. However, the public doesn't want to see some plump, Santa Claus–type character as a romantic lead . . .

"At one point in radio I was playing romantic leading men with a figure that tipped the scales at 340. And even at 6'2" that kind of weight doesn't exactly qualify you to snare the pretty leading lady."

Financially, he was secure. Despite the big bucks he claimed to lose by leaving the country to entertain the troops, he still was one of Hollywood's highest-paid supporting players. By the late 1950s, Raymond was raking in over $100,000 a year from his movie work alone—and another combined princely sum from his television and radio work. He appeared frequently on television (*Lux Video Theatre, Climax!, Playhouse 90*), and in 1956 he lent his pipes to the lead role of Captain Lee Quince in forty episodes of the CBS radio drama *Fort Laramie*, which aired Sunday nights.

If he didn't quite have the fame yet, Raymond certainly had the money, and he spent lavishly. He showered gifts on friends and, in the mid-1950s, bought a house on a bluff in Malibu, overlooking the Pacific Ocean. There he could hold his famous dinner parties and indulge his interest in nature. He began cultivating his lifelong love of flowers, especially orchids, by cross-pollinating different strains and developing his own hybrids. He stocked the yard in Malibu with a variety of animals, including dogs (Australian Silky terriers and Saint Bernards), cats (Siamese and Himalayan), and ducks, geese, and chickens, which he kept penned up.

The mini-zoo would eventually swell to accommodate other animals: pheasants, peafowl, a burro, pigeons, and two sheepdog brothers—one of them deaf. Raymond tried un-successfully to have a hearing aid fashioned for the hard-of-hearing hound.

The house in Malibu was in a picturesque setting, but it wasn't ostentatious. That wasn't Raymond's style. The lack of pretense didn't mean, though, that it wasn't stocked with the finest artwork, furniture, and doodads from Raymond's travels abroad. The kitchen, where Raymond gleefully cooked his culinary concoctions, dominated the downstairs part of the house.

"He had a great big bedroom upstairs in that Malibu house that had varnished floors and windows looking out over the whole Pacific," recalled Raymond's old friend Bungy Hedley. "He had a great big bed in the middle of this room with a side table with a reading lamp on it. And on that little cabinet sat a little photograph of me holding my first daughter. That's the only thing he had in there. He didn't have any pictures on the wall."

Raymond bought the house from Sylvester Samuel Pierce, a member of the famous Boston grocery family. Pierce had built the structure with his own two hands, and after he died, his widow, Yvette, and her sister, Mrs. Andree Floyd, were frequent guests. "Ray has the oddest relationship with those people," said *Perry Mason* executive producer Gail Patrick Jackson. "He acts as though he didn't buy the house, but just borrowed it."

Not only did the sisters frequently stay for the weekend, but they also chipped in with household chores, washing dishes, dusting, and helping Raymond chop onions for one of his many gourmet meals. It even went beyond that; if Raymond wanted to change something in or around the house, he did so only after running the idea past Mrs. Pierce. "They're family," he said.

The stucco house was located about forty miles from Hollywood, past Malibu Beach. It was roomy and comfortable, and the spacious kitchen, which Raymond added on to, was dominated by a huge stove and oven, offset by a table that easily sat sixteen. The forty-foot-long living room led to Raymond's bedroom, with a guest bedroom at the other end and a third room with a liquor cabinet and a pantry. Raymond built a stone pathway leading to the house from the driveway and also built and tiled a patio. "It's the kind of home I like . . . kind of Grecian-Tahitian," he said. "Post-peasant and pre-provincial."

Raymond could also count on spending time at the house with his parents. In 1954, after twenty-seven years apart, Minerva and Bill Burr reconciled and remarried. The romance was rekindled when Raymond's brother Edmond was drafted into the service, and his parents—Minerva in Los Angeles and Bill in New Westminster—began corresponding with each other. Minerva was still teaching music in the late 1940s when she was temporarily blinded, and Bill reached out to her. The bond between the two grew even closer then.

"I always hoped we would get back together someday. There had never really been anyone else for either of us," Minerva explained simply. "We decided we wanted to be together. It wasn't as difficult readjusting as you might imagine because we both set our minds and our hearts to it. Few things in life worth having come easily."

Raymond was preparing to set off for a lengthy USO tour and about to bid his mother good-bye at the airport when she said she wanted to tell him something. "I'm going to trade my old car in and get a new one," she said. "And then I think I'm going to take a trip." Raymond knew immediately what she meant. Minerva and Bill Burr were remarried a short time later at the Brighton Presbyterian Church in Seattle, with a reception afterward at the home of Raymond's nephew Dr. Leonard Rich. Minerva returned to Los Angeles to pack up her belongings and move back to New Westminster with her new/old husband. The happy couple declined Raymond's invitation to move in with him.

———

Despite all of his work in television throughout the 1950s, the prospect of regular work in a weekly series wasn't on Raymond's radar. He was a movie actor, and while the explosion of television as a cultural medium coincided with Raymond's busiest years in Hollywood, why would he have even given it a second thought?

A guest shot on television here and there was one thing, but few movie actors made the full-time transition from the big to small screen successfully—or at least did so willingly. Red Skelton, Jack Benny, Groucho Marx, and Lucille Ball were all well-known movie personalities embraced by the television audience. But their segue to television had more to do with necessity than choice, once their big-screen roles dried up and radio's influence began to wane.

Raymond, though, had reached the point of no return in his movie career. He was about to turn forty and was an established actor who could continue making good money playing villains. But he wanted something more. He wanted to play the good guy for once. And a proposed television series he heard about, while working on *Fort Laramie*, had possibilities.

CHAPTER FIVE

Enter Perry Mason

Perry Mason had already gone through several pop-culture incarnations by the time producer Gail Patrick Jackson, a former actress, and her husband, Cornwall "Corney" Jackson, pitched the fictional defense attorney to CBS as a weekly television series. The creation of self-taught lawyer Erle Stanley Gardner, Perry Mason began life as the pulp-novel hero of *The Case of the Velvet Claws,* which was published in 1933.

Gardner, bored with practicing law, had begun writing his hard-boiled prose for various pulp magazines, taking the same literary path traveled by contemporaries including Dashiell Hammett and Raymond Chandler. Gardner discovered a knack for short, straightforward storytelling, coloring his tales with shadings of the legal system he knew so well.

Gardner found steady work churning out crime stories, creating a stable of characters including Lester Leith and Ken Corning. His work appeared in magazines with names like *Black Mask, Argosy, Dime Detective,* and *Detective Fiction Weekly,* all of which kept pace with the public's fascination with crime and all its seedy glory.

It was with the character of Perry Mason, though, that Gardner hit the jackpot. Mason was a defense attorney intent on proving his clients' innocence—through any means necessary. He was assisted by his devoted personal secretary, Della

Street, and his private investigator, Paul Drake. Together, the trio solved crime after crime, with Perry inevitably triumphing over hapless district attorney Hamilton Burger in the courtroom. Gardner took great pains to paint Mason as an honorable attorney who was earnest in his pursuit of justice yet not above bending the rules to prove his case. In all his *Perry Mason* stories and novels, he never once provided a physical description for Mason, leaving that up to the reader's imagination.

By the time Gardner's third *Perry Mason* novel, *The Case of the Curious Bride,* was published in 1934, Perry was making his first big-screen appearance in *The Case of the Howling Dog,* produced by Warner Bros. with Warren William starring as Perry and Helen Trenholme playing Della Street. That was followed in quick succession by *The Case of the Curious Bride, The Case of the Lucky Legs,* and *The Case of the Velvet Claws,* all starring Warren William as Perry. Warner Bros. produced two more Perry Mason features before calling it quits in 1937, with Ricardo Cortez playing Perry in *The Case of the Black Cat* and Donald Woods doing the honors in *The Case of the Stuttering Bishop.*

Gardner, who was initially pleased with the *Mason* movies, grew increasingly irate as Warner Bros. began tinkering with his tried-and-true formula. The studio pulled the ultimate blasphemy by having Perry propose to Della in one movie and then showing them as a married couple in *The Case of the Velvet Claws.* The married Gardner, who was rumored to have a wandering eye, was intent on keeping his fictional characters chaste (definitely a case of art *not* imitating life). Then, in *The Case of the Dangerous Dowager,* Perry suffered the ultimate indignity. He was written out altogether, and the movie was released as *Granny Get Your Gun*, a western starring May Robson. Gardner told friends he was through with Hollywood.

Yet while Gardner continued churning out *Perry Mason* novels, his intrepid defense attorney and his trusty companions Della and Paul made the transition to CBS, starring in a radio series that began in 1943. The franchise expanded into comic books and even a short-lived *Perry Mason* comic strip, which ran for two years (1950–52).

The fifteen-minute *Perry Mason* radio episodes aired daily on CBS. Over its twelve-year run, the *Perry Mason* radio series featured Bartlett Robinson, Santos Ortega, Donald Biggs, and John Larkin as the voices of Perry, and Gertrude Warner, Jan Miner, and Joan Alexander as Della. Gardner wrote many of the radio scripts for the first three seasons and provided original *Perry Mason* stories during the course of the series's run. Still, he griped about the show's quality and never thought fifteen minutes was enough time to tell his stories.

When the *Perry Mason* radio series ended, it morphed into the daytime television soap opera *The Edge of Night,* which used crime, rather than personal melodrama, as its thematic framework. Gardner was originally slated to create and write *The Edge of Night* but got into an argument with CBS and pulled out of the project. *Perry Mason* radio writer Irving Vendig took over and launched *The Edge of Night,* which ran on CBS and ABC for nearly thirty years.

All during *Perry Mason*'s radio run, Gardner resisted moving the series to the fledgling medium of television. After being burned by Warner Bros. on the *Perry Mason* movies, he was in no mood to deal with Hollywood again. He was so adamant about Perry Mason not moving to the small screen that in the early 1950s he turned down a $1 million network television offer. He was more content to hammer away at his typewriter churning out *Perry Mason* novels.

But Gardner's agent, Thomas "Cornwall" Jackson, thought differently. He talked Gardner into joining him and his wife, former actress Gail Patrick Jackson—known for her steely roles in *My Man Godfrey, Stage Door,* and *My Favorite Wife*—in a partnership. Together, they would capitalize on the popularity of *Perry Mason*. The trio formed Paisano Productions (named after Gardner's spread, Rancho del Paisano) and also hoped to develop several of Gardner's other characters for television, including Bertha Cool and Donald Lam, who were portrayed in a *Climax!* television special by Jane Darwell and Art Carney.

But while Paisano Productions had its fingers in other pies, its first priority was to turn *Perry Mason* into a television series, giving Gardner strict control over the show's content and direction. There would be no studio interference this time around.

For Raymond, the role of Perry was a dream job. Here was a character who fought for truth, justice, and the American way—with a pretty sidekick, to boot—and who was not some violent sleazeball. "Perry Mason has to be the equivalent of the knight on the white charger riding to rescue damsels in distress," Gardner wrote in a memo to Gail Jackson outlining the proposed television show. Perfect.

It didn't matter to Raymond that *Perry Mason* was a television job; at this point, he was so fed up with playing heavies and malcontents that he was willing to take a "step back" (as it was considered then) into the young and unpredictable

LEFT: Newborn Raymond William Stacy Burr, already a hefty bundle in mother Minerva's arms shortly after his arrival in May 1917. (*Photofest*)

BELOW: A cherubic Raymond, around six months old. (*Photofest*)

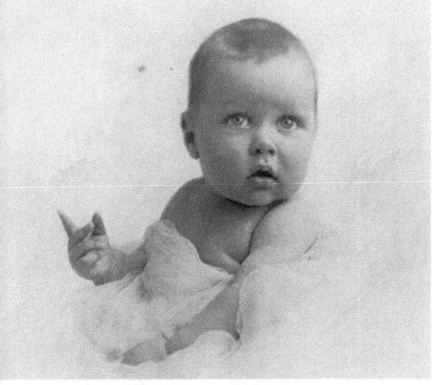

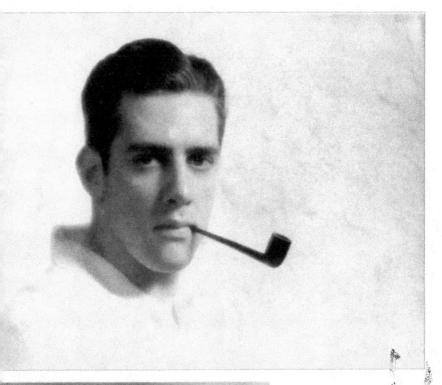

OPPOSITE: Raymond with his doting father, Bill Burr. (*Photofest*)

ABOVE: The young hopeful strikes a thoughtful pose. (*Photofest*)

LEFT: A high school photo of Isabella Ward, Raymond's first and only wife. (*Photofest*)

ABOVE: May 1948: Raymond and Isabella costarred in the Pasadena Playhouse production of *Gauguin*, written by Catherine Turney (right). Their marriage dissolved shortly thereafter. (*Huntington Library*)

OPPOSITE: Raymond took this publicity shot around the time he signed his RK◦ deal. "He has traveled around the world five times, lived in the Orient and has six years of education at three universities," gushed the studio's press machine◦ None of it was true. (*Photofest*)

THIS PAGE: Raymond Burr, Hollywood heavy
a familiar sight in B-movies and noir dramas
beginning in the late '40s.

OPPOSITE, TOP: Raymond's first credited role
was in the 1946 RKO potboiler *San Quentin*
starring Lawrence Tierney (center) and Joe
Devlin.

OPPOSITE, BOTTOM: Raymond's ample waistli
and sad, moonish eyes, on display here in
Desperate (1947), were reminiscent of his
hero, actor Laird Cregar. He and Cregar wer
often mistaken for brothers.

OPPOSITE: Menacing Lizabeth Scott in *Pitfall* (1948). (*Photofest*)

ABOVE: And . . . action! A rare shot of Raymond as the quintessential villain, cameras rolling.

LEFT: If Raymond's on-screen heavies weren't getting shot, beaten, or stabbed, there was always strangulation: *Abandoned* (1949).

OPPOSITE, TOP: Raymond was pegged as the bad guy even in a comedy like *Love Happy* (1949), starring an apple-biting Harpo Marx in one of his final screen appearances.

OPPOSITE, BOTTOM: A rare good-guy role (sort of): That's Raymond, far left, in *M*, in which he played a small-time hood who helps apprehend a child molester (David Wayne, grimacing) in a remake of the 1931 Peter Lorre classic.

ABOVE: In his most violent on-screen role, Raymond played pyromaniac mobster Rick Coyle in *Raw Deal* (1948), directed by Anthony Mann and costarring Dennis O'Keefe (left). (*Photofest*)

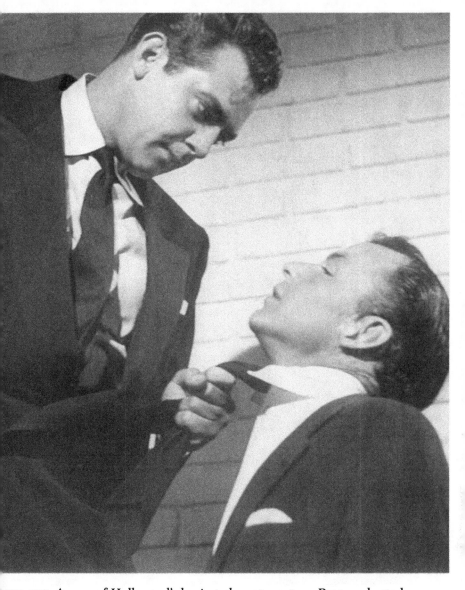

SITE, TOP: As one of Hollywood's busiest character actors, Raymond acted
;side a bevy of screen greats, including Clark Gable in *Key to the City* (1950).
ofest)

SITE, BOTTOM: *Stick 'em up*: Mobster Pete Ritchie menaces government
ts Johnny Macklin (Fred MacMurray) and Gladys LaRue (Claire Trevor)
rderline (1950).

E: Raymond claimed he lost the chance to act opposite Frank Sinatra in *From
 to Eternity* because he was traveling. He got his chance to harass Sinatra here
eet Danny Wilson (1952).

ABOVE: Dogged district attorney Frank Marlowe hectors murder suspect George Eastman (Montgomery Clift) in *A Place in the Sun*. Raymond garnered critical kudos for his role in the 1951 classic, directed by George Stevens. (*Photofest*)

OPPOSITE, TOP: As an RKO contract player, Raymond had to adapt to a variety of genres, including costume dramas like *Serpent of the Nile* (1953) with Rhonda Fleming (left).

OPPOSITE, BOTTOM: Raymond as evil town elder Stanley in *A Man Alone* (1955) opposite Lee Van Cleef (left) and Grandon Rhodes (right).

LEFT: Raymond as wife-killer Lars Thorwald in *R[...] Window* (1954), his best-known movie role. Direct[...] Alfred Hitchcock suppose[...] modeled Thorwald's phys[...] look on studio nemesis David O. Selznick.

BELOW: *Nice to meet you*: Thorwald throttles wheelchair-bound photographer L. B. Jeffer[...] (Jimmy Stewart) in the penultimate scene of *Rea[...] Window*.

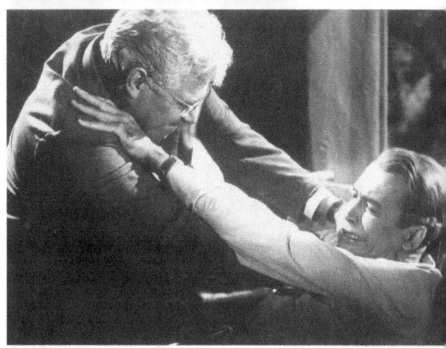

medium. And it wasn't like he hadn't already tried, and failed, to land a regular television job. He'd been turned down by CBS to star as Marshal Matt Dillon on the television version of *Gunsmoke* (James Arness won the role), and now he really had nothing to lose. If he didn't get the *Perry Mason* job, he still had his movie work; if he was hired, and the show succeeded, he could be seen by thirty to forty million people each week. That would also mean more scrutiny, of course—and more probing questions about the details of the tragic private life he had whipped up. But he would cross that bridge when he came to it.

Raymond, however, wasn't on the Paisano Productions radar. Gail Jackson had acted opposite Cary Grant and William Powell on the big screen and envisioned a tall, slim, handsome Perry as the crusading legal knight. Gardner, on the other hand, never once described Perry's physical attributes and relied on instinct. He would know Perry when he saw him.

Raymond was tipping the scales at nearly three hundred pounds while making *Fort Laramie*, and he knew that winning the *Perry Mason* job would be a daunting task. If he had any chance at all, he would have to go on one of his crash diets and slim down before taking the leap. Paisano had already tested over one hundred actors for the role, including Fred MacMurray, William Holden, Efrem Zimbalist Jr., William Hopper, Richard Egan, Mike Connors, and Richard Carlson. Raymond could not go into his audition a chubby mess. He had to look like a leading man.

By the time Lester Salkow talked the Jacksons and Gardner into testing his client for the show, Raymond had shed about thirty pounds on his cottage cheese, fruit, and cigarette diet. The weight loss sharpened his features; they were more chiseled now, which, in turn, exaggerated his big, penetrating blue eyes and sturdy frame. His booming voice complemented the package.

But the Jacksons and Gardner, recalling Raymond's portrayal of Frank Marlowe in *A Place in the Sun*, envisioned him in the Hamilton Burger role. By April 1956, Gardner assumed MacMurray had won the job and that the search for Perry was over. "Apparently Fred MacMurray is the person who will probably be selected" as Perry, he wrote in a memo to Gail Jackson. He was also completely unaware of just who Fred MacMurray *was*.

So the deck was stacked against Raymond winning the lead. He was disappointed, especially after shedding all the weight, but he agreed to audition for Burger with one stipulation: that he also be allowed to audition as Perry. "All right, we'll humor him," Jackson remembers telling her partners. "If he'll test for Burger, we'll test him for Mason, too."

The rest, as they say, is history. The stories, which were repeated ad nauseam after Raymond became famous, had several variations. In one, Gardner was in a projection room watching Raymond audition as Perry when he leaped to his feet and shouted, "That's Perry Mason!" In another, Gardner was walking through the studio while Raymond was auditioning and stood transfixed, watching the magical scene unfold. "In twenty minutes, you captured Perry Mason better than I did in twenty years," the author supposedly said to actor. In yet another scenario, Lester Salkow bribed the projectionist to screen Raymond's reading as Perry Mason first, before Gardner could watch him as Hamilton Burger.

Gardner explained his enthusiasm with typical terseness. "Burr had the authority," he said. "His other assets are obvious, but the thing I wanted most in my Perry Mason was authority."

Raymond had the job. He signed on for a three-year commitment, with an option for an additional two years—*if* the show lasted that long.

After the long search for Perry, casting the show's supporting players proved to be much easier for the Paisano Productions triumvirate.

For the role of Perry's loyal secretary, leggy Della Street, former RKO contract player Barbara Hale got the call. Hale already had something of a comfort level with Raymond, since they knew each other from their RKO days. She was also good friends with Gail Jackson, who designed and sold children's clothing in her Beverly Hills shop, Enchanted Cottage (catering to a large celebrity clientele). Hale had designed a doll she was hoping to sell in Enchanted Cottage, and while the project never came to fruition, she and Gail became close friends.

"She called and said, 'Barbara, I think you should be Della Street,' and I said, 'Gail, I just can't. I have my three babies. I'm happy. I can't take on a series," Hale recalled. "She said, 'We're only going to do eighteen,' and I said, 'Eighteen, huh?' And I talked to my husband, Bill, and decided eighteen shows, what the heck! That would be a nice thing to do."

For the role of the hapless Hamilton Burger, "the world's worst D.A.," the producers chose William Talman, a forty-one-year-old character actor (*One Minute to Zero, Two-Gun Lady*). Talman had a colorful past tinged with real tragedy, unlike the sob stories contrived by the star of his new show. The son of a wealthy industrialist, Talman attended Dartmouth College, where he was involved in a car crash that killed a friend. Talman, who was driving, swerved to avoid a truck and hit a tree. The car turned out to be stolen, and Talman served some time in jail before being booted from Dartmouth. He was eventually invited back a year later.

After college, Talman boxed as an amateur (a skill he honed while being picked on in school, he said) and embarked on a short-lived evangelical career before settling on acting (he also wrote and directed). Talman's boxing background would come in handy for Burger's weekly pummeling by Mason. Still, he was the perfect choice for the role. "Bill Talman is really a wonder," Gardner said. "He actually looks as if he expects to win a case."

Since his arrival in Hollywood, Raymond's biggest cheerleader in the press had been powerful Hearst gossip columnist Hedda Hopper, who wrote about Raymond frequently, and always in glowing terms. Hopper, who had no problem writing slyly about "confirmed bachelors," was extremely discreet when it came to Raymond's dalliances. It was Hedda who led the press pack in detailing Raymond's "romance" with Natalie Wood. He, in turn, reciprocated with insider gossip items.

If Hedda had some sort of payback in mind, she called in her chit when it came time for Gail Jackson to cast Paul Drake, the wolfish gumshoe who spent almost as much time leering at Della Street as helping Perry crack a case.

The role went to Hedda's son, William Hopper, whose father was acclaimed stage actor DeWolf Hopper. Hedda, twenty-seven years younger than DeWolf, was his fifth wife;

the couple divorced when William was seven, and mother and son moved to California. William chased an acting career but, unlike his father, did so halfheartedly. "I became an actor because it seemed the easiest thing to do and because it was expected of me," he said. "But it stunk." It's easy to imagine him as Paul Drake, delivering those lines in his deadpan style.

William Hopper loafed around Hollywood, snaring minor roles in a few forgettable movies, and after serving in World War II he chucked the acting business altogether. He detested trading on his mother's powerful name, much to Hedda's chagrin, and he sold cars for eight years before getting the acting bug again. This time around, he was more successful, landing a role opposite John Wayne in *The High and the Mighty* and appearing in *The Bad Seed*. Like Barbara Hale, William had a personal connection to Raymond. He'd played Natalie Wood's father in *Rebel Without a Cause*.

In casting the role of Hamilton Burger's favorite homicide detective, Arthur Tragg, the *Perry Mason* brain trust deviated a bit. In Gardner's novels, Tragg was described as "slender," "suave," and "sophisticated," with "wavy hair and thoughtful eyes"—quite a stretch from craggy Ray Collins, a veteran of Orson Welles's Mercury Theater who had appeared in *Citizen Kane*, *The Grapes of Wrath*, and *The Desperate Hours*, among other noteworthy roles. Casting Collins was a shrewd move; white-haired and sixty-seven when *Perry Mason* began, Collins became one of the show's most popular characters.

With the *Perry Mason* cast set, a pilot, *The Case of the Moth-Eaten Mink*, was filmed in October 1956. "We had a great time with it and it went very well and we felt pretty good about it," recalled the pilot's first assistant director, Art

Marks. "One of my best friends edited it, and he told me how good that pilot was. And of course CBS had been, for a long time, trying to get the Erle Stanley Gardner properties off the ground."

It was NBC, though, that first showed interest in the pilot once Gail Jackson began shopping it around Hollywood. But CBS made the big offer to Paisano: $500,000 for the series and half the profits. It also gave Gardner complete creative control—which was more important to him than the money—*and* the power to veto scripts.

The network set a budget of $100,000 per episode, a huge sum in those days and the highest per-episode budget in television at that time. Raymond demanded to be paid his entire per-season fee upfront, eschewing a potentially lucrative syndication deal. He considered the "glories" of syndication overrated, anyway. "The money aspect of it is often just a myth," he said. "After the tax bite, what've you got? A lot of taxable money."

Perry Mason would be filmed in black and white in and around Los Angeles as television's first one-hour crime drama. While Gardner never bothered to describe Perry's physical attributes in his books, he now became a stickler for detail regarding the show's legal overtones once it moved to television, and he hired a staff that was schooled in the letter of the law. Writer/producer Ben Brady had practiced law for ten years before entering show business, and story editor Gene Wang had a law degree. Producer Gail Jackson studied law at the University of Alabama with an eye toward becoming an attorney before she made the trip to Hollywood.

Raymond, meanwhile, continued to line up movie projects, blissfully unaware of the extent to which *Perry Mason* would come to dominate his life. He was, more likely, just hedging his bets in case the the show flopped. Publicly, he put on a brave face—"I'll be playing the role for a long, long time," he told reporters—but privately, he was concerned. Would viewers, so used to seeing him as a villain, accept him in his new incarnation as a legal do-gooder? He quickly signed on for a role in *The Long Haul*, which was scheduled to film in England with leads Diana Dors and Victor Mature, before plunging into the filming of *Perry Mason*.

The question of where CBS would put *Perry Mason* on its prime-time schedule was made easier by Jackie Gleason. Stung by the less-than-stellar reception of *The Honeymooners*, which had replaced *The Jackie Gleason Show* for the 1955–56 season, Gleason folded up his tent and skulked away after taking a Saturday-night ratings pounding from crooner Perry Como. (Ironically, those same episodes of *The Honeymooners* would later become one of the most beloved sitcoms in television history.)

With Gleason gone, CBS penciled in *Perry Mason* for an 8:00 p.m. Saturday time slot—where it would butt heads with Como, whose top-rated NBC show was still going strong after seven years on the air. That decision in itself raised eyebrows, since the province of most television dramas were the later time slots. *Perry Mason* at 8:00 p.m.? Unheard-of.

CBS made further waves when it landed a lucrative sponsorship deal with bleach manufacturer Purex, which offered to sponsor *Perry Mason* every other week . . . but only if it began a half hour earlier, at 7:30, in order to get a jump on *The*

Perry Como Show. "We hope to have viewers so intrigued by clues in the first half hour that they won't dream of touching that dial," Raymond said. CBS quickly agreed to the sponsorship deal.

ABC, meanwhile, was using the same 7:30 p.m. strategy against CBS—hoping their new James Garner western series, *Maverick*, could make a dent against *Perry Mason*. "Question is, can Mason jar Como?" Raymond joked to Hedda Hopper in April. "We can hope."

Raymond was ready to fill the void left by Jackie Gleason on the airwaves, but the weight department was another matter. With *Perry Mason* set to premiere in September, he worked hard to keep off the pounds he had shed for his audition. "He loved food and he loved wine," said close friend Art Marks. "And then he would go into the [sufferance] bit of trying to lose fifty or one hundred pounds. He did that a couple of times and he got very ill from it."

But unlike Gleason, who would check himself into the hospital to lose weight quickly, Raymond used self-restraint—and sheer willpower. "I've reformed," he said at the time. "No more candies, no more baked potatoes drowned in melted butter . . . just cottage cheese salad for a while." To keep everyone honest, Gail Jackson took matters into her own hands. "She brought a big scale and sat it by the front door of the set, and we would have to weigh in," the petite Barbara Hale remembered.

CBS, meanwhile, began laying the groundwork for the show's debut. Items were planted in all the major gossip columns, including those of Hedda Hopper, Sheila Graham, and Dorothy Kilgallen. "If the pilot is any criterion, this series will be one of the greatest," Hopper crowed in support of her son's new venture. Raymond joined Gardner in a promotional tour with stops in New York, Chicago, Washington, D.C., and Boston. "I'm enthusiastic about *Perry Mason* because great care is being taken with the stories," he said. "Erle Stanley Gardner has script approval, and there are six top writers and six good directors working on this series. I don't see how we can miss with that combination."

Gardner was an enthusiastic promoter and did most of the talking. But not everyone was sold on the idea. "If the series were opposing any program except *The Perry Como Show,* I'd have no hesitation about predicting high success for it," wrote *Washington Post* critic Lawrence Laurent. "Against Como? I just don't know."

While Raymond, Barbara Hale, William Hopper, and the rest of the cast shot the first season's worth of shows on Stage 8 at the Twentieth Century Fox lot, Gardner's latest *Perry Mason* serial, *The Proxy Murder,* was launched into national newspaper syndication. It was accompanied by a photo of Raymond hyping the show's September 21, 1957, premiere on CBS. A national magazine campaign was also launched, featuring one of Gardner's *Perry Mason* stories illustrated with likenesses of the television cast. "This was a year or six months before the show started," Hale said. "And on the *Perry Mason* books, the paperbacks, they changed the people to look like Raymond and me and Bill Hopper."

So after months of promotion, *Perry* was ready to battle Perry. *Perry Mason* premiered on Saturday, September 21, with "The Case of the Restless Redhead"—and was met with a resounding yawn. "In its translation to the TV medium the mystery series is faithful to the taut and compact Gardner style of presentation," Jack Gould wrote in the *New York Times*. "It also has an advantage in its hour-long format—the extra time does permit more attention to detail, particularly in the courtroom.

"But beyond that the premiere was not so long on distinction as to suggest serious competition for Mr. Como," Gould wrote. "Raymond Burr is playing Mr. Mason very straightforwardly. The lawyer-investigator, as a matter of fact, seemed a wholesome resident of suburbia on his way up the executive ladder. The volatile Mason of the printed page was not very evident."

"Mr. Burr [appears] to do his best acting in opening shots of the titles," huffed *TV Guide*. "[He] always seems . . . to have about as much color as a corporation executive on the way to, and slightly late for, the 4:12 club car from Grand Central."

Variety thought the show "was deftly handled, never far-fetched and unraveled with simple clarity."

"Simple clarity" became the hallmark of *Perry Mason* and was the one element, in particular, that led to the show's eventual success. Each episode, titled "The Case of . . . ," was predictable in its structure, but that was okay; the fun for the viewer lay in guessing who the *real* murderer was (since Mason's clients were always innocent). "The makeup of the show was very simple," said Art Marks. "There were five new characters that came into the show. Five suspects. And each suspect had to have equal time . . . so that they all stood out . . . so when eventually you got to the courtroom, they stuck in your mind."

The first fifteen minutes or so of each episode were spent setting up the murder. The victim's body was usually discovered slumped over a desk or lying dramatically on the floor and was always found after the fact (all *Perry Mason* corpses were remarkably free of bullet wounds, knife wounds, blood splatter, or gore).

In the world of *Perry Mason*, Detective Arthur Tragg, played with laconic élan by Ray Collins, worked in a remarkably small homicide division for a city the size of Los Angeles. It was always Tragg who inevitably materialized at the crime scene, and it was always Tragg who arrested the suspect—either at the crime scene or in Mason's office. He usually stopped to banter with Perry, Della, and sometimes Paul Drake before dragging the suspect downtown to the realm of DA Hamilton Burger.

The second half of each episode featured Perry, Della, and Paul (whose office was just down the hall from Perry's) piecing together the scenario—with Perry often going to questionable lengths to prove his client's innocence. "Lawyer Mason counts on the D.A.'s being stupid enough to miss catching him in misdemeanors," *Time* magazine sniffed. But they were right. One of the show's biggest unsolved mysteries was how Burger was ever elected in the first place.

The first-act murder and Perry's piecing together the facts culminated in the second act: *Perry Mason*'s trademark courtroom scenes. It was here that Perry pulled out his weekly bag of tricks to defeat frustrated DA Burger, using his machine-gun interrogation style and his laserlike stare to elicit a confession from the witness box (or from the guilty party, conveniently seated in the courtroom). Perry swooped in for the kill, verbally battering the witness, his voice rising in crescendo with each accusation. *"And you took that gun, didn't you?! And you shot him?! Didn't you?! DIDN'T YOU?!"*

That was the signal for the Big Confession, which was usually something along the lines of: "You're right, Mr. Mason. I did it. I killed (so-and-so)." Any plot points left dangling were then explained by Perry, Della, and Paul as they discussed the case in Perry's well-appointed office, always stocked with food and coffee, or as they hung out in a restaurant after Perry elicited his confession. The episode usually ended with a corny joke before the fadeout to Fred Steiner's jazzy *Perry Mason* theme (titled "Park Avenue Beat").

The *Perry Mason* shooting schedule was brutal. CBS had ordered thirty-nine episodes the first season, with each episode requiring six- to nine-day shoots. The cast and crew were working six-day weeks, with little to show for their efforts. Despite the prelaunch publicity, the numbers were static, and the show plodded along throughout the fall.

And then, like someone flicking a switch, something clicked: viewers began to take notice. "You could tell because we got so much [feedback] from the bridge clubs, the gals that had their charity work," Hale said. "They would all be talking about *Perry Mason* and who did what to whom in the story. And we were told about that."

There was also intrigue, at least on the part of viewers, about whether there was any romance between Perry and Della, who were together constantly and were always giving each other knowing looks. Perry, though, was always the perfect gentleman; the closest he came to touching Della was draping his jacket across her as she lay sleeping on his office couch in one episode.

Still, in Eisenhower-era America, when sex was only hinted at, their relationship was a subject often discussed among the show's fans.

"It was audience participation," Barbara Hale said. "See, the secretaries that wanted [there] to be something between Perry and Della were probably fooling around themselves, and the straitlaced young ladies and women who weren't [fooling around] just said, 'Oh, Della is a true-blue, good, hard worker.' But Raymond and I got great kicks out of trying to sneak looks and what have you."

By January 1958, *Perry Mason* was making serious headway, both in the ratings and against *The Perry Como Show*. *TV Guide* now weighed in with a ringing endorsement: "There's no reason why Mason shouldn't go on enjoying its popularity."

That was the good news. The bad news, at least in Raymond's purview, was the attention now focused on *him*—and the inquiries that began to arise about his personal life. After over ten years in Hollywood, Raymond Burr was becoming a household name as he neared his forty-first birthday. But the attention came with a steep price tag.

CHAPTER SIX

Howdy, Partner: A Little R&R

The number of magazine features and newspaper interviews focusing on Raymond's personal life grew as *Perry Mason* became more and more popular. The public was interested in this veteran actor who, save for what was portrayed in the media as his brief dalliance with Natalie Wood, had one of those faces everyone knew but couldn't quite match with a name.

That was all changing now. Certainly Raymond's face was familiar, but now the tragic tale of his dead wife and dead son assumed a life of its own. Once *Perry Mason* took off, the dead-wife-and-son story was repeated time and again. Raymond could have ended it all right then and there, blaming the mix-up on an overeager studio publicist or on his youthful showbiz naïveté. But he chose to continue perpetrating the fabrications by refusing to address them. He would answer the inevitable queries about his supposed marriages by reciting the facts of his brief union with Isabella Ward. If the questioning went any further in relation to Annette Sutherland or, God forbid, son Michael, he begged off with a terse "I don't discuss that." Reporters who were cowed by his presence followed his lead and quickly changed the subject. He repeated the "I don't discuss that" mantra so many times that writers eventually gave up asking him about it and relied on rehashing the story of his dead wife and son as fact.

"I know he was genuine in liking and disliking people; I don't think he hid that," recalled *Perry Mason* producer Art Marks. "But I just know he was putting on a show for the other things about wives and children. That was my gut feeling. I think the wives and the loving women, the Natalie Wood thing, were a bit of a cover."

Even Barbara Hale, one of Raymond's closest confidantes, had trouble piercing his protective armor. Or, if Raymond did confide in Barbara, he swore her to secrecy. According to Hale, "He had a great love for Barbara Stanwyck and for Natalie Wood . . . but he said, 'I was too old for [Wood], but oh, my gosh, Barbara.' And he said, 'My wife and little one, that was tragic,' but he said it was 'something I don't talk about that much.' And that's about as much as we talked about it."

Raymond's grueling *Perry Mason* shooting schedule would have made it difficult for him to have a romance with a member of *either* sex. So he used his long hours on the set as a convenient excuse whenever the subject of remarrying was raised. "I am an unmarried man, as opposed to a single man," he lectured one reporter in November 1957. "A bachelor, according to the dictionary, is a man who has never been married. An unmarried man is not married at the moment. Many of these terms have fallen into disuse."

Okay, the reporter, pressed, but there's no wife waiting for you when you return home from the studio?

"That is correct and it's a good thing because I'm working eighteen hours a day and sometimes don't come home from the studio at all," he answered. "I don't want to seem to avoid giving direct answers"—which is exactly what he was doing—

"but I've played attorneys so many times I'm getting to be a curbstone lawyer."

Raymond was sleeping at the studio, and doing so was now part of his weekday routine while shooting a *Perry Mason* episode. Because of his backbreaking work schedule, it was often easier to sleep on the lot instead of making the hour-long drive back to Malibu or arising at 2:30 a.m. to make the drive from Malibu to Sunset-Western Fox Studios so he could get there in time to learn his lines for that day's shooting. Barbara Hale went home to her husband and kids at the end of the day. That wasn't an option for the show's star, who carried an enormous workload on his broad shoulders.

Unlike his costars, Raymond was in nearly every *Perry Mason* scene, and he was often memorizing fourteen or more pages of dialogue each day. The courtroom scenes alone were killers. To make his hectic schedule a little easier, he would often sleep at the studio during the week and would rise around 3:30 in the morning to go over that day's script. His companion in these wee-hours script readings was often Paul Kennedy, a young actor who described himself, rather strangely, as being "at liberty" to work with Raymond as a dialogue director (whatever *that* meant). Raymond averaged around four hours of sleep a night. Six-day workweeks were common, and weekends off were rare. Such was the life of a television star.

As *Perry Mason* grew in popularity and CBS realized it had a hit on its hands, the network went to great lengths to appease its newest meal ticket. Raymond didn't sleep in just any old room at the studio; CBS furnished a three-room bungalow for him on the lot, complete with all the amenities.

The renovated space, which was originally built for Shirley Temple, included a full kitchen, a combination living room/ bedroom, a large dressing room with a cedar-lined walk-in closet, a modern bathroom, and a foyer used by his secretary, Bill Swann—an ex–concert singer and "a helluva good guy and rather fey in his way," according to Art Marks.

Midway through the first season of *Perry Mason,* CBS announced it was renewing the show. But Raymond was already beginning to sound the alarm. It had been a year since filming began on the first episode in April 1957. It was a period Raymond had devoted to working insane hours on a television show that not only put the reticent actor front and center, but kept him from entertaining the troops for the first time in years.

"Let's just say that the part isn't conducive to leisurely living the way I once knew it," Raymond said. "I only hope that I can regain my own identity, once I decide that Perry Mason and myself have come to the parting of the road.

"Perry Mason has become a career for me . . . all I know is that I work, eat and sleep Perry Mason. It's a lucky thing I'm not married now. No woman would understand my work schedule."

It's a good bet that *had* Raymond been married, his wife would have had a difficult time understanding his growing relationship with Robert Benevides, a young actor Raymond met on the set of *Perry Mason.* The handsome Benevides, thirteen years Raymond's junior, had a small role in the 1957 sci-fi flick *Monster That Challenged the World* (billed as Bob Benevedes) but was having trouble finding steady work. He and Raymond hit it off immediately, reportedly after Robert delivered a script to Raymond, and their attraction to each other grew. Before too long, Robert—"a nice fellow and very cordial all the time," said Art Marks—was running errands for Raymond.

"Benevides started hanging around the set with Raymond. I didn't know who he was at the beginning, but I thought he was a friend of Ray's, and I asked Bill Swann . . . whether Benevides was gay, and he said he didn't know," said Marks.

"But I know Ray liked [Benevides] and was supporting him in some things he wanted to do . . . Benevides was writing a script or something and Ray was in his corner, so to speak. He was like Ray's flunky. He would run errands, fly to Phoenix for him, pick something up and come back. Ray needed people like that, because he didn't have the time to do it."

Besides sharing the same initials, Robert and Raymond had somewhat similar backgrounds, geographically.

Robert was born in Visalia, California, in February 1930. After graduating from Exeter Union High School, he studied theater at the University of California, Berkeley, Raymond's old stomping grounds, and served in the army during the Korean War. Stationed in Japan, he spent two years as an army combat engineer and reentered UC Berkeley after his discharge from the service, graduating with a Bachelor of Arts degree in 1955. After knocking around Lake Tahoe, he hooked up with agent Sid Gold, who got him the job in *Monster That Challenged the World* and roles on television in *West Point, Navy Log,* and *Death Valley Days.*

Raymond and Robert were discreet in their relationship, and the *Perry Mason* cast was an extremely close and tight-knit group—ensuring that the relationship would stay insulated "within the family," even if no one was exactly sure if

Raymond and Robert were lovers. Even though Raymond's homosexuality was known within the industry, the scandal magazines of the time, including *Confidential*, hadn't been sniffing around. They had bigger fish to fry, including Raymond's *Horizons West* costar Rock Hudson, who was one of their favorite targets.

Future movie director Arthur Hiller was behind the camera for several early *Perry Mason* episodes. He was chatting with Raymond on the last day of filming one of those episodes when Raymond mentioned he wanted to renovate his house in Malibu but couldn't find a good contractor. Hiller, who was adding on a few bedrooms to his own house in West Hollywood, recommended the two men who'd been doing the work—one of them a huge Raymond Burr fan—and arranged for the men to drive out to Malibu on a Sunday.

"When the workers came to my house on Monday, I asked them how the meeting went on Sunday and they said 'fine,' but I could sense something was off-base," Hiller said. "They didn't have the enthusiasm that they had before, or which I expected. I kept at them, 'What's the matter?' Turned out they were going to do the work, but when they knocked and Raymond opened the door, he was wearing a pink bathrobe. And that put the one who just loved him away."

Raymond had been living a closeted life in Hollywood for over a decade without even the whiff of anything "untoward" about his lifestyle. Part of that had to do with his status as a supporting actor in the shadows, out of the spotlight's direct glare. Leading-man types—Cary Grant, Randolph Scott, and Errol Flynn among them—were grist for the rumor mill, but Raymond had always flown under the radar.

Until now.

His much-publicized relationship with Natalie Wood helped his straight-arrow image, and he was well liked among the major gossip columnists, especially Hedda Hopper. And with her sonny boy making a name for himself on *Perry Mason*, Hedda had extra incentive to ensure Raymond's name was kept away from "those" rumors. They could destroy a career. Hedda's devotion to Raymond is illustrated in a story told by one of his intimates. One of Raymond's male conquests wrote a letter to Hedda, threatening to expose the actor's secret. Hedda, in turn, wrote to Raymond to apprise him of the situation—and to tell him that his secret was safe. She would, she told him, "stand up and swear anything" for him.

For all intents and purposes, he was hiding in plain sight. In September 1954, Raymond attended the star-studded premiere of Judy Garland's *A Star Is Born* at the Pantages Theater in Hollywood. It was considered a huge event, even by Hollywood's jaded standards, and nearly every A-list celebrity was there.

Not only were there the usual newsreel cameras, but NBC also aired the gala red-carpet premiere live, for the first time ever. Jack Carson, who was featured in the movie, hosted the festivities, with emcee George Fisher asking questions of the two-hundred-plus stars in attendance. A crowd estimated at twenty thousand strong screamed, and flashbulbs popped as the stars, decked out in tuxedos and evening gowns, stepped up to the microphone to share a quick hello with Fisher.

Raymond, who was just back from another USO tour of Korea, followed Hedda Hopper up to the microphone as Fisher wiped his brow under the hot television lights. Fisher introduced Raymond, who was there with his date, USO cast-mate Evelyn Russell—and with a dark-haired, nervous-look-ing young man wearing a dark naval uniform, with a white sailor's cap angled jauntily on his head. Raymond introduced him to the television cameras as "Frank Vitti, a boy that's with us tonight right back from Korea." No one asked why young Mr. Vitti was attending a Hollywood movie premiere with two virtual strangers he seemed to have just met minutes before.

Three months later, the "Film Events" column in the *Los Angeles Times* had a few paragraphs about Raymond's upcom-ing visit to the Sixth Army Area in the western States. Once again, he was joined by Evelyn Russell, Bungy Hedley, Para-mount's Donna Percy, and Frances Lansing—and Frank Vitti. Frank's name would pop up every now and again in magazine stories about Raymond throughout the next several years. He was described in magazine features as "Burr's nephew," who was living with Raymond in the Malibu house (where, appar-ently, he had his own bedroom). Later, he became the curator of Raymond's Beverly Hills art gallery.

The mainstream press, though, respected Raymond's pri-vacy, even as *Perry Mason* took off and he became a household name. The few interviews Raymond did grant after 1957 fo-cused on the show and on his burdensome workload. Several publications sent reporters to spend a day on the *Perry Mason* set, their stories complemented with the obligatory timeline illustrating Raymond's horrendous work hours. If a publica-tion did delve into his personal life, it was a "Raymond Burr at home"–type feature highlighting the petting zoo at his Malibu ranch or the gourmet meals he cooked for close friends. He was, of course, always "too busy" to date anyone steadily.

"It's true that I could like to be married and after this series is over, perhaps I can take time to find someone," he told *Screenland* magazine in a 1959 article titled "No Time for Marriage." The article contained one of Raymond's longest published discourses on the subject of matrimony.

"So far I haven't met anyone and with an average fifteen-hour workday schedule, I hardly think it's probable . . . For the sake of my making my point, however, let's stretch our imagination and believe that the damn girl does exist," he said. "When would we go through the period of courtship, which is very important to a woman, especially—and to marriage? And when would we have time to get the marriage license?

"Seriously—quite seriously—I firmly believe that marriage is to be enjoyed and shared," he said. "Now I have a beautiful home at Malibu beach, but I'm lucky if I get to be in it over a weekend. So if I had a wife, I'd probably only get to see her over a weekend—unless of course she moved in here with me."

Raymond's talk of marriage was a smokescreen, but there was no denying the enormity of his *Perry Mason* workload and the effect it was having on his life. He wasn't the only television star carrying a show on his shoulders, but with *Perry Mason*'s one-hour format and its signature courtroom scenes, he *was* on camera for a staggering 90 percent of each episode. And the *Perry Mason* cast and crew were shooting thirty-nine episodes per season in the early years—seventeen more episodes than today's standard one-hour television drama.

These work demands made outside employment nearly impossible, and while Raymond talked of movie projects, the show took over his life. *Affair in Havana*, the last movie he made before shooting the *Perry Mason* pilot, opened in October 1957, and he was making plans for phantom movies that never materialized. One project for which he had high hopes was Robert Blees's book *Naked Is the Flesh*. Raymond and agent Lester Salkow bought the rights to Blees's book with plans for turning it into a movie, which Raymond envisioned would be shot in Italy. The project died a quick death.

It would be three years before Raymond had the time or energy to act in another movie. He didn't entirely abandon stage work, though. In November 1959, he appeared with *Perry Mason* castmates Barbara Hale and William Hopper in a benefit performance of *The Happiest Millionaire* at the San Gabriel Mission Playhouse in Alhambra.

By the end of its second season, *Perry Mason* was firmly entrenched in the public *zeitgeist*. It was averaging thirty million viewers a week and had cracked the Nielsen top twenty—which was ominous news for *The Perry Como Show*. By February 1959, Como was talking about leaving his Saturday-night perch to replace Milton Berle as the host of *Kraft Music Hall*, which aired Wednesday nights. He made the move in September.

Perry Mason's popularity expanded into other areas. Gardner continued to crank out his *Perry Mason* books, but the television franchise took on a life of its own. There were *Perry Mason* lunchboxes and board games. Sponsors began lining up to buy time on the show, and Raymond, in one instance, complained about the abundance of on-camera smoking when a cigarette company bought a chunk of time. Lawyers' groups began inviting Raymond to speak at their meetings, and he surprisingly accepted many of their invitations. That added weekend travel, often out of town, to his already-grueling schedule.

"He made a lot of speeches, and he became an officer of the Freedom Foundation in Washington and would travel there occasionally," said Art Marks. "He was very involved with law enforcement with the Los Angeles Sheriff's Department. He was very much into who he was as a character. Bar associations gave him all kinds of awards . . . and he spoke to them, whether it be in Kansas or Texas. He would fly in for one night and fly back and be shooting the next morning. I said, 'Ray, why do you put yourself through these things?' and he said, 'Because it's such a relief to get away. And I love it.' And he did enjoy it."

The *Perry Mason* cast grew extremely close and was known as one of the tightest-knit ensemble groups in the business. Raymond, Barbara Hale, William Talman, Ray Collins, and William Hopper all hung their personalized coffee mugs on a shared rack near the back of the set. Practical jokes abounded; sadness and joy were shared among cast and crew. "We saw children grow up and marriages and divorces," Hale said. "It was just amazing. We became very good friends. It was an extended family."

Raymond hosted dinners for the cast and crew out in Malibu, featuring sumptuous spreads of the best food and wine. An invitation to a Raymond Burr dinner party was a sought-after commodity, with the host whipping up dishes in his huge kitchen. A writer who was invited to one of Raymond's dinner parties described his host as "sitting at the head of the huge table like some lustily benevolent medieval squire, tossing his head with raucous laughter at some guest's joke."

Jokes, too, were used on the set to ease the tension and the long, boring hours. *Perry Mason* was, in essence, an hour-long movie being filmed each week. Tempers flared often, and Raymond used practical jokes to lighten the mood and to fend off the stifling boredom between shots. More often than not, he was the jokes' instigator. And more often than not, Barbara Hale was his target.

The stories are legion: Raymond putting a baby alligator in a drawer on the set, awaiting Barbara's inevitable shriek; Raymond filling Barbara's entire dressing room and bathroom, floor to ceiling, with flowers; Raymond enlarging one of Barbara's old studio beefcake shots showing her in a leopard-print bikini and placing it behind the judge's chair; Raymond camouflaging Barbara's car under some lumber; Raymond filling Barbara's commode with green Jell-O. And on and on.

"It went on for weeks. He just never stopped playing gags," Hale said. "He once took everything out of my dressing room. He had a truck come and get it. It went on for two weeks [and] then I said, 'Raymond, this is enough. You get those things back to me or I am going to get a real lawyer.' And he said, 'Nobody beats Perry Mason!' Anyway, he brought it back, and they called me from the set and a moving van was at the gate. He had given me the bill."

The closeness wasn't limited to the *Perry Mason* costars. Raymond treated everyone on the set as family. The stories about his practical jokes were matched only by the stories of his acts of kindness and benevolence. When he heard that veteran character actor George Stone was ill—nearly blind and unable to find steady work—Raymond, who didn't know Stone, hired him as the *Perry Mason* court clerk. The role required nothing more of Stone than to sit in a chair at a desk and look busy.

When *Perry Mason* makeup man Irving Pringle collapsed on the set from a hemorrhaging ulcer, Raymond "took him to the hospital, checked him in and was up all night with him," according to Gail Patrick Jackson. When he heard from his secretary Bill Swann that a little girl in Massachusetts, who'd been horribly burned, preferred an autographed photo of her hero Perry Mason to a letter from President Eisenhower, he flew to the hospital to visit her. He was furious when photographers showed up to document the occasion and refused to let his picture be taken.

"There were no secrets about the show. We were an open book," said Art Marks. "There were no actor problems, really. There was no animosity between one actor, one director, or any of that kind of crap. First of all, we wouldn't allow it. If an actor was a problem, that actor was written off, or told off, or corrected. And Ray was the first to say, 'I don't want any of that around. I want a family.'"

Raymond lent money to anyone who asked, grew close to Barbara Hale's children (including future costar William Katt), and contributed generously to charitable causes. He threw lavish dinner parties for friends, sponsored foster children from Korea and Italy, and puttered around the house in Malibu on his days off, tending to his menagerie.

And, along the way, he invented another wife.

CHAPTER SEVEN

A Confidential Matter

This time Raymond named his wife Laura Andrina Morgan (or Morga, in some accounts), and she started to appear in his tragic personal history around 1959. The story, always told in hushed whispers, was that Raymond married Laura in 1955 (or 1953). She died shortly thereafter, losing her brave battle with cancer just before the couple's planned honeymoon in the Bahamas. "I worked with Ray through much of 1955. I never heard him mention a wife, either one who was ill or one who had recently passed away," a friend told *Inside TV* magazine. "And I think he would have mentioned it."

Had anyone bothered to check Raymond's story, they would have realized that the timeline made no sense at all. If Raymond married Laura in 1955, that would mean the courtship began shortly after the death of his "son," Michael Evan—*and* during a time when Raymond was spending well-documented months in Korea entertaining the troops. If he married Laura in 1955, it would mean he was married while he was wooing Natalie Wood. And if he married Laura in 1953, as some articles claimed, Michael would still have been alive.

Current Biography, and that bastion of reliability *Life* magazine, even went one step further, listing the marriage date as 1950—and *that* would have meant that Raymond was a bigamist, having wedded Laura while he was still legally married to Isabella Ward, who wasn't granted a divorce until 1952. And by 1950, Raymond was firmly established as a supporting player in the movies. Surely there would have been a published account of his new bride *somewhere*. There wasn't. "Please, we don't talk about that" was his familiar refrain to the *Life* reporter when he was asked about the chronology of his private life.

He did, apparently, discuss Laura Andrina Morgan with his costars. "He said, 'I married that young lady because she was dying, and I knew it,'" Barbara Hale recalled. "He said, 'She just wanted to be married, and I did it for that reason.'"

For those keeping score at home, Raymond had racked up an impressive laundry list of personal misery in the years between 1943 and 1955: two dead wives, a dead son, one ex-wife, and a star-crossed romance with Natalie Wood that was destroyed by powerful studio chiefs. He was nothing if not unlucky.

As the lies about his personal life increased, Raymond immersed himself in work. *Perry Mason* occupied nearly every waking hour of his day, six days a week, nine months out of every year. By the beginning of the show's breakthrough second season, even Raymond, with his bull-like strength and powers of concentration, was feeling the strain. He still slept at the studio and still rose at 3:30 a.m. every day to fire up a pot of coffee and go over that day's script. But into his life on the *Perry Mason* set entered a new love, otherwise known as the actor's best friend: the TelePrompTer.

The device had been around since the early 1950s and was designed specifically for television actors, performing live, who were forced to learn large amounts of dialogue in a short time. If they stumbled, they had a fallback. Popularized by *I Love Lucy* star Lucille Ball (the show's producer, Jess Oppenheimer, held the patent on the machine), the TelePrompTer, in its rudimentary form, was simple: the machine, which was placed out of the picture frame, scrolled a piece of paper on which dialogue was printed. If the TelePrompTer was placed properly in the actors' sight lines, they could appear to be looking at each other—while actually glancing at the words scrolling over the shoulder of their costar(s).

Raymond quickly mastered the TelePrompTer and grew increasingly reliant on its mystical powers. The TelePrompTer proved especially valuable during the courtroom scenes, in which Perry delivered verbose soliloquies crammed with technical jargon.

"The TelePrompTer took the curse off hours and hours [of memorizing dialogue]," says Marks. "Raymond was probably the best actor I've ever worked with using a TelePrompTer, because, in most cases, the actor's eyes do focus in and . . . they are really playing to the prompter. So they have a dead feeling in their eyes. Ray never lost it."

Raymond's reliance on the TelePrompTer could be off-putting to the other actors, including Fay Wray, who guest starred on a 1958 episode of *Perry Mason*. "He always read his material on camera and that was dismaying to me," she said. "I couldn't understand how anyone could depend on reading rather than memorizing. He had so much to do, perhaps you can't really blame him."

Three TelePrompTers were placed strategically around the *Perry Mason* courtroom set, allowing Raymond a clear view no matter where he turned. The machine came in especially handy when the intrepid attorney used his laserlike stare to bore into his prey on the witness stand. Raymond was so proficient at using the TelePrompTer that he made Perry's rat-a-tat, hectoring style seem natural while he was really reading his lines off a machine. This doesn't mean Raymond was growing lazy—on the contrary, he still memorized a good chunk of each week's *Perry Mason* script, and he used the TelePrompTer more as an aid than a substitute, once the cameras began rolling in the courtroom.

By the end of the 1958–59 season, *Perry Mason*'s audience had grown to forty million viewers each week, and the series leapfrogged into the Nielsen top ten.

Not all the critics were enamored of the show. "At least a half-dozen characters . . . are so suspicious that we don't trust them even after [Perry] has told us at the end that they didn't do it," sniffed *TV Guide*'s Cleveland Amory. "And the suspicious characters are made so saintly that even after we've been told which one of them has done it, we can't believe it." But there was no doubt the show was a smashing success.

The Television Academy took notice of *Perry Mason,* and in early 1959, Raymond and Barbara Hale received their first Emmy Award nominations. In May, they walked off with Emmys, Raymond for Best Lead in a Dramatic Series and Barbara for Best Supporting Actress.

The show seemingly could do no wrong. The strongest complaints about *Perry Mason* emanated not from television critics, but from the legal community. Some attorneys went public with their dissatisfaction about Perry winning every one of his cases, while others questioned the legitimacy of an actor like Raymond addressing legal groups. In one of the more drastic moves, Superior Court Judge Frank Armstrong protested Raymond's speech to the North Carolina Bar Association, refusing to attend. "Perry Mason's program bears no semblance of the correct and proper means of administering justice, or the proper conduct of the lawyer in trial of a criminal case," he huffed.

Another common complaint was that Perry never lost a case, and Raymond, Gardner, and Gail Jackson were vociferous in defending Perry's spotless courtroom record and his sometimes dodgy legal ethics. Their defense often took on philosophical overtones, rather than simply explaining that Perry was a *fictional* character. And did anyone *really* think there could be a DA as incompetent as Hamilton Burger? Maybe, as Raymond joked, Burger won all of his cases during the week—losing only on Saturdays.

"Basically, Perry Mason is a symbol of human morality and responsibility," Jackson said. "He's a contemporary hero in the classic sense, and this kind of hero must never lose. If he does, both he and one of life's great philosophies—that good eventually triumphs over evil—are destroyed."

Those were pretty heavy words for a fictional television character, but Raymond echoed her sentiments.

"He always defends innocent men. He is always ethical," he said. "Please remember that we have put in special scenes in which the District Attorney says that winning or losing a case is not important. What is important is to see that justice is done."

With *Perry Mason* providing him financial stability, Raymond pursued other interests outside of the show. He established a flower business, which he named Sea God Nursery, that enabled him to import exotic flora to his Malibu ranch. At the ranch he began developing orchids and pursued his lifelong passion for cross-pollinating different strains of the delicate flower (blue was his favorite color). "He raised a lot of weird stuff," recalled partner Robert Benevides. "To import a lot of this stuff he needed a license, so he got a license for Sea God Nursery." Raymond and Robert eventually created over two thousand orchid hybrids, registering two hundred of these in the American orchid hybrid catalogue.

Raymond also went into the art business, buying into the Hilda Swarthe Gallery on Santa Monica Boulevard in Beverly Hills and further etching his image as a sophisticated bon vivant. The gallery, which he eventually renamed the Raymond Burr Gallery, was managed by his furtive "nephew" Frank Vitti—the jittery sailor Raymond introduced at the 1954 premiere of *A Star Is Born*.

"I've always been interested in art; there's nothing unusual in this," Raymond said. "But I've been fortunate enough to be able to do more than visit galleries. I've enjoyed collecting works of art, and I find enormous enjoyment in this first step I've taken that lets me be a participant in art by presenting the work of painters who deserve the attention of the public."

The gallery exhibited an eclectic "cross section of the works of contemporary American and European artists," including Sheldon "Shelley" Schoneberg, Richard Kozlow, Natalie Krol, and Luis Somoza. Raymond wasn't at the gallery very often— his work schedule precluded too much involvement—and Vitti ran the day-to-day operations. Fred Astaire's daughter Ava, a painter, worked there for a while.

"It was very large and dignified. People really came there and bought," recalled Shoneberg, whose works Raymond featured often in the gallery. "It was exclusive, which I liked a lot, and he had a very special relationship to the community in Beverly Hills and Los Angeles. And people liked him, as far as I could tell. He was used to having his own way and that was fine."

"He did not pretend to draw or paint or do anything in the arts except act," said Robert Benevides. "But he certainly loved it all."

But if Raymond had his own way on the public stage, privately it was another matter. He was fiercely protective of his private life, and by now the lies he'd told over the years were repeated so often that he could have done nothing to correct them. The "confirmed bachelor" still griped about his long hours prohibiting a relationship while he conveniently ignored how other ostensibly straight male actors, working just as hard as Raymond, found time to step out on the town with a lovely lady or two. To the general public, the hulking *Perry Mason* actor was still dealing with the tragedy of two dead wives and a dead son; to those "in the know," he was hiding in broad daylight.

"It was an open secret . . . that he was gay," says Bob Thomas, who covered the Hollywood scene for the Associated Press. "He had a companion who was with him all the time. That was a time in Hollywood history when homosexuality was not countenanced. Ray was not a romantic star by any means, but he was a very popular figure . . . if it was revealed at that time in Hollywood history [that he was gay] it would have been very difficult for him to continue."

In the early 1960s, Robert's name began appearing in articles written about Raymond. He was always described as Raymond's "business manager" and/or close friend, although the amount of time they spent together spoke volumes about the true nature of their relationship. They shared their life and their love of flowers; in Raymond, Robert had found his soul mate.

"I was an actor, I did a lot of television plays. The last thing I did was in 1963 on stage in Hollywood. It was a play called *Seidman and Son,*" Robert said. "That was when I decided that I no longer wanted to do that. I came home one day to talk to Raymond (we had been together about three years) and I saw how easy it was for him and how much he enjoyed being in front of the camera, but it was so difficult for me. It was just agony.

"He said, 'Well, you don't have to do that anymore.' I'd never thought of that, and it was such a load lifted off my shoulders. Raymond told me, 'You've been doing production stuff for me already. You've been working on my scripts, you've been doing it all, why don't you just go into the production side?'"

It was as easy as that. Raymond set Robert up as a producer, and together they founded Harbour Productions in Universal City as a vehicle to develop projects for Raymond and for others. But just when everything was going smoothly, *Confidential* magazine came sniffing around, threatening to blow the lid off Raymond's secret gay life thanks to a talkative drag queen named Libby Reynolds.

The scurrilous scandal magazine was loathed (and devoured) by Hollywood glitterati and housewives alike. "Everyone reads it but they say the cook brought it into the house," Humphrey

Bogart said, only half-jokingly. By the time it grabbed Raymond in its tentacles, *Confidential* was wobbling, thanks in large part to actress Maureen O'Hara. She brought the magazine to its knees in 1957 with a damaging lawsuit after it ran a typically sensational story detailing her alleged Hollywood sex romp with a Latin lover in the balcony of Grauman's Chinese Theater. O'Hara's subsequent courtroom victory and multi-million-dollar settlement left *Confidential* reeling. But it was still capable of delivering the occasional knockout blow.

In the middle of 1960, Raymond flew from Los Angeles to New York to visit a burn victim who wanted to meet his hero, legal eagle Perry Mason. In typical fashion, Raymond refused to publicize the goodwill mission, preferring, as usual, to visit the sick boy in anonymity.

It's anyone's guess how one of the biggest stars in television figured he would *remain* anonymous in the world's biggest city. But Raymond, who was always so careful, was hell-bent on throwing caution to the wind this time. After arriving in Manhattan he checked into the Plaza Hotel, then sauntered down to Greenwich Village, where he'd made his home during his first stints on Broadway nearly twenty years before. He eventually landed in the Main Street Lounge, where he sat down and ordered a rye and water. Ray Reynolds was tending bar that night, filling drinks and making small talk with his customers to earn money for his other job—as female impersonator Libby Reynolds.

"My back was toward him at the [cash] register, but I knew exactly who it was when I heard his voice," recalled Reynolds, who was wearing everyday street clothes when Raymond entered the bar. "He was very friendly."

Raymond hung around and had a few drinks. Reynolds, along with another bartender and a few other staffers, were closing up for the night when Raymond approached them. "He wanted to know if we would like to go to breakfast, and if we knew of any places to go," Reynolds said. "I said, 'I think I'll take you to Mulberry Street.' It was after four o'clock in the morning, but you could eat there. It was strictly all Mafia. And [Raymond] was thrilled about the idea of going there.

"There were about four or five of us, and we piled into a cab and went down there, and naturally when we got there they treated us like royalty. In fact, they took us on a tour of the kitchen, just me and [Raymond]. Because he loved food. He was a complete food addict."

The group chatted away and ate their breakfast. When it was over, everyone went their separate ways—except for Raymond and Ray/Libby.

"He drove me to where I was staying with this other kid, Joey Tone, who was up in the Catskill Mountains working in what they called the 'Italian Alps,'" Libby said. "I mentioned a nightcap, and he had the cab wait for us. So we went up to the room and had a drink, and he just grabbed me and kissed me and shocked the shit out of me, you know? And then he said, 'Well, you are the first boy I ever kissed,' and I wanted to burst out laughing. How cornball can a movie star be, giving me that fucking line? So I just laughed it off and he said, 'Well, okay,' and I took him down to his cab."

As they got off the elevator, they ran into Libby's roommate, Joey, who was returning early from the Catskills. "We introduced each other, and I sent [Raymond] off to the cab and he went back up to the Plaza," said Libby. "Joey and I went upstairs, had a couple of drinks, and decided to go to sleep. No sooner had we put the lights out and bang—Burr calls. He said he couldn't sleep. Would I come up to the Plaza? he wanted to know. Oh, and he said not to worry about anything."

Libby got out of bed, got dressed, and took a cab up to the Plaza. "Sure enough, the doorman took care of everything, and I went up to the room," he said. "We talked for a while, and then we went to bed. He was very laid-back and didn't make any advances or anything—he just laid there . . . just like a piece of dough. No grunting, groaning, nothing. I don't know how to put it. It was like I wasn't even there. So I got on top of him and we did our little thing."

Libby spent the night. Raymond was scheduled for a flight the next morning and asked Libby to accompany him to the airport. "I was helping him pack his bags while he showered, and then I showered," Libby said. "His sponsor at the time was Parliament cigarettes, and he had about four or five cartons of Parliaments and he gave me a carton. On the way to the airport he gave me the phone number of a family member, a cousin or something, who lived in Wisconsin, and asked me to call them to let them know he would be late. We went for coffee and sweet rolls at the airport, and all the people were screaming, 'Perry! Perry!'"

And that was that . . . or so Raymond thought. Libby, who was struggling to establish himself as a female impersonator and needed money, sold the story of his tryst with Raymond to *Confidential*. There was a bit of irony involved in all of this; in the 1950 movie *Unmasked*, Raymond played the murderous publisher of a scandal rag not unlike *Confidential*.

The April 1961 cover of *Confidential* boasted a composite photo of Raymond and Libby—the actor glancing furtively at the drag queen—over the headline "TV's Perry Mason Gets Fooled: The Case of the Miss Who Was a Mister-Y."

The accompanying three-page article, though, told a different story. "The 'lawyer' who never lost a case lost his heart to a 'girl' who wasn't one," it blared. The ensuing narrative erased any hints of Raymond's tryst, at least from a homosexual angle.

In *Confidential*'s version of that evening in the Main Street Lounge, bartender Ray Reynolds introduced Raymond to a "cute barmaid," disappeared for about ten minutes, and reappeared in full drag as Libby Reynolds. After all, as he supposedly told *Confidential*, "If I can put on a performance that would fool a star, then my act is good. If not I'll need more polishing up." Raymond, though, didn't hit if off with the barmaid, but he *was* quite taken with Libby. He and Libby, along with the others, left for that breakfast on Mulberry Street. And, according to the Libby's *Confidential* account, Raymond still never realized that "she" was a "he."

In the magazine's sanitized version, Raymond kissed Libby up in the apartment then and again in the lobby of the Plaza: "Suddenly Libby broke away and ran out, jumping into a cab two steps ahead of the passion-bent Mr. Burr."

Libby, who was now dressed again as Ray, wanted to confess to Raymond that "the woman Burr had apparently fallen in love with and had pained and pined over was really a man dressed as a girl," but he couldn't get the Plaza operator to rouse Raymond out of his deep sleep. So, according to the *Confidential* version of events, he called Raymond the next morning and told him that Libby was unavailable for break-fast—but that she was sending Ray over to make amends for the previous night.

The rest of the story—the packing, the trip to the airport, even the phone call to Wisconsin—remained unchanged. The real part of the story, Raymond's one-night stand with Ray Reynolds, was completely omitted.

Raymond had dodged a potentially career-ending bullet.

It's not clear why *Confidential* changed the story. In all probability the magazine's editors contacted Raymond and told him what they had, and both parties reached a cash compromise.

"It was a total fucking lie," Reynolds said, still steaming about the story "revisions" forty-five years later. "I would imagine that *Confidential* got in touch with him and gave him the whole layout of what I had told them, and to avoid anything further, they came to an agreement where they would sort of 'pretty it up' to the drag queen thing. They changed the story."

Reynolds said that after the story ran in *Confidential*, he was contacted by other female impersonators who told him similar stories of being approached by Raymond. "I knew about four or five people that had run into him," he said. "He was obviously a closet queen. I guess back then you had to be [in the closet]. I'm surprised he never did come out. I guess he just had that phobia."

The incident, however, didn't go unnoticed by the American Bar Association (ABA). In the wake of his *Perry Mason* success, Raymond frequently spoke at ABA conventions and other functions. After the *Confidential* article appeared, several prominent ABA members sent letters to Whitney North Seymour, the organization's outgoing president, urging him to refrain from using Raymond as a speaker because, as one letter stated, "Unfortunately this actor is a noted sex deviate." The letters to Seymour were, in turn, forwarded to the FBI—catching the attention of director J. Edgar Hoover, who kept copious top-secret files, brimming with incriminating information, on hundreds of celebrities. He now opened a file on Raymond.

Hoover used his files as leverage if he needed a favor in Hollywood; more likely, he used them for his own form of emotional blackmail. "The Director," as everyone called him, was a feared and powerful figure who, if the gossip was to be believed, had plenty of skeletons in his own closet. There were whispers about his personal life, particularly about his relationship with his longtime companion Clyde Tolson, the bureau's number-two man. Tolson never left Hoover's side, and they ate lunch and dinner together nearly every day. Long after Hoover's death in 1972, stories about his alleged cross-dressing lifestyle were still circulating but never proven.

Hoover, surprisingly, had never opened a file on Raymond until the Libby Reynolds story ran in *Confidential*. The director vetted anyone and everyone who had anything to do with his beloved bureau. And that included show-business personalities associated with FBI-related projects (movies, radio series, television shows). Raymond's costarring role as a hood in the 1951 movie *FBI Girl* didn't trip any alarms, but the *Confidential* story took care of that.

On November 14, 1961, the FBI's H. L. Edwards sent a memo to his superior, a Mr. Malone, regarding the letters from alarmed ABA members to Whitney North Seymour vis-à-vis "sex deviate" Raymond Burr. The memo rehashed the *Confidential* article and ultimately dismissed it out of hand. "Bureau does not support this allegation," Edwards wrote. "I do not feel the Bureau should ask Los Angeles to try through confidential sources to get information on Burr. Burr has been very popular at ABA meetings because he is a drawing card although some elements in ABA resent him since he is not a lawyer and because Perry Mason's show always portrays defendant winning."

Edwards attached an addendum a week later on November 21, saying he had spoken to one of the men (not identified) who had sent a letter to the ABA complaining about Raymond's affiliation with the organization in the wake of the *Confidential* article. Edwards's words shed some light on how Raymond reacted to the *Confidential* story when it was first published.

"He said that he had talked with Raymond Burr about the *Confidential* article and had asked Burr why he didn't sue *Confidential*. Burr said that he had presented the matter to his lawyers and his lawyers, after thinking the thing over and considering it from all angles, advised Burr against suing because they felt that it would do more harm than good. It would create a lot of adverse publicity and they felt that the nature of *Confidential* magazine would place Burr pretty much in the position of being in a 'contest with a skunk' and that he could only come out second best anyway."

But the allegations spurred by the *Confidential* article refused to die, at least in the eyes of the FBI. Several months later, in February 1962, an internal FBI memo was sent to bureau bigwig Cartha "Deke" DeLoach. Raymond was scheduled to narrate the television and radio coverage of a Freedom Foundation presentation to Hoover; when the obligatory background check turned up the Libby Reynolds saga, nervous field agent M. A. Jones sent DeLoach a memo.

"The April, 1961, issue of *Confidential* magazine relates an incident at Greenwich Village bar in which Burr, who is unmarried, made a date with a man dressed as a woman, thinking the person was a woman," Jones wrote. "The female impersonator allegedly committed hoax as practical joke and Burr did not discover the impersonation. ABA member reported matter to Bureau because of complaint, apparently based on this article, that Burr was a 'noted sex deviate.'"

The memo, which was filled out with some of Raymond's biographical data, exonerated him of any wrongdoing (or at least as that was defined by Hoover's FBI). But just for kicks, Field Agent Jones threw in the fact that "the 1948 report of California Senate Fact-Finding Committee of Un-American Activities listed Burr as endorser of the American Youth Congress, which has been cited by Attorney General as communist." If Hoover couldn't get Raymond on the allegations of cross-dressing, there was always the reliable "he's a communist!" approach.

DeLoach copied the memo to Tolson with a scribbled, "Suggest no objection."

"Objection." "Object." They were words Raymond said so often in each *Perry Mason* episode that he was beginning to despise them. Obviously, these were words that were necessary for a courtroom drama, and Raymond never, well, *objected* to uttering them. But with increasing regularity, and more to keep himself amused than anything else, he began experimenting with different ways to say "I object!" or "Objection!" He was sounding the alarm that the series was beginning to get old.

"A perceptive performer makes professional use of seeming inconsequential details in order to inject subtle differences in his reactions," he explained in a read-between-the-lines reply when asked about the sameness of the show's format. "After all, when you've won every single case for five years, you've got to clutch at all available straws to give new values to your performance. A simple thing like approaching the witness stand or the phrasing of a question must always be considered . . . I do things for the sake of this series that I never before would have done as an actor. I call attention to myself in ways I wish I didn't have to use."

They were signs he was growing weary of the series, weary of cranking out thirty episodes every season—and weary of Perry's infallibility. In earlier seasons he bristled at the suggestion that *maybe* Perry should lose a case every now and then, to prove he was human. Now it rankled him that Perry never lost. "Any person who makes a living with his mind must make mistakes," he said.

In an effort to keep the show fresh and to keep Raymond focused, the *Perry Mason* cast and crew often traveled outside Los Angeles and away from the stifling studio atmosphere. "We would take him down to San Diego or do a show in Arrowhead to give him more variance in his role and more challenging things to do," said Art Marks. "We did this, we did that, to break the monotony of courtrooms. It sometimes helped to get the actors away from their domain. Ray enjoyed that."

But even changing the show's locales and filming on location was beginning to lose its luster. It took a sex scandal involving *Perry Mason* costar William Talman, who played woeful DA Hamilton Burger, to spice things up a bit.

Talman was among eight people arrested on March 13, 1960, when the Los Angeles narcotics squad raided a "wild marijuana party" in Richard Reibold's Hollywood apartment. The recently divorced Talman was naked (along with all the others) when the cops broke in, and he was booked on suspected possession of marijuana and vagrant, lewd conduct. He immediately pleaded his innocence. "We just dropped into a friend's house for a drink—and suddenly we find ourselves in the middle of a rumble," he said, conveniently neglecting to explain why he preferred to have that drink in the buff.

"What can I say? This is going to ruin me," Talman said, and it looked for all intents and purposes that he was right. CBS chief William Paley loved his *Perry Mason* show and was aghast at the arrest. Executive producer Gail Jackson, who had to answer to Paley, wasn't thrilled, either. "I don't think it will help his career any, if the report is true," she said after Talman's arrest.

It was also unfortunate timing. Talman's March 13 arrest dovetailed with the March 19–25 edition of *TV Guide,* which featured Raymond and Barbara Hale on its cover. The inside feature on *Perry Mason* was headlined "The Case of the Handy Helpers: How a hard-Hitting Cast Keeps 'Perry Mason's' Winning Streak Alive."

Talman was fired March 18, five days after his arrest, for violating the morals clause of his $1,500-a-week contract. CBS president James Aubrey said that "another actor" would be hired for the Burger role, but he didn't go into detail. Officially, CBS gave no explanation for axing Talman, but it was obviously because he'd violated his contract's morals clause.

"CBS took the stand," said Gail Jackson. "We miss Bill; we were all very fond of him. The whole company was shook [sic] up by the affair. But we're continuing with the series. Morale is still high."

Raymond considered Bill Talman a good friend and immediately went on the offensive, lobbying behind the scenes to get him his job back. He fired his first salvo in mid-April, about a month after Talman was fired.

"The present situation involving William Talman is one of the most unfortunate I have ever encountered," he said. "I feel very strongly that the incident has been magnified all out of proportion . . . Mr. Talman is an exceptionally fine actor. He has been an equally fine friend for a number of years . . . I am sure that in the final analysis matters will not turn out to be as serious as newspaper stories would indicate."

Talman's trial began in June, but it was interrupted on the third day when Judge Adolph Alexander dismissed the morals charges against him. "It isn't against the law to go around a house without clothes on," the judge explained. Talman was visibly relieved. "It was a clear-cut case of invasion of privacy," he said. "But now that it's over, I hope I can get on with my career." Since his arrest, he'd lost custody of his children and he'd lost his house in Sherman Oaks, where his ex-wife lived.

Talman's firing stuck a dagger into the heart of the *Perry Mason* family, and Raymond continued his campaign to get his friend rehired. Five episodes that Talman filmed before his arrest filled out the season, and *Perry Mason* was airing in reruns all summer. So, to the show's viewers, it was as if Hamilton Burger had never left.

Although Raymond lobbied CBS on Talman's behalf, the network refused to budge. Hollywood also unofficially blacklisted Talman, making it difficult for him to find acting jobs. Since his arrest he'd earned only $3,000, and that was from selling television scripts under a pseudonym. Raymond, meanwhile, talked him up to anyone who would listen. He pressed the network affiliates who carried *Perry Mason,* and who carried clout with CBS, to pressure the network into rehiring his pal.

Raymond's loyalty also extended to the set, where he insisted that Talman's coffee mug remain on the rack. He forbade Talman's dressing room to be cleaned out or his space on the studio parking lot to be reassigned. He also personally answered all fan mail in favor of rehiring the actor.

"Talman was a horse's ass in many ways. When Ray was off the set, Bill Talman liked to be a prima donna," said Art Marks. Despite that behavior, Marks added, "It wasn't only Ray, but Gail [Jackson] also fought for him. I think we all fought to keep him on the show."

CBS finally relented and, in December, hired Talman back for "occasional appearances," ostensibly to be once every three weeks. Eventually, he was back to his weekly appearances and still losing case after case. "It's the first argument Talman ever has won on the show," quipped one wag. Talman credited Raymond with playing a key role in his reinstatement.

"It was principally Ray who made them change their minds," he said. When he returned to work on December 9, 1960, the lot was plastered with signs reading "Welcome Home, Bill." It was Raymond's doing.

CHAPTER EIGHT

Your Slip Is Showing

Despite the on-set camaraderie, *Perry Mason*'s slip was beginning to show. On the surface, things couldn't have been better. The show's popularity was growing each season, and it continued to draw forty million viewers a week who enjoyed the inevitability of Perry Mason's courtroom triumph. Artistically, it was held to a higher standard and continued to feature good writing and strong production values. In May 1961, Raymond won his second Emmy Award as Best Actor in a Drama.

He was earning $150,000 a year now, making him one of television's highest-paid actors, and had survived the *Confidential* scandal. He was the highest-paid star on the summer-stock theater circuit and was wealthy enough to send agent Lester Salkow and his wife on a ten-day trip to Nassau in the Bahamas—with a stopoff in New York, where they saw several plays, all paid for by Raymond.

He joined a group of Hollywood elitists who called themselves Black Tie International. Their sole function was to get together each month, fly in a famous gourmet chef, and gorge on a meal. Gregory Peck, Jack Warner, Richard Boone, and Jack Cummings were some of the group's other members.

Raymond even (finally!) found time to make another movie. In *Desire in the Dust* (1960), a sweaty southern-fried drama à la *Cat on a Hot Tin Roof,* he played an evil, wealthy businessman bent on destroying his daughter's ex-con boyfriend. "Burr gives another of his subtle performances," wrote *Los Angeles Times* critic Charles Stinson. "He uses his big, dark, hooded eyes and his soft, dark-timbered voice with a superbly villainous effect." Louella Parsons even threw Raymond a bone, writing about how he and his costar, Martha Hyer, were "gazing into each other's eyes" over dinner.

But behind the scenes, Raymond was threatening to quit *Perry Mason.* He had one more year remaining on the original contract he'd signed in 1957, and that would be it, he said. The threats, which he made in the press and through his pal Hedda Hopper, were really only half serious. They were bargaining chips, with Raymond taking a cue from CBS stablemates James Arness and Richard Boone, the stars of *Gunsmoke* and *Have Gun—Will Travel,* who used similar ploys to get raises.

"Raymond Burr has had to engage another secretary to take care of the protesting mail that's poured in after the announcement there'll be no more *Perry Masons,*" Hopper wrote. "He can't do that to us." Even acclaimed Broadway and Hollywood writer Morrie Ryskind weighed in with a tongue-in-cheek piece, "The Final Caper for Perry Mason: The Case of the Forgotten Speech."

To emphasize his dissatisfaction with his contract status and with the show, Raymond called in "sick" three times during the 1960–61 season. In October, he checked in to a Los Angeles hospital for a "checkup and diagnostic tests" to treat an undisclosed ailment. His absences from the set weren't any longer than a few days, and he always returned to shoot his scenes. The show's directors, including Art Marks, worked around the missing star using his stand-in, Lee Miller.

"Sometimes Ray got into a snit where he felt that CBS was screwing him in some way, contractually, or wasn't giving his dressing room the added attention it deserved," Marks said. "And Ray would say, 'I don't feel well' . . . and this always happened, it seemed, when I was directing the show. He did those things only to prove a point to CBS."

The situation reached a breaking point by late spring, with rumors circulating that Raymond was demanding part ownership of the show, a bigger salary, or both. Lester Salkow leaked word to the press that he'd told CBS Burr wouldn't return for the 1961–62 season. Raymond was about to leave for a tour of Australia to publicize the launch of *Perry Mason* there. "Ray has stated flatly that he will not be on the show next season," his assistant, Bill Swann, said. "He leaves June 10 for Australia . . . After that he hopes to devote his time to his principal concern—using television to work for world peace."

The turn of events didn't please Gail Jackson; she and Burr had been butting heads behind the scenes for some time but managed to keep their mutual disgruntlement out of the press. Raymond was pushing for a lighter workload, better scripts, and at least *some* control over the writing.

"If he's unhappy with us, I'm extremely sorry," Jackson said. "But we start the Perry Mason show for the next season on July 13—and I *hope* it's with Ray. Everybody else's contract's been picked up."

Raymond's hardball tactics worked. CBS got the message. In late May, shortly after his Emmy victory, Burr signed a two-year contract extension, taking him through the 1963–64 television season, with an option for a third year. CBS also agreed to provide his company, Harbour Productions, with a "development fund" to be used toward producing new television shows.

The new agreement was amiable on the surface; in private, though, the contract situations often grew tense in what Marks described as the "triangle" linking Raymond, Gail Jackson, and CBS.

"Gail Jackson had no use for CBS and the people running it," Marks said. "Ray Burr was the third party in this triangle, and, in turn, he had to negotiate with CBS in order to get . . . the money, and Gail, as the executive producer, was the force that always objected to him getting a raise.

"CBS controlled the purse strings of the show . . . so having the creative end, and then getting a show that was a hit, Gail would force her issues on CBS. And then CBS would say to Ray, 'Well, we can't do that because Gail feels this way.' You can understand how that antagonism was always there under the surface."

Instead of soothing Raymond's feelings, the new contract, and the prospect of at least three more seasons of *Perry Mason,* seemed only to irritate him. In the four years since the show's premiere, Raymond was loathe to ever criticize it publicly. He always defended his on-screen alter ego and the show's writing, which fell under the aegis of Erle Stanley Gardner. The author, still churning out his *Perry Mason* mysteries, remained plugged into the television series and had final script approval. A knock on the writing was, in effect, a knock on Gardner.

Subtle dissatisfactions crept in, though, as *Perry Mason* headed into its fifth season. Where in the past Raymond had shrugged off questions about the density of each *Perry Mason* plot, he now seemed defensive when probed about the complexities of his on-screen character. "I've never managed to solve any of the cases until I read them through," he told *TV Guide.* "In fact, I've often been puzzled about who committed the crime *after* we finished shooting the script." He loved the fame, he admitted, but was being crushed by the workload.

Raymond was not alone. Costar William Talman, who should have been thrilled to even *have* a job after his arrest, displayed some major-league chutzpah by criticizing the *Perry Mason* characters. "I know more about Burger than Erle Stanley Gardner does," he said. "Erle detested Burger and drew him as the prototype of the loud, blustering sorehead, like the one who used to plague *him* as a young lawyer." Gardner wasn't thrilled with Raymond's criticisms, but he let them pass. Talman was a different story. Behind the scenes Gardner griped about the costar, whose criticisms stung more, since Gardner had rushed to Talman's defense after his arrest and continued to support him and to push CBS to rehire him. And these were the thanks he received?

There were other changes. Raymond, who had never missed an episode, was forced to bow out for a month in December 1962, this time for real, when he underwent surgery to remove some intestinal polyps that turned out to be benign. The surgery was scheduled for just before Christmas, and Raymond pulled one of his famous practical jokes on the hospital staff. He sent his secretary, Bill Swann, to get some

Mercurochrome, which he grabbed, and then he disappeared into the bathroom. He reappeared a short time later and climbed back into bed.

"The doctor scrubbed and got ready for the operation," said Barbara Hale, "and when they pulled back the sheet to operate, across his tummy Ray had written, 'Do Not Open Until Christmas.' They fell apart in the operating room."

Raymond's absence meant he would miss four episodes of *Perry Mason,* and CBS wasted no time in filling the void. Legendary actress Bette Davis was hired to replace Mason for one episode as "a modern-day Portia," according to Gail Jackson. Davis was followed by Hugh O'Brian, Walter Pidgeon, and Michael Rennie—all winning their respective cases and holding down the fort until Raymond's *Perry Mason* return in March. Even Perry's *fill-ins* were victorious.

But Perry's real-life alter ego couldn't lay claim to winning all his cases. "The Case of the Unpaid Debt" was played out in September 1963, when Raymond was dragged into court by someone named George Shaheen. Shaheen claimed he lent Raymond $1,085 back in 1949, when Raymond was still struggling in Hollywood, and was never paid back. Raymond lost the case, forking over the cash and more money to cover court expenses. And several months later, he closed the Raymond Burr Gallery in Beverly Hills because of a lack of business. "It was not supported by the public," he said.

But the court of public opinion was still heavily on Raymond's side, his fans blissfully unaware of the facade he'd constructed to protect his private life. While his relationship with Robert Benevides continued to flourish, Raymond publicly spoke of his desire to get married and even to have children. And if he couldn't have his own children, he said, he would adopt.

"I have great plans for the future," he said in a July 1962 magazine interview shortly after he turned forty-five. "Not only in my public life but in my private life. I would like to get married tomorrow if I found the right girl . . . or if she found me.

"Since I am not assured of getting married tomorrow, I'm not assured of having children. So I'm planning to adopt some. I'm adding eight rooms to my house in Malibu Beach—it's going to be a wonderful place for children."

The talk of marriage was bogus, and having biological children was not an option. But Raymond always had a soft spot for kids, and they for him. He loved to have kids running around the Malibu spread and had Barbara Hale's children wrapped around his finger.

"When we started [Perry Mason], my youngest baby was nearly three. I took her to the set and oh, my heavens! She went to Raymond like he was her mother!" said Hale. "She would not leave him; he held her and walked around the set . . . I said, 'Why do you like him?' and she said, 'He has big fat eyes!' So he was called 'Big Fat Eyes' for a few years as a joke between the crew and everybody on the set."

He became a foster parent to several of the children he met throughout his travels to Korea and the Far East in the 1950s; according to one widely published estimate, Raymond sponsored twenty-seven children through the Christian Children's Fund. He proudly showed off pictures of two war orphans, a boy and girl, whom he sponsored in Italy, and he would become a foster parent to four Vietnamese children orphaned by the war there. His television colleague Steve Allen also sponsored two children in Vietnam.

There were changes in the *Perry Mason* family, as well. Lovable Ray Collins, a regular since the show's premiere and the oldest cast member, was forced to leave midway through the 1963–64 season because of illness. He died in 1965 from emphysema at the age of seventy-five. Collins was replaced by the much younger Wesley Lau, who played Lieutenant Anderson for the 1964–65 season; he, in turn, was succeeded in the final season by Richard Anderson, Raymond's costar from *A Cry in the Night*.

Perry Mason's popularity, which had been a sure thing since 1957, was now beginning to show some cracks in its armor. CBS continued to show faith in the series by extending its life, but in September 1962 it moved the show to Thursdays at 8:00 p.m. *Perry Mason* was roundly thumped in its new time slot by NBC's *The Donna Reed Show* and *Leave It to Beaver* on ABC. It never really recovered.

In September 1963, CBS moved the show back an hour to 7:00 p.m., hoping to counter ABC's new *Jimmy Dean Show* and NBC's combination of *Dr. Kildare* and *Hazel*. But that move also failed. *Perry Mason* dropped out of the top-twenty-five-ranked shows, and the writing was on the wall. If CBS could take any solace, it was in the fact that *Perry Mason* was its most widely distributed show overseas, where it aired in fifty countries. The lucrative international syndication dollars would fill the network's coffers for years to come.

Raymond still had a year to go on his *Perry Mason* deal, but he startled everyone in the summer of 1964 by announcing he would star in a new drama series, *The Power*, in which he would play the governor of a large state. *The Power* would be produced by Don Fedderson, the man behind *My Three Sons*, and it would begin production the following summer. The next season of *Perry Mason*, Raymond told the Associated Press, "will wind it up."

It didn't.

CBS renewed *Perry Mason* for the 1965–66 season and began formulating a backup plan if Raymond balked at returning after his contract expired (in April). The network talked of replacing him with Mike Connors, who'd subbed for Raymond on a *Perry Mason* episode that season. And Connors was a familiar commodity, having starred a few years earlier in the CBS series *Tight Rope*.

Plan B wasn't necessary. CBS threw $2 million at Raymond to come back for another season of dreadfully long hours, tired press interviews, and boring affiliates meetings. It was a no-brainer of an offer that he readily accepted. "I've always told myself I'd like to go out on a good year. This year was a bad year," he said. "Sometimes the plots got so involved even I couldn't understand them. But next year can be a great one."

His deal to star in *The Power* was conveniently forgotten and brushed under the rug. "It had some of the same things going for it that *Perry* did," he said of *The Power*. "It was the best damn thing I ever read, the best new show presentation anybody in this business had ever seen. The heads of CBS decided that with another year of *Perry* in the offing they didn't want to convert at that point . . . I went along. I'm a paid actor. Once having signed a contract, I had a certain obligation."

In eight seasons of *Perry Mason*, Raymond's per-season fee had risen from $100,000 to $2 million. That was incentive enough to stick around for one more season. And he wasn't shy in admitting it.

"Money, that's why," he told columnist Sheila Graham. "It is as simple as that. CBS offered me so much money, I would have been a fool to turn it down."

There was another reason, "a bit of ego," he said, connected to his returning to the show for another season. CBS was moving *Perry Mason* back to Sunday night, where it would directly battle *Bonanza*. Five years before, *Perry Mason* had forced *Bonanza* off Sunday nights, and Raymond was girded for battle again (or so he claimed). But in those five years the television landscape had completely changed. *Bonanza*, which aired in color (a rarity), was now the top-rated show on television—and *Perry Mason* was about to get whupped yet again.

By late fall it was obvious the show could no longer continue. It was being steamrolled weekly by *Bonanza*. In mid-November, Gail Jackson announced that CBS would drop *Perry Mason* at season's end. "CBS figures we are worn out. But this season the show is getting more mail than ever before and so is Raymond," she told the *New York Times*—which viewed *Perry Mason* as "a sacrificial lamb in the twilight year of its television practice."

The cancellation, in and of itself, was no great shock. Still, it caught Raymond by surprise. It wasn't so much that CBS was canceling the show—Raymond didn't need the money, and it would be a relief to be free of Mason after all these years—but it was the way in which he found out that would rankle him for years.

Raymond said that CBS approached him early in the fall of 1965, asking if he would do a final season of *Perry Mason*. This time, the show would air in color for the first time. "They guaranteed the quality of the show and said, 'Let's go off with a big bang.' This was all of the people at CBS," he said. Three weeks later he picked up the trades to read that *Perry Mason* was canceled. "I would have thought that any one of them would have had the decency to just pick up the phone and say, 'We came out, we persuaded you, but we have now reconsidered and it's not a great idea,' and I would have said, 'Wonderful.'"

Raymond and the crew did shoot one color episode of *Perry Mason*, "The Case of the Twice Told Twist," because "[CBS chief] Bill Paley wanted to see the show in color," said Art Marks. But the network just couldn't justify spending millions, a good chunk of that going to Raymond, for another season of a show that had lost much of its ratings luster.

"CBS felt that they had enough shows that they didn't have to make anymore because the syndication would make them rich," Marks said. "I was told the show just didn't warrant spending X amount of dollars over thirty shows, when they had nine years of it. They were probably quite right, as far as dollars and cents—but the show could have gone on for another five years."

The final *Perry Mason* episode, "The Case of the Final Fadeout," aired on May 22, 1966, and featured several in-jokes and some actual crew members and inner *Perry Mason* family members (including a Gail Jackson cameo). William Hopper played Paul Drake for the last time on crutches, after slicing a tendon in his foot (he'd stepped on a piece of glass).

The finale also featured a judge no one had seen before: Erle Stanley Gardner, who was making his acting debut.

But if any sentimental feelings were emanating from CBS, they were few and far between. "Nothing about the end was nice," Raymond said. "I remember finishing my last scene at 10 in the morning and going to my dressing room to take my makeup off. I had a watch on that they'd bought for Mason five or six years before, which I wore on the show, and I was in my dressing room for no more than 10 minutes before they came over and asked for the watch . . . I gave them the watch and never saw any of them again."

The final line on *Perry Mason* totaled nine seasons and 275 episodes, including the four episodes Raymond missed in 1963 after his surgery. The show made millionaires of Cornwall Jackson and wife Gail Jackson and padded Erle Stanley Gardner's already substantial bank account. According to one estimate, Paisano Productions, which owned 60 percent of the show, had "salted away" $10 million when all was said and done.

Perry Mason had also transformed Raymond Burr from a B-movie villain into a pop-culture hero and a household name. He was the highest-paid actor in television history, and he didn't have to work another day in his life.

And after the grueling six-day work weeks and eighteen-hour days, who could blame him if he didn't?

CHAPTER NINE

It's a Jungle Out There

If flowers were Raymond's first passion, then his love of travel ran a close second. He and Robert traveled constantly during breaks in the *Perry Mason* schedule; they'd even named their company, Harbour Productions, after one of their favorite places in the Bahamas.

Raymond continued his visits to Vietnam, and as the war in Southeast Asia escalated, his trips there became more frequent. On each sojourn he added several more orphaned Vietnamese youngsters to his growing stable of foster children from around the world, until their numbers reached thirty by the mid-1960s. "If I send money to them, they don't spend it on themselves," he explained. "They share it with other children and parents, if they have any. They don't know the meaning of the word 'greed' or hoarding.'"

He didn't go out of his way to publicize these trips, but he garnered attention nonetheless. The press had a long memory for selflessness and remembered Raymond's many visits to Korea in the 1950s. And the fourth estate was eager now to chronicle his treks to Vietnam, particularly as ripples of dissent began to roil the sociopolitical waters back home. Perry Mason, that paragon of American values, visiting the troops? It was too good a story to pass up.

"The first time I went, there were no more than a few hundred Americans there serving as advisers to the South Vietnamese forces," he said. "I went simply because they were there and because I thought they would appreciate seeing someone from home. And they did—much more than I expected."

In March 1967, Raymond was on a troop visit to Vietnam when America got its first look at his new television character: San Francisco chief of detectives Robert T. Ironside.

For all his grousing about *Perry Mason* robbing him of a personal life, Raymond was surprisingly eager to get back into the game after the show wrapped up production. He had some assistance in finding new work from his old friends at CBS, which had helped him set up Harbour Productions several years before as an added incentive to continue *Perry Mason*. Now, with Raymond a valued free agent in demand, he and agent Lester Salkow used Harbour Productions as a home base to field offers for his next project.

He was hoping to jump-start his movie career, which had been dormant since 1957 with the lone exception of *Desire in the Dust*. But that was already six years earlier, which was an eternity in Hollywood. "He was elated that he was going on to other things," recalled Art Marks, but disappointment set in when the movie roles failed to materialize.

Raymond was a prisoner of his own success; he was so ingrained in the public consciousness as Perry Mason that the movie colony found it difficult to look past that image, despite his impressive big-screen résumé peppered with names like Alfred Hitchcock and George Stevens. Today, movie stars such as Tom Hanks and Glenn Close move freely between

LEFT: By 1955, Raymond was tiring of the bad-guy roles, even if he played them for laughs as he did here opposite Jerry Lewis in *You're Never Too Young*.

BELOW: After a decade in Hollywood, Raymond finally earned his first starring role as a lovestruck defense attorney blindsided by a scheming murderess (Angela Lansbury) in *Please Murder Me* (1956).

ABOVE: Raymond was thirty-eight and Natalie Wood only seventeen when they "fell in love" after costarring in *A Cry in the Night* (1956). Raymond blamed the breakup on pressure from the studio.

OPPOSITE, TOP: "The Raymond Burr Hollywood Christmas Show" entertains the troops at the Yuma Test Station in Arizona (1954). Leggy actress Marla English plays the coquette.

OPPOSITE, BOTTOM: Raymond at home in Malibu with "nephew" Frank Vitti. The woman on the left is identified as Raymond's niece Phyllis Zillo. (*Photofest*)

The original cast of *Perry Mason* (left to right): William Talman, Ray Collins, Barbara Hale, Raymond, and William Hopper.

...shful thinking, pal: Hapless DA
...milton Burger (William Talman)
...er could defeat his wily adversary,
...ry Mason.

ABOVE: Raymond shares a laugh on the set with *Perry Mason* executive producer, writer/director Arthur Marks. (*Courtesy Arthur Marks*)

OPPOSITE: *Perry Mason* viewers were left to wonder what those meaningful glanc between Perry and his loyal secretary, Della Street (Barbara Hale), really meant. (*Photofest*)

ᴏsɪᴛᴇ: Perry counted on crack private detective Paul Drake (William Hopper)
ᴇlp him prove his clients' innocence. Hopper's mother, gossip columnist Hedda
per, helped protect Raymond's image.

ᴇ: Perry bores in on his prey with "the stare," which always led to a sudden
ession.

LEFT: Raymond in Vietnam with some of his foster children. (*Photofest*)

BELOW: Raymond won critical kudos for his portrayal of Pope John XXIII in *Portrait: A Man Whose Name Was John* (1973). Raymond considered Pope John the greatest person he'd ever met.

SITE, TOP: Raymond and Barbara clutch their Emmy Awards for *Mason* while sharing a laugh with w Emmy winners Bob Hope and Benny (May 1959).

SITE, BOTTOM: Raymond's troop to Vietnam formed the basis of NBC special *Raymond Burr Visits am*, which aired in 1967 and was ized by some as a preachy vanity ct. (*Photofest*)

ᴏꜱɪᴛᴇ: Back home in New Westminster in 1966 with parents Minerva and Bill,
had divorced and remarried after a long separation.

ᴇ: Raymond returned to series television in *Ironside* with costars (clockwise
left) Barbara Anderson, Don Galloway, and Don Mitchell. (*Photofest*)

ᴏꜱɪᴛᴇ: Wheelchair-bound tough-guy Robert T. Ironside takes aim. The series
ᴅ almost as long as *Perry Mason.* (*Photofest*)

ᴇ: Raymond and Barbara Hale reunited for a series of highly rated *Perry Mason*
ɴovies in the late 1980s—with Hale's son, William Katt (left), playing Paul
ᴋᴇ Jr. (*Photofest*)

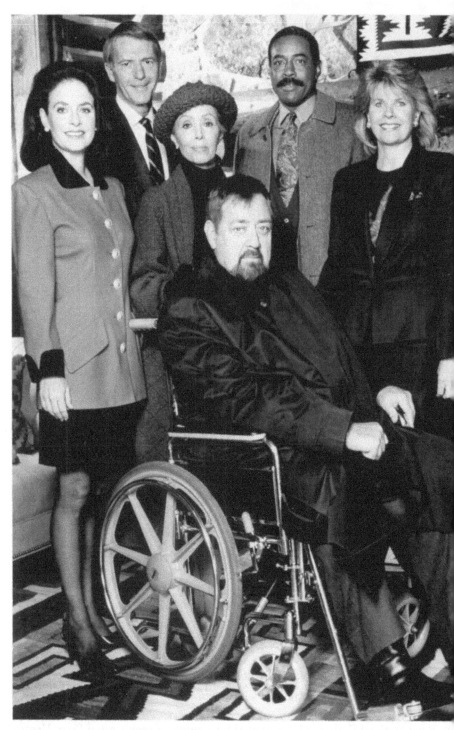

Raymond knew he was dying when he reunited for *The Return of Ironside* with (
to right) Elizabeth Baur, Don Galloway, Dana Wynter, Don Mitchell, and Barba
Anderson.

big-budget movies and television; in the mid-1960s, the Hollywood elite still looked down upon their television cousins.

"Raymond did not want to go right into another television series; he was hoping he was going to get some big movie parts," said producer Paul Mason, who would play a big role in Raymond's next small-screen success. The money certainly wasn't a deciding factor, but he did crave the public acclaim. The man who went to such great lengths to hide his private life reveled in the public spotlight—and by now he was accustomed to that spotlight shining very brightly on his corpulent frame.

Ego was involved, too. Jackie Gleason, his former CBS stablemate, insisted on being the highest-paid variety star on television, and Raymond followed his lead. He departed *Perry Mason* as the highest-paid series star in television, and he was determined to retain that status.

As he turned forty-eight, Raymond found himself a wealthy man who'd saved wisely and invested in a number of profitable side businesses. But *Perry Mason* was over, and he wouldn't see any of the show's huge syndication profits. Unlike the Paisano Productions triumvirate, he'd eschewed that end of the business in favor of being paid upfront, reasoning that he'd be overtaxed on his syndication profits. Now he needed another big payday to retain the elegant lifestyle to which he'd grown accustomed.

Part of that lifestyle was anything but elegant, at least on the surface. In 1965, with an eye toward life after *Perry Mason*, Raymond began searching for a retreat far away from the questioning, prying eyes of Hollywood. He found his nirvana just northeast of Fiji in the South Pacific: a four-thousand-acre slice of island paradise called Naitauba (pronounced

"Ny-*tum*-ba") for which he paid the previous owner, an eighty-three-year-old German woman named Elizabeth Henning, anywhere from $150,000 to $300,000 (the amount varied depending on the source). He promised Mrs. Henning, who'd lived on the island with her late husband for sixty-two years, that she could continue living there, which she did until her death in a car accident several years later. Raymond buried her on Naitauba beside her husband.

Raymond hoped the island was an investment in a lifetime of happiness he couldn't find in the United States. And with Naitauba being nearly six thousand miles away from San Francisco, it really *was* the other side of the world.

"Raymond was looking for a place to get away and we were looking at Hawaii," his partner Robert recalled. "It seemed like every time he found a little beachy place he wanted, the property next door was always being considered for a large hotel of some kind." Exasperated, the couple looked at a map of the world, and Raymond encouraged Robert, who doubled as his business manager, to write to the Fiji Chamber of Commerce to see if anything was available there.

"Of course there was no Chamber of Commerce in Fiji, but somebody there, a shady Australian . . . got the letter and mailed me back and said they had an island of about ten acres," Robert said. "When we got there, this gentleman said, 'Oh, I'm sorry, but that island has been sold. But, there is another island that just came on the market, but I'm almost ashamed to bring it up to you because it is so difficult to get to.'"

The "shady Australian" went on to explain the harrowing transportation route to Naitauba—a plane ride to another island, followed by a forty-five-minute taxi ride and then a six-hour boat ride. "As he was telling this to us, Raymond's eyes got bigger and bigger and he said, 'Oh, we've got to see that.'

"We went out to the island in the little boat. I get seasick, so I was taking Dramamine and it was putting me to sleep," Robert said. "Raymond shook me and said, 'We're getting close!' and he opened a bottle of champagne. A shaft of light came down on the island—it was very cloudy and stormy— and he said, 'It's a sign.' So we drank the champagne, stayed there for a day or two, and he fell in love with it."

After the purchase of Naitauba officially went through—he learned via shortwave radio that he'd closed the deal—Raymond sold the house in Malibu Beach and donated his menagerie to the Los Angeles Zoo. "I never really *lived* in Malibu in the ten years I was building onto the house," he said. When he was asked where he spent most of his time while in Los Angeles, he answered cagily, "I live around."

Raymond quickly established Naitauba as his home away from home and traveled there whenever he could. He and Robert lived in an eighty-year-old house built by Mrs. Henning's husband (and eventually overrun by termites), and there was an adjoining guest cottage. Communication with the outside world was strictly through two-way radio, since there were no phones on the island and, more important for Raymond, no television. "We had a radio telephone which twice a day we could call in on," Robert said. The closest neighboring island was Kanathea, which was twenty-eight miles away.

Raymond got right to work in trying to modernize the island. He paid to have electricity brought to Naitauba and financed the construction of a hospital to service the local population. He also established an island newspaper and provided other services for the 167 natives. He "adopted" several island children and eventually brought a handful of them to the States and paid for their schooling here. Jacob Temo, one of the Naitauba natives who came to America, became a lifelong friend and employee of Raymond and Robert's.

"There's an entire village in the middle of the island," Raymond said proudly. "The people expect respect and they give it . . . we import flour, salt and pepper: everything else we grow ourselves, and by using breadfruit and taro we could get along without flour." But even now, with all the success, old habits died hard. "When I first went to Fiji, one of the first men I saw was a man I knew during the war at Guadalcanal," he told the *Los Angeles Times,* adding a new detail to his non-existent war record.

Some of Raymond's friends ventured to Naitauba, but it was a daunting task. The flight from Los Angeles to Suva, the Fiji capital, was eighteen hours, and the entire trip took anywhere from twenty to twenty-two hours. "It's a hard place to get to, and I won't put an airstrip on it," he said. "So the last part of the journey is by boat. And it's a private island, so you can invite whom you wish."

Raymond's old pal Bungy Hedley was up to the challenge. Her marriage was in shambles, and Raymond invited her to visit Naitauba with her four children, one of whom was confined to a wheelchair.

"We had to fly from the main island in a little six-seat plane to another island and then a boat met me there," she said. "We had to ride eighty miles with them out in this little fourteen-foot boat . . . we arrived about two in the morning and there was a lot of coral in the water and we signaled with our lights so Ray knew we were there.

"Well, Ray walks all the way out to the boat and grabs me and carries me over the water to the shore. He arranged a tutor for the two oldest kids, arranged a nursemaid for the six-month-old, and for the one in the wheelchair he arranged for a really strong guy to take care of him and exercise him. He told me I could be the administrator of the island . . . he was going to take care of me and the kids and everything . . . but I stayed about a week, and my life was such a mess that I said I had to go back and try again. So I didn't do it."

Being the lord-master of his own private island was nice, but it was time for Raymond to get back to work. When the hoped-for movie offers didn't materialize, he turned his attention to television. Within months, he signed a deal with Universal Studios. "I have to finance my outside interests," he explained.

"His agent thought that he would never play anything besides Perry Mason after that. This is his agent!" Robert Benevides said. "He never turned down a challenge."

Raymond was intrigued by Collier Young's script for *Ironside,* which was built around gruff San Francisco chief of detectives Robert T. Ironside, who was paralyzed by a sniper's bullet in a failed assassination attempt. Ironside, now confined to a wheelchair, returns to work as a special consultant to the SFPD and is given his own staff and a specially outfitted van enabling him to travel to crime scenes. It would be the first television series featuring a handicapped protagonist—if it sold. "There's more latitude for showing a *human being* because he is not tied down to a courtroom,"

Raymond said in response to the inevitable comparisons to *Perry Mason*.

What was left unsaid at the time was Raymond's personal connection to the character of Robert T. Ironside. In 1966, his mother, Minerva, underwent three operations at St. Mary's Hospital in New Westminster to treat varicose veins in her leg. The surgery was a success, but several months later, while Raymond was shooting the *Ironside* pilot, she'd fallen while out for a walk. Her hip was severely damaged by the fall, and although she wasn't a paraplegic like Ironside, her doctors doubted that Minerva, who was now seventy-three, would ever walk again. Raymond was crushed.

Minerva spent months laid up in bed, but she was determined not to live out her days confined to a wheelchair, especially when Bill Burr was still spry at eighty-two. "I've always told my children they must look on the positive side of life—so what kind of mother would I be if I didn't practice that philosophy?" she said. Minerva relearned how to walk after undergoing months of rigorous physical therapy. Her cane was now the only reminder of her accident.

When Collier Young created *Ironside* for Universal Television, he envisioned Melvyn Douglas in the role of the cantankerous chief. "But [Universal chief] Sid Sheinberg wanted Raymond Burr," said *Ironside* producer Paul Mason. "They had just signed a new contract with Burr to star in movies, and they told him he was going to be a movie star *and* a television star. His manager, Lester Salkow, said to him, 'Raymond, it's a movie, maybe it will sell, maybe it won't. Who is going to buy a series about a crippled cop?'"

Filming on the *Ironside* pilot began in late 1966, shortly after *Perry Mason* was launched into syndication. Raymond was now working for NBC, home of his former nemesis, *Bonanza*, which had helped put *Perry Mason* out of business.

The two-hour *Ironside* movie premiered on March 28, 1967, as part of NBC's "World Premiere" movie programming slate. Raymond, who was in Vietnam visiting the troops, missed the premiere and the next day's largely noncommittal reviews.

"Although NBC called it a major motion picture, the show was a routine whodunit that would have comfortably occupied an hour on TV, but which was padded with all sorts of irrelevant odds and ends," wrote the Associated Press. "Whirling around in his wheelchair, Burr plays Ironsides [*sic*] as a sort of combination Lionel Barrymore and Nero Wolfe, with some colorful and un-Masonish flourishes like dropping his G's, cussing mildly, and belting bourbon steadily."

The *Ironside* cast included Don Galloway and Barbara Anderson as Ed Brown and Eve Whitfield, Ironside's chief investigators. Don Mitchell played Mark Sanger, a young, angry, militant black man and former delinquent who grudgingly accepts Ironside's offer to become his driver and aide-de-camp. With the race riots in Newark, New Jersey, exploding that summer, and the riots in Watts still a fresh memory, Mark's relationship with Ironside became a focal point for the show, which prided itself on mirroring the country's sociopolitical climate.

Ironside had another element of coolness in its favor: its jazzy theme music, written by Quincy Jones, which was the first theme music in television history to utilize a synthesizer.

The *Ironside* movie did well enough in the ratings to warrant a series pickup, and by the summer of 1967, cast and crew began filming on the Universal lot in Los Angeles. Seven episodes were filmed, but something didn't feel right, and Raymond was unhappy. And that wasn't ever a good thing. "I was ready to blow someone's brains out," he said, until NBC brought in Frank Price as the show's executive producer. Price listened to Raymond's vociferous complaints about the quality of the first seven episodes and decided they would shoot all seven episodes over again. From scratch. "I don't think it's ever happened in TV," Raymond said, a hint of admiration in his voice. "It cost a lot of money."

NBC spent the rest of the summer hyping *Ironside* throughout July and August and announced it would rerun the pilot on September 2 in anticipation of the series premiere on September 14.

For Raymond, back on the lot, it was an all-too-familiar scenario: Up at 4:00 or 4:30 a.m. to read through the script, followed by an all-day shooting schedule and crashing in his apartment on the studio lot.

But he was fifty now, and the weight he'd lost to win the *Perry Mason* job over ten years earlier had crept back with each successive season. He now topped the scales at around 275 pounds, although NBC's generous press department had him 45 pounds lighter. His long hours spent sitting in Ironside's wheelchair didn't help. His hair, once jet black, was now flecked with gray, and his hound-dog eyes were underscored by puffy black bags. He was fleshy and jowly but was still a commanding presence with his booming voice and bearish demeanor. Costars meeting him for the first time were cowed. Raymond Burr demanded respect. And he usually got it.

"I certainly have an ego, but I don't have the kind of ego that demands constant attention," he told *TV Guide* on the eve of *Ironside's* premiere. "If I dug a good ditch, I'd like someone to say that's a pretty good ditch.

"I've given a good deal of my life to pleasing people, and I'm glad they're still pleased," he said. "And there's satisfaction in the knowledge I'm going strong still. But 'thrilled' is not the word I'd use."

It also wasn't the word most critics used to describe their feelings about *Ironside* after the show's premiere. "Raymond Burr scored in his portrayal of a paraplegic San Francisco detective, but the script didn't," Don Page wrote in the *Los Angeles Times*. "Somehow, despite the failures of the first show, you get the feeling that *Ironside* will be a hit and there are enough values to be salvaged in the coming weeks."

New York Times critic Jack Gould described the premiere as "a tepid whodunit of very modest interest," while, according to *New York Post* critic Bob Williams, the script "surrendered any pretensions of suspense."

But despite the critical yawns, *Ironside* opened to strong numbers, and NBC had a bona fide hit on its hands. The network quickly dismissed all the hand-wringing over whether Raymond would be accepted by the public as someone other than Perry Mason. And in Raymond's opinion, Robert T. Ironside really wasn't all that different from the crusading defense attorney he'd played for nine seasons: "In *Ironside* I've switched from the defense to the prosecution," he said.

What *was* different this time around was his insistence on establishing his own ground rules vis-à-vis the *Ironside* production schedule. He still undertook a tremendous workload, but he had his limits—and he wasn't afraid to voice his displeasure. Unlike his situation on *Perry Mason*, which was owned by Paisano Productions and CBS, Raymond owned 51 percent of *Ironside* through Harbour Productions. *He* would dictate how and when he wanted to work. And once the series established itself as a Thursday-night beachhead on NBC, he had all the leverage he needed.

"I think it was about our sixth episode when he walked into the office, which was always a bad sign, and we chatted," recalled *Ironside* producer Paul Mason. "As he got up to walk out, almost like [Peter Falk's] Detective Columbo, he turned around and said, 'By the way, I don't want to work outside anymore. I'm in the wheelchair, I look up into the sun, and it's too difficult for me.' I said, 'Raymond, we'll put silk screens over you' and he said, 'No. I don't want to work outside anymore.' And then he turned, looked back again, and said, 'Oh, and I don't want to work Fridays.'

"So I ran upstairs to my boss [Frank Price] and said, 'He doesn't want to work outside and he doesn't want to work on Fridays.' He looked at me and said, 'So, work it out.' That was television."

It was clear that the Universal Studios politics were plain and simple: do not ruffle Raymond Burr's feathers. Not that anyone dared. He could be funny and charming one minute, surly and brooding the next, his huge blue eyes boring into his target with a steely glare. "Raymond was enigmatic . . . He was a very charming, bright, witty guy . . . who made the greatest mai tais I ever had in my life," said *Ironside* producer Joel Rogosin. "But he was also careful and contained."

"Careful" and "contained" could, at least initially, describe Raymond's opinions on the subject of the war in Vietnam. He'd been visiting there since the early 1960s, talking to the troops and lending his support, usually on his own dime. He was one of only a handful of celebrities, including Bob Hope, Martha Raye, George Jessel, and George C. Scott, who cared enough to make the long trip to Southeast Asia. Vietnam, unlike World War II or Korea, was a war of a different color. It was an undeclared war, unpopular and polarizing and being fought in an unfamiliar, faraway place most Americans had never heard of. Celebrities accustomed to glitzy press conferences announcing their visits to the troops were sorely disappointed, because they didn't exist. Neither did welcome-home receptions from an adoring public.

Stars like Raymond who did make the trip to Vietnam went at their own peril. Unlike the big USO troupes of wars past, the Vietnam performers traveled in small groups of five or six. Their safety was not guaranteed in the uncharted, unpredictable jungles of Southeast Asia. Hollywood's lack of enthusiasm in the war effort was so glaring that the government eventually pressured the USO into forming a Hollywood Overseas Committee to recruit celebrities into making the trek to Vietnam. It was a campaign doomed to failure.

Raymond's trips to Vietnam didn't go unnoticed by the press, and neither did the change in his attitude in 1965 after returning from yet another trip there. Previously he'd kept his mouth shut about the situation in Vietnam, but he now embarked on a public speaking tour in which he preached an intensified war effort as the only way to beat the Viet Cong. Raymond's crusade was taken up by Charlton Heston, who wielded influence among his peers as the president of the Screen Actors Guild. Even the apolitical "fence-sitter" Bob Hope started voicing displeasure at the antiwar effort back home. As Bob Dylan sang, "The Times They Are a-Changing."

Raymond's opinions on the war were also changing. The *Ironside* premiere in the fall of 1967 dovetailed with the escalation of the conflict in Vietnam and with the growing antiwar movement back home. Raymond had spent parts of seventeen years visiting war zones in Korea and Vietnam. And by now he wasn't shy about expressing his opinion when he was asked the inevitable questions about America's involvement in the war.

"My only position on the war is that I wish it were over," he said when pressed. "Actually, we should have been taking positions before we became involved to the extent that we now are. Today, all we can do is strive for peace within the framework of the ultimate goals which brought us there in the first place.

"As far as questioning the war is concerned, however, I am inclined to pay a good deal of attention to it. Boys who have lost arms or legs or were otherwise wounded in Vietnam naturally wonder whether their sacrifice was worth it. And sometimes I wonder, too."

Raymond brought a piece of Vietnam into America's living rooms in October 1967. He'd been accompanied by an NBC camera crew on his trip there the previous winter, and that footage, together with his narration, provided the backdrop for *Raymond Burr Visits Vietnam*, which aired two weeks after the premiere of *Ironside*.

Not everyone was pleased, and not everyone was interested in hearing Raymond's take on the situation. Many critics viewed the Vietnam special as a preachy, self-involved vanity project, or as NBC's cynical attempt to capitalize on its new prime-time star. "If I want to hear about Vietnam, I'll listen to James Reston, not some actor," an anonymous detractor sniped in *TV Guide*. "Ray takes it all so damn seriously," one of his former press agents chimed in.

They had a point. When it came to discussing his trips to Vietnam, Raymond could be pedantic and overbearing. He even took a swipe at Bob Hope, the patron saint of GI Joe. "The Bob Hope Show's fine, but they can't get to the men and the men can't get to *them*. I've got a reputation in Vietnam second to none because I've covered so many places," he said—failing to add that his own war record was completely fabricated.

"The impressions he came up with are neither weighty nor particularly revealing," *Chicago Tribune* critic Clay Gowran wrote in his review of *Raymond Burr Visits Vietnam*. "Saigon's citizens seem to spend all of their time in the streets, traffic there is heavy, the war seems far away. 'I was with one soldier when he died,' Burr says at one point. If that soldier had been my son, I'd have wanted doctors, a chaplain, maybe a kindly nurse with him—*not* a video actor."

Los Angeles Times critic Hal Humphrey was a bit kinder: "Burr's presence certainly adds to the hour. His questions asked of people he met were intelligent and elicited some interesting replies . . .Burr's 10 previous visits to Vietnam (plus a dozen to Korea during the conflict) gave him a knowledge and some reason to be shown on TV in this capacity."

Raymond Burr Visits Vietnam wasn't a ratings smash, nor was it completely ignored. Footage from Vietnam was a regular part of the evening news, and nothing about the country seemed so surprising anymore, not even the occasional grousing from a soldier. When Raymond asked one GI on camera to name the "worst thing" about Vietnam, his reply was swift and telling: "Being here!"

NBC intended to use the prime-time special to publicize its new star and to stick it to Raymond's previous employers at CBS. But it wasn't necessary. Despite all the internal hand-wringing and *agita* among NBC executives, Raymond made a seamless transition from *Perry Mason* to *Ironside* and was as popular as ever, if not more popular. As fall 1967 segued into winter, it was becoming obvious that Raymond was the first actor in the twenty-year history of television to star in back-to-back hit dramatic shows.

And if a segment of television viewers disagreed with Raymond's views on escalating the war, they certainly didn't take it out on Robert T. Ironside, who was anchoring NBC's Thursday-night schedule with thirty million viewers each week.

In hindsight, it's clear that *Ironside* creator Collier Young hit on a winning formula with impeccable timing. The show premiered as Richard Nixon announced his candidacy for president, pledging his "law and order" commitment to cleaning up America's streets and appealing to the country's massive "silent majority" for support.

Ironside was, in essence, a fictitious microcosm of Nixon's platform unfolding every Thursday night on NBC—with beneficent, handicapped Chief Ironside leading his interracial team of investigators (all young and clean-cut—no hippies) on their quest to clean up the streets of San Francisco.

Nixon couldn't have scripted it better.

"I think our younger generation has a lot going for them," Raymond said in response to his youthful costars. "Their insistence upon telling it as it is, that I'm all for. If there's anything I can't tolerate, it's being lied to. I have a great respect for the truth and that's what I want to hear." Apparently the "truth" applied only to others.

During the *Perry Mason* years, Raymond complained, often and bitterly, of how the show eventually took over his life. Part of that was true, and part of it was his own doing. No one forced him to fly all over the country on his treasured days off to address various bar associations and legal groups. No one forced him to pontificate in print on the American system of jurisprudence. The *Perry Mason* fame fed his ego and vice versa; complain as he might, he had only himself to blame.

Once *Ironside* became a hit, the familiar pattern of personal appearances resurfaced, this time with a new commitment to a new cause: the physically disabled. "Those handicapped must realize they can still go on living full, worthwhile lives after they have accepted certain adjustments," Raymond pronounced. "Those around them must learn to help them not by pitying, but by encouraging them."

Raymond's lectures to legal groups were replaced by speeches on behalf of the physically challenged; the pronouncements to the press now focused on Ironside's physical and emotional makeup, as opposed to Perry Mason's ethical compass.

"The things I do as Chief Ironside are not wish fulfillments. Everything has been thoroughly researched and tested for credibility," he said. "What he can't do physically, he doesn't do. He's learned to throw aside false pride and get help from others. Instead, he has the *real* pride of knowing that he's still in there doing a job."

Raymond took the role seriously, but that was in his nature. He got completely lost in whatever it was he was focusing on, be it cooking, growing his orchids, or tending to island business on Naitauba. It was no surprise that he became so passionate about the plight of the physically handicapped that when the *Ironside* writers broached the idea of having Chief Ironside walk again after a miraculous operation, he quickly nixed the idea.

"There is no way I would ever allow a scriptwriter to come up with a fiction miracle just to get publicity, viewers or anything else," he said. "We're not about to give false hope to the thousands of paraplegics who have so bravely made new and rewarding lives for themselves. It is important that he [Ironside] function, and function well, in his wheelchair. He's showing millions of people this can be done."

He devoted his time and financial resources to his new cause and became politically active on behalf of the physically handicapped (still often referred to as "cripples" in late-1960s parlance). "The handicapped are one of the biggest minorities in the country," he told reporters. "We're trying to call attention to some of their problems . . . We've started legislation to widen entrances to public buildings. We're campaigning for ramps instead of curbs at crosswalks. And there should be a percentage of rooms in apartment houses and hotels built so people in wheelchairs can get around."

Ironside, meanwhile, continued to hum along, and in the spring of 1968 Raymond was nominated for two Emmy Awards, one as Best Actor in the *Ironside* pilot, and one as Best Actor in the series. He didn't win, but costar Barbara Anderson walked away with a statuette as Best Supporting Actress in a Drama.

After only a season on the air, the show was winning kudos for its topicality. Against the backdrop of the Civil Rights movement, *Ironside* won the NAACP's first-ever Image Award for its sensitive treatment of the Mark Sanger character, played by Don Mitchell. Mark grew steadily from an angry young man into a thoughtful, well-rounded individual—without losing his strong views and outlook (he eventually attended law school). "I said to the NAACP guy, 'I can't believe you're giving us an award for having a black guy push a fat white guy around in a wheelchair,'" recalled *Ironside* producer Paul Mason. "And he said, 'But it's an honest job, and [Mark] is going to college.'"

"Millions of people watch a black man doing something important in *Ironside*," Mitchell said at the time. "Mark is not a token negro in Ironside's world. He is an important, needed human being with emotions inside of him and being given a chance to express them."

Like Perry Mason, Robert T. Ironside never lost a case and was always on the side of truth, justice, and the American way. He wasn't as eloquent as Perry; he had a saltier tongue and displayed many more foibles. "Our show is about a winner," producer Cy Chermak explained. "The anti-hero doesn't work with today's TV audience—it believes in superheroes . . . we do small stories about small people—plausible stories."

The long sedentary hours in the wheelchair were wreaking havoc on Raymond's physique. He always returned to the set after an invigorating trip to Naitauba tanned and slimmer than when he'd left. But eventually the bloat returned. Raymond was now closing in on three hundred pounds, which didn't make life any easier for Don Mitchell, whose job it was to push Chief Ironside around in his wheelchair (there should have been a medal for *that*).

The extra weight sapped a good amount of Raymond's energy, and his refusal to shoot on location forced *Ironside* directors like Jeff Hayden to contrive some creative filming techniques, including a rear-projection process, to work around that problem. Outdoor scenes on location were filmed with Raymond's stand-in, Lee Miller, and the footage was then brought back to the studio, where Raymond and his wheelchair were positioned in front of the movable "wild wall" on which the existing footage was screened. The scene was then reshot, this time with Raymond delivering his lines.

"When they told me about it, I thought they were crazy, but it worked," Hayden said. "Ray had a stand-in who was a good double from the back. Since Ray wouldn't go on location, we'd shoot many of the scenes from across the back of Ray's double with other people. We did this on other shows, but never because the star didn't want to go out on location. But Ray spent a lot of years in television, and he knew what it was all about. It's a terrible grind for a leading character—and he wasn't a young man anymore."

Raymond also claimed that the long hours in the wheelchair were affecting his eyesight. Because he was constantly looking up at the other characters from his seated position, he also was looking directly into the bright studio lights, which he said were damaging his vision. Benevides said later that Raymond's eyes were "burned" by the studio lights.

"He claimed that was the case and spoke about that occasionally, which is one of the reasons he said he needed to work less," said *Ironside* producer Joel Rogosin. "And he didn't want to be sitting outside with big panels reflecting the sun onto his face, which I think became a factor."

Raymond had all the sun he could handle on Naitauba. His Fiji hideaway was evolving into a bustling island where "the boss," as the natives referred to him, ran a tight ship. Raymond spent about two months a year in Naitauba. The plan was to spend six months a year there, or perhaps even make it his permanent residence after he retired, which he figured would be around 1975. As early as 1969, when he was into the third season of *Ironside,* he was already talking about throwing in the towel on his performing career. "I'm getting closer to that time in my life when I don't want to do a television series," he said.

He'd transformed his island into a profitable business venture and, five years into his investment, had more than doubled the land's value. All of the Naitauba natives worked for "the boss" in one capacity or another. It was "a feudal setup and Burr is lord of the manor," was how Cindy Adams described it for *TV Guide.* "He doesn't buddy with the peasants or drink with them . . . He blesses the children. He receives the elders. He is King Raymond the First."

Naitauba's chief source of income was its production of dried coconut meat, called *copra.* Raymond invested heavily in copra-producing machinery, and by the early 1970s

Naitauba was producing about three hundred tons of copra a year. It wasn't the island's only output—macadamia nuts and, of course, orchids were also exported—but the copra plantation was Naitauba's bread and butter. Raymond put whatever profits he made right back into feeding Naitauba's livestock, repairing and purchasing new copra and agricultural equipment, and maintaining living quarters for the locals. He launched an evening newspaper in Suva called the *Suva Sun*, partnering with Hong Kong and New Zealand newspaper owners in a bid to compete with the long-established *Fiji Times*.

Health care was a major concern for the Naitauban natives. Getting sick on the island could be a dangerous proposition. The medical clinic that Raymond financed and built didn't have a doctor on the premises, and in extreme cases, doctors in Suva, 160 miles away, had to be contacted by radio. Medical supplies were scarce, and those that were on-site had to be airlifted to the small island. In April 1968 a rare strain of influenza infected nearly all of the island natives, forcing Raymond to appeal via radio to an airline for help in getting supplies dropped onto Naitauba.

He also used the island to his advantage, persuading NBC to film parts of an *Ironside* episode, "Vacation in Fiji," in various South Pacific locations while he and Robert vacationed there during the summer 1970 hiatus (only Raymond appeared in the footage). A quick stopover in Naitauba while on the shoot revealed that termites had overrun his eighty-year-old house, creating a dangerous scenario, with the rotting floorboards threatening to give way under Raymond's enormous weight. The house was demolished, and Raymond hired an architect to plan a new, palatial residence to be built on the other side of the island.

Raymond's lifelong battle of the bulge was no laughing matter, and his bad eating habits and sedentary lifestyle were beginning to take their toll. He didn't exercise, and much of his working day was spent on the set, sitting in that damned wheelchair.

Still, despite his obesity and his heavy smoking habit, he'd been relatively healthy the past fifteen years. He'd missed the four episodes of *Perry Mason* in 1963 after having the benign polyps removed, and he was treated for various bumps and bruises after that, including an infected hand, ripped shoulder tendons, and a stomach bug from his various trips to Vietnam. He'd suffered the shoulder injury while in a helicopter that undertook emergency maneuvers to avoid Viet Cong gunfire.

He told friends he wanted to quit smoking, but he didn't, even though lung cancer had claimed the life of his *Perry Mason* pal William Talman, who'd made a highly publicized antismoking commercial that aired posthumously (Yul Brynner would do the same sort of ad years later). "It's not so much the medical pronouncements, although I know they're true," Raymond said about his smoking habit. "It's the fact that I know what smoking does to me. It's beginning to slow me down. I tramp up and down those hills and valleys and get short of breath. I don't like it at all."

As he neared his midfifties, his body began to rebel. Filming on the sixth season of *Ironside* had begun in August 1972 when Raymond, who was speaking a line of dialogue, stopped suddenly in midsentence. He felt his throat fill with blood and quickly grabbed a towel as the blood came out of his mouth. Worried crew members called for help and he was rushed to the hospital, where it was discovered that a blistered vocal cord had burst. It was a painful condition, but not life-threatening. He underwent surgery to have the blister removed and missed several weeks of work. Once again his stand-in, Lee Miller, worked overtime as the *Ironside* cast and crew shot around Raymond until his return.

The *Ironside* set was friendly enough, although the close rapport Raymond enjoyed with his *Perry Mason* costars never developed there (insiders said his *Ironside* costar Don Galloway addressed Raymond as "sir"). Barbara Anderson, an original cast member, left at the end of the 1971 season, frustrated at not having enough to do. She was replaced by Elizabeth Baur. Raymond seemed to almost resent the show's success, and insiders complained how his moodiness created an often tense atmosphere on the set. He was earning $20,000 per episode, a huge sum in those days, yet even that didn't seem to stanch his dark moods.

If Raymond was in a good mood, he could be delightful; more often than not, he was isolated, removed, and curt. Much to the displeasure of the NBC brass, he began talking about ending *Ironside* after the 1972–73 season when his contract ended. NBC, though, felt that *Ironside*'s shelf life hadn't yet expired, and they were right. After all, Raymond was nominated for yet another Emmy Award in 1972 (he lost again), and *Ironside* continued to be a ratings winner.

For some inexplicable reason *Ironside* was a huge hit in Israel, where a survey showed it was the country's most popular television show. But then again, Raymond contributed heavily to Jewish causes, a practice he continued for the rest of his life, which might have had something to do with his popularity among Israelis.

NBC had other reasons to keep *Ironside* around for a while. The previous season, a two-hour *Ironside* episode called "The Priest-Killer" helped launch George Kennedy's series *Sarge*. *Ironside* was then moved to 9:00 p.m. to dispatch a pesky newcomer, ABC's *Longstreet*, an *Ironside* ripoff in which James Franciscus played a blind insurance investigator with a loyal secretary and a seeing-eye dog. *Longstreet*, which was produced by ex–*Ironside* producer Joel Rogosin, lasted one season. *Sarge* met the same fate.

Yet despite his squawking about ending the series, which was an old habit carried over from his *Perry Mason* days, Raymond agreed to return for the 1973–74 season. But that was only after wrangling an unheard-of two-year deal under his new company, R.B. Productions (formed "as a Raymond Burr/ Robert Benevides Enterprise"). R.B. Productions replaced Harbour Productions, with Robert becoming vice chairman of the new company. Guy della-Cioppa, a former assistant to CBS chairman William Paley, was brought aboard as president. Raymond's agent, Lester Salkow, was named executive consultant.

The new two-year deal with Universal and NBC included two television specials and a planned big-screen adaptation of *Portrait: A Man Whose Name Was John,* a television movie Raymond starred in for ABC the previous year. He played Pope John XXIII, who reigned from 1958 to 1963 and whom Raymond considered one of the greatest men he'd ever met. The movie's focus was on then-archbishop Angelo Roncalli's efforts to save a boatload of 647 Jewish children from being shipped from Istanbul back to Nazi Germany and certain death. Don Galloway costarred as Roncalli's loyal secretary. Raymond, asked by reporters about his first meeting with Pope John XXIII years before, remembered it vividly: "He looked at me and said, 'Ah, yes, Perry Mason.'"

The Universal/NBC deal also included the promise to film a series that would be set in Fiji, and Universal laid out a bundle to send Joel Rogosin and a small group to the South Pacific to come up with ideas for the show.

"A bunch of us went to Fiji to scout locations and I wrote episodes for a proposed new series, *Raymond Burr in Fiji*," Rogosin said. "Ray hosted us in Fiji and introduced us to the local dignitaries, including the Fijian prime minister. The series was going to be about a character, based on Raymond, who ran a newspaper enterprise and other interests including a hotel, and [the series] presumably was going to be shot there. The studio sprung for quite a bit of money to send us there and develop the show, which, needless to say, never got made.

"Raymond was the king in Fiji," Rogosin said. "The response he got, from the people on the street on up to the prime minister, was incredible."

Filming on the seventh season of *Ironside* began in June 1973, shortly after Raymond's fifty-sixth birthday. The season was fraught with problems, both professionally and personally, from day one.

During a scheduled shooting break in early August 1973, Raymond and Robert flew to the Azores on business. On August 10, they boarded a Portuguese airliner for a flight back to Boston and were seated for takeoff when Raymond felt a sharp stabbing pain in his chest.

It took both of the airliner's pilots to hoist Raymond from his seat and drag him out of the plane. He was rushed to the Lajes Field Air Force Base Hospital, which was only half a mile from the airstrip. After undergoing a battery of tests, he was told the next day that he'd suffered a heart attack.

"He is improving, but is under observation. He can't be moved for a couple of weeks," Robert told a reporter from *Photoplay* magazine, which called the hospital after learning about Raymond's condition—and was finally connected four hours later. After Robert's initial comments he paused, and then continued with what *Photoplay* described as "forced levity." "The electrocardiograms seem to be satisfactory," he said. "Yes, it was a heart attack . . . but he's doing very well. You know how strong he is. He bounces back."

Raymond remained bedridden at Lajes for another two weeks before he and Robert returned to the States, where Raymond secretly checked in to UCLA Medical Center for more tests. He left the hospital on August 24 and refused to comment on his condition, instructing the hospital to follow his lead and remain mum.

There was soon more to worry about. Feisty Minerva Burr, who was now eighty-one, was battling cancer, and her prognosis wasn't good. Raymond was glad that he'd persuaded his parents to sell the historic Burr house in New Westminster in 1971 and move into his old house in North Hollywood. It was a nine-room place just blocks away from their famous son. Raymond's brother Edmond, who was married with seven children, was also close by. Their sister, Geraldine, was living in Alaska.

There were concerns, too, on the set of *Ironside*. Raymond returned to the show after resting for several months following the heart attack and was under strict orders from his doctors to work only half a day. But that was long enough for trouble to start on the set. He'd been griping for months over the quality of the show's scripts and had clashed with several directors. Now, back on the set, he began jawing with director Barry Shear and then fired him halfway through an episode. Shear told reporters that the entire *Ironside* cast and crew was afraid of Raymond's volcanic temper.

The string of bad news continued. In December, Raymond lost a $95,000 court case against his former attorney, Donald Leon, and a group of Leon's associates. Raymond claimed Leon and his partners gave him the bad advice to invest in a land deal that went belly-up. Whether Leon did anything wrong was moot, since the judge ruled that Raymond waited too long to file the lawsuit (the case had a five-year statute of limitations). While Perry Mason never lost a court case, in real life Raymond couldn't lay claim to the same unbroken string of judicial brilliance.

In late January, Minerva Burr died, and Raymond was crushed over the loss. "They sedated him for three days. He wasn't even able to go to the funeral," recalled his sister, Geraldine. "He took that awfully hard."

He also wasn't pleased a short time thereafter when his father, still going strong at eighty-five, announced that he was moving back to New Westminster. The stubborn Bill Burr always *was* happier in his native Canada. Once asked if he would ever consider retiring to Naitauba, Bill responded with typical alacrity: "Not me. I like New Westminster."

The run of bad luck continued into the fall of 1974. In October, Raymond was rushed into surgery to have his gall-bladder removed. He returned to the *Ironside* set just in time to learn that NBC was canceling the series, which was losing the ratings race to ABC's *The Streets of San Francisco*. *Ironside* would be replaced in January by *Archer*, a new detective show starring Brian Keith. *Ironside's* eight-season run was over. Production on the series ended in mid-December, and the last original episode, appropriately titled "The Faded Image," aired on January 16, 1975.

Raymond, though, wasn't heartbroken to see the show die. He experienced much the same sense of relief that he'd felt when *Perry Mason* met the same fate in 1966. "I hated that wheelchair," he said. "I'm not a good sitter at the best of times. I prefer being vertical or horizontal. Sitting down is agony. I never had back trouble until I started doing *Ironside*. It was the most uncomfortable job in the world."

Aside from the minor gripes, there were no public protestations from Raymond, no postcancellation interviews blasting NBC for axing the show and reneging on a promise to keep it going. For Raymond, the last few seasons had been a struggle, anyway, a seemingly endless battle over scripts and directors mollified only by his trips to Naitauba and the relief of working for ABC on the Pope John movie. And money certainly wasn't an issue now.

Eight seasons of *Ironside* had padded Raymond's already substantial bank account, and this time he'd taken a cut of the profits, selling his share of the syndication rights for a reported $1.5 million. Like *Perry Mason*, *Ironside* was launched into syndication almost immediately after its final original episode aired. The syndication package included three episodes produced, but never aired, before the series left the air.

CHAPTER TEN

Raymond and the Misses

Raymond and Robert bought a new house in North Hollywood and settled in for life after *Ironside*. The house, an understated ranch-style dwelling, was built into a hillside and was partly situated on the old Mary Pickford estate. It was surrounded by a long retaining wall with built-in niches, each adorned by brilliantly colored orchids. The top of the property line backed up onto the Hollywood Bowl.

Part of the property housed Raymond's flower collection, and he bought a four-wheel-drive vehicle to travel up and down the sloping grounds. "The first time I walked into the house, it was amazing," said friend Don DeLano. "He had six to seven different refrigerators in the kitchen for cheeses, condiments, meats, etc. He would cook a whole lamb and make enough lasagna for about one hundred people."

Raymond had been working on two highly successful television series for almost eighteen years straight and needed a rest. So he did what Raymond Burr did to relax.

He went back to work.

Shortly after returning from yet another trip to the Azores to check on his newest investment, a seaside inn on the volcanic island of Fayal, Raymond tackled the script for *Mallory*. The NBC pilot cast him in the familiar role of a brilliant lawyer once again outwitting the district attorney.

It was a not-so-subtle reminder of *Perry Mason,* but it was now ten years later.

In the *Mallory* scenario, however, the DA, angry at Mallory, sullies his reputation by charging him with perjury. Mallory, now down on his luck and looking for clients, is forced to defend a kid (Mark Hamill, a year away from his *Star Wars* fame) who's in jail for supposedly stealing his uncle's (Robert Loggia) car. For some inexplicable reason, Raymond wore a ridiculously curly wig for the role, which elicited laughs from the *Tonight Show* and *Merv Griffin Show* audiences after clips from *Mallory* were shown while Raymond was on those talk shows to promote it.

NBC had high hopes for *Mallory,* and it scheduled the two-hour television movie for a prime 9:00 p.m. spot in the ultra-important February sweeps period, which is used by networks to determine advertising rates. But most critics weren't impressed; *Mallory* was described as "talky" and its plot "impenetrable" when it aired on February 6, 1976. Its ratings were mediocre, and while Raymond garnered generally good reviews ("his intelligence and authority . . . [hold] everything together," opined the *Los Angeles Times*), NBC passed on turning *Mallory* into a series.

Universal was determined to find something—*anything*—in which to showcase its very expensive star, so it went back to the drawing board. In late spring, Raymond was cast in another series pilot, called *Kingston: Power Play.* In this one he played R. B. Kingston, a hard-charging (despite his girth) freelance investigative reporter working for a powerful newspaper chain called the Frazier Group. Raymond shot the *Kingston* pilot over the summer, and it premiered on September 15. A confident NBC was already penciling in *Kingston* as a midseason replacement for early 1977.

"Burr is back with a winner in *Kingston: Power Play*," wrote *Los Angeles Times* television critic Kevin Thomas. "*Kingston* is escapist TV fare at its sleekest . . . made persuasive by sharply delineated characterizations. Burr is in fine form."

NBC was encouraged by *Kingston's* critical and public reception and went forward with its plans to make it a regular series. The show was retitled *Kingston: Confidential* and was slated for a March 1977 debut. R. B. Kingston was now upgraded to the owner of the Frazier News Group, which also included television stations. The immense Kingston still went out into the field when duty called, and Pamela Hensley returned as Kingston's public relations aide, while actor Art Hindle was hired as Frazier News Group reporter Tony Marino.

Kingston: Confidential premiered on March 22 and bombed. "Raymond Burr looks and acts about as much like a crack investigative reporter as Farrah Fawcett-Majors looks like the new school marm," sniped one critic. "*Kingston* has the look of an old, rather tired show that's been around a long time," sniffed the *Los Angeles Times*, while the *Washington Post* said it was "a little too much for all but [Raymond's] most faithful fans to believe in." Viewers agreed, and the show premiered to low ratings and only passing interest. With *Mallory's* failure months before, Raymond and NBC were cooking their second consecutive turkey.

Although *Kingston* just wasn't very good, it was also hampered by its time slot and never really stood a chance. NBC scheduled *Kingston: Confidential* directly against ABC pow-

erhouse *Charlie's Angels* Wednesday nights at 10:00 p.m.—
which was the first indication that NBC officials weren't too
high on the series having a long shelf life. *Charlie's Angels*,
which premiered the previous fall with the aforementioned
Farrah Fawcett, had steamrolled everything in its path—
including *Kingston: Confidential*'s predecessor, *Tales of the
Unexpected*.

"I don't need to say anything else. *Charlie's Angels* was the
hottest thing, even though we had Pamela Hensley, who was
pretty sexy in her own right," Hindle said.

Raymond's workload on *Kingston: Confidential* was heavy,
but it wasn't anywhere nearly as demanding as the ones he'd
shouldered on *Perry Mason* and *Ironside*. Still, his reliance on
using the TelePrompTer was so ingrained into his television
acting style by now that it was second nature. And during the
short run of *Kingston: Confidential* he used the machine to
his advantage.

"Burr was totally in control of that series," Hindle said.
"If he said 'jump,' you jumped, of course. He was as big as a
refrigerator . . . and he was the best I'd ever seen using the
TelePrompTer. He had those huge, widely spaced blue eyes,
and he just worked it so that he could be thinking or looking
and somehow he could find that TelePrompTer and look away.
He was a genius at that. He hired all his cronies as directors
and the guys that knew how to work with him. I think that's
one aspect he wanted to control. And he was very concerned
with his privacy."

Hindle heard the stories about Raymond being gay. One
day, he was standing around waiting to shoot a scene with
Raymond and Pamela Hensley, just before the show broke for

the Christmas holiday. Raymond had called in sick a few days before and went for a series of gastrointestinal workups to determine the problem. Hindle figured he'd make small talk during a break in the shooting and asked Raymond how he was feeling. "He said, 'I feel so much better, because I had a GI a couple of days ago.' The only GI I knew was the military kind, and I thought I got caught off guard."

Kingston: Confidential ran for thirteen weeks before it was unceremoniously dumped by NBC. For the week ending August 7, 1977, it was the least-watched show on television. The news of its cancellation barely registered a blip on the Hollywood radar.

After carrying two of the most successful shows in television history, which he followed with two flops, Raymond's career as the star of a weekly television series was over. And he knew it. "I hated to lose that one," he said of *Kingston: Confidential*. "I'd wanted to play a crack journalist for years. The problem was, our stories simply weren't good . . . the worst experience I ever had in my life . . . the show should have been cancelled after we filmed four episodes . . . not one of the thirteen episodes was any good."

He took a brief hiatus and spent five weeks in Naitauba. And he focused now on his flower business.

He had greenhouses on his estate in North Hollywood and in Naitauba, and he was making personal appearances to promote his line of orchids. Raymond and Robert's flower business, Sea God Nurseries, was generating a profit, which was reason enough to put some effort into maintaining their investment. Raymond also bought into a business that was designed to send flowers via telephone, a commonplace practice now (enhanced by online computer technology) but still a revolutionary concept in the late 1970s. The business, called Teleflora, grew to become a giant in the flowers-by-phone industry and padded Raymond's already huge bank account.

"I'll make personal appearances for the [flower] company at flower shows and the like," he said. "I may even make TV commercials for them. I haven't decided. The fact is, flowers are my passion. I believe that by enabling people to send flowers instantly by telephone, we're helping the country, I hope aesthetically and culturally."

He was a frequent visitor to California State Polytechnic Institute in Pomona (known as "Cal Poly") after donating his collection of three thousand orchids to the school. One estimate had Raymond's gifts to Cal Poly worth well over $100,000, including the orchid collection, two greenhouses he paid for, and the equipment to run those greenhouses. He'd also gotten involved in the school's fund-raising efforts and was a featured commencement speaker. He and Robert later donated a $1.1 million art and antique furniture collection to the school.

Cal Poly's Don DeLano was Raymond's liaison at the school and remained a friend until the actor's death. "He tried to find a school with a hands-on approach, and he picked Cal Poly and also sent over some greenhouses that were assembled by the students," DeLano recalled. "I gave he and Robert a tour of the facility, and most of our corridors were narrow. We had to open both doors for Ray to get through, and he was walking with a cane."

Raymond's self-imposed hiatus from television didn't last for long. In September, he inked a deal to play an underworld boss in a six-hour television miniseries, *79 Park Avenue,* an adaptation of a Harold Robbins novel, costarring Lesley Ann Warren. He followed that with a guest-hosting gig on *Saturday Night Live* in February 1978 and then took his third stab at a post-*Ironside* television series.

This time it was a pilot for CBS called *The Jordan Chance* and was written by the talented Stephen J. Cannell, who'd written several episodes of *Ironside* and would later find fame as the creator of *The Rockford Files* and *The A-Team. The Jordan Chance* cast Raymond as Frank Jordan, who'd spent seven years behind bars for a crime he didn't commit. He was now a lawyer running a foundation to help other wrongly accused people prove their innocence. The show recalled *Perry Mason* in several ways, not the least of which was its plot, which bore a strong resemblance to Erle Stanley Gardner's NBC series *Court of Last Resort,* which premiered in 1957 alongside *Perry Mason* and was based on Gardner's real-life organization fighting for the wrongly accused. And once again, Raymond was playing a crusading lawyer.

The Jordan Chance also marked Raymond's first time back at CBS in a series role since *Perry Mason.* But the reunion proved short-lived after *The Jordan Chance* aired in December 1978 and no one cared.

It was becoming increasingly obvious that series television no longer had a place for Raymond and, at sixty-one, his movie career had long since passed him by. He'd made only one big-screen appearance in the years following *Perry Mason*— playing the devious millionaire Orbison in 1968's *P.J.*—and there wasn't much call for a three-hundred-pound actor who had trouble lifting himself out of a chair.

Raymond's weight gain had shifted into overdrive as he reached his sixties. His once-handsome face was now jowly and bloated, a triple chin adding to the unflattering portrait. He also continued to smoke, and the combination of the obesity and his cigarette habit was making his doctors and friends uneasy. Still, he insisted he didn't overeat, and he grew testy when he was questioned about his gargantuan girth, using fuzzy logic to explain his enormous waistline.

"I don't overeat—I only eat one meal a day, really, except when I'm traveling or living it up on weekends or something like that," he said at the time. "But my body has been one of those that has almost perfect assimilation, so everything I eat is assimilated, not lost in the whole process. I can eat just a little bit and gain, because my body works too well, all right?"

Raymond's weight, like that of his equally huge colleague Orson Welles, had become fodder for the late-night comedians. Johnny Carson teased him mercilessly in his *Tonight Show* monologues, to the point where Raymond refused to do the show, even when he was technically an NBC employee while he was starring in *Ironside*.

"I have been asked a number of times to do his show and I won't do it," he said. "Because I like NBC. He's doing an NBC show. If I went on I'd have some things to say, not just about the bad jokes he's done about me, but bad jokes he does about everybody who can't fight back because they aren't there. And that wouldn't be good for NBC."

Raymond's enormous size didn't help his employment prospects, and with regular series work and movie roles drying up, he was reconsidering some moneymaking options he'd previously scoffed at. He once considered television commercials beneath him, unless they related to publicizing the floral industry; now he signed a deal with the Independent Insurance Agents of America to star in a series of commercial testimonials and to appear in print ads plugging their services.

His television roles were reduced to guest shots (*The Love Boat, Eischied, The Misadventures of Sheriff Lobo*) and roles on bad made-for-television movies (*Disaster on the Coastliner, The Curse of King Tut's Tomb*). He talked about starring in Jay Broad's play *Conflict of Interest,* and eventually taking it to Broadway, but those plans went nowhere. He made brief appearances in two big-screen bombs, *Out of the Blue* and *Airplane II: The Sequel,* calling *Out of the Blue,* directed by his old pal Dennis Hopper, "the worst film I ever worked on and the worst experience of my life." His career was, for all intents and purposes, stuck in neutral.

Raymond put up a brave front, but the times were changing, and it was clear that television audiences weren't interested anymore in seeing an older, extremely corpulent Raymond Burr as a weekly series presence. He wouldn't, or couldn't, admit that fact. Full of the typical Burr bluster, he blamed the "financial setup of the studios" as the reason *he* no longer wanted to do a series, though no one was beating down his door with offers. "The public doesn't get a chance to voice their opinion before a show is canceled!" he said— conveniently forgetting that low public interest killed *Mallory, Kingston: Confidential,* and *The Jordan Chance.*

Even Naitauba no longer held much allure. Raymond was sixty-six now, with one heart attack already under his huge belt, and making the twenty-hour-plus trek to the South Pacific was just too much. His dream of retiring there faded until it was no longer realistic.

He put Naitauba up for sale in April 1983 but decided to keep some land in Fiji, including an orchid farm, as well as his ownership stake in *The Fiji Sun*. In September, he sold the island for a reported $2 million, or nearly ten times what he'd paid Mrs. Henning eighteen years earlier.

The Fiji government put a bid in for the island but couldn't match the winning bid submitted by self-proclaimed guru Adi Da Samraj. Born Franklin Jones, he'd founded a religion, Adidam, and formed a commune. According to the *Washington Post*, one of the commune's members during the 1970s was Joan Felt, daughter of Mark Felt—better known as Watergate informer "Deep Throat."

CHAPTER ELEVEN

Redux and Cover

Try as he might, Raymond never really could escape the large shadow of überlawyer Perry Mason. He had a nice run on *Ironside,* but it was *Perry Mason* with which he was most closely identified in the public consciousness. He found himself still talking constantly about Perry in interviews, nearly twenty years after the show's demise. And while he complained bitterly about the huge bite the show had taken out of his life, it was clear Raymond would be forever linked to Erle Stanley Gardner's maverick lawyer. The older he grew, the more he seemed ready to embrace his legacy.

That legacy hadn't gone unnoticed by Fred Silverman, the onetime wunderkind of ABC whose programming genius landed him on the cover of *Time* magazine in 1977. Silverman's jump to NBC in 1978 wasn't as smooth, though, and he lasted a rocky three years at the Peacock Network. He oversaw a string of flops at NBC, most notably the ridiculously expensive series *Supertrain,* which hastened his departure.

After his ouster from NBC, Silverman formed his own production company. Looking around for projects, he cast his keen programming eye on Raymond. It was nineteen years since *Perry Mason*'s cancellation, and Raymond wasn't working regularly anymore. Nostalgia seems to come in twenty-year cycles, Silverman thought; maybe, in 1985, *Perry Mason* was ripe for a revival.

It wouldn't be easy. The idea of reviving *Perry Mason* was an uphill battle. CBS had tried in 1973 by casting Monte Markham as Perry in *The New Perry Mason,* but the series failed miserably. Markham tried desperately to distance himself from Raymond's Perry Mason, but when the series premiered, all the critics could write about was how Monte Markham was no Raymond Burr. And apparently the public agreed, by ignoring the show.

The Erle Stanley Gardner estate also made it difficult for anyone trying to revive the series. "People had talked about [creating new *Perry Mason* shows] from time to time, ever since we stopped making them, but the [Gardner] estate made it so tough," Raymond said. "The terms were very difficult, so I was told."

No one, though, bothered to tell that to Silverman, who had the connections, the tenacity, and the moxie to get a deal done.

"I just thought it was a good idea to bring it back," Silverman recalled. "I was looking for kind of an angle. How do you make some noise? Even back then it was a crowded television environment. And I thought the idea of bringing *Perry Mason* back in the two-hour movie form made a lot more sense than a weekly series, as a kind of event."

Although Silverman was gone from NBC, he certainly wasn't persona non grata at the network, especially in his new role as a television producer. He called his replacement at NBC, programming chief Brandon Tartikoff, and pitched him the idea of bringing Raymond back as Perry.

"He said, 'Get Raymond Burr and you've got a deal.' It was that simple," Silverman said. "So I picked up the phone and called a friend of mine, an agent named David Shapiro, who happened to represent Raymond, and we set up a lunch. Raymond was intrigued by the idea. He had come off *Ironside,* and he wasn't doing a helluva lot. He said, 'Put it together and you have me on board.'"

"It took me twenty seconds to agree," Raymond said. "I'd been saying all those years, since we did the pilot in 1957, let's do a two-hour program. One hour never did justice to the scripts. We had to simplify too much, leave out clues and some of the good writing. We barely had time to do the show."

Silverman hired Dean Hargrove, who was over at Viacom working on *Columbo,* to help him hammer Perry Mason's prime-time return into shape. They struck a coproduction deal with Viacom, which in turn got permission from the Gardner estate to proceed with the television movie.

"We turned the first draft of the script in to NBC on a Friday, and on Monday afternoon a Viacom executive walked into my office and said, 'Well, we're picked up for production,'" Hargrove said. "They liked it, and they saw the potential."

"Raymond was at an age where the offers weren't coming in every day," Silverman said. "Even back then, it was a kind of youth-oriented society, particularly so in television. But you could take only so much of a South Pacific island, and it was a reasonably short, four-week production schedule, with Raymond working about two weeks. It was a good gig for Raymond."

With Raymond on board and the movie a go, the next step was to hire a cast. With production set to start in Toronto that summer, time was of the essence. Except for Raymond and Barbara Hale, all of the original *Perry Mason* stars were dead (and original executive producer Gail Patrick died in 1980). But Silverman didn't see that as a problem. "We wanted to simplify it a little bit," he said. "I felt, in looking at the original series, that there were almost too many regulars."

Raymond refused to do the movie, which was now being called *Perry Mason Returns,* without Barbara, who, at the age of sixty-one, was semiretired and working only sporadically, content to watch her son, actor William Katt, achieve television stardom on ABC's *The Greatest American Hero.* Little did she suspect she'd be costarring with him—in a *Perry Mason* movie, no less.

"When they came to me . . . I said, 'Well, how are you going to manage that? The boys, God love 'em, are gone,'" Hale said. "And they said, 'Well, we're going to work with a younger group; we're going to have Paul Drake have a son, and that will be for the younger audience, because it's a different show now and a different time.' I said, 'Well, that sounds reasonable,' and they said, 'Yeah, we have somebody in mind. He's a blond kid, and he's doing something about a hero or something—he happens to be in Kansas City doing *The Music Man* right now. I said, 'Well, I changed his diapers!'"

Barbara was reluctant, at first, to do the movie. She was recovering from a broken hip and didn't know how or if she could handle the workload. "When we first got the project, I called Raymond and said, 'Tear up the script!' He said, 'Why?' I said, 'I'm in the hospital. I just broke my hip.' He said, 'Well, you've got to do the show. You've got to do the show!' I said, 'How am I going to do it?' and he said, 'I don't know, but you'll do it. I know you, Barb.' And I did it. They flew me up there, wheeled me on the set, and I would stand up by the table and hang on like crazy!"

"I think she was a very important part of the mix," Silverman said of Hale. "Because the other people were not going to be on the show, and it would be nice—and [she] was also somebody Raymond could interact with."

William Katt, though, had reservations from the very beginning that would manifest themselves later on. "Bill didn't really want to do it when we first approached him," Hargrove said. "But Raymond had been a sort of surrogate father to him . . . so Bill came along, kind of reluctantly, although he fell into it. But he was never totally happy doing it."

In Hargrove's script, Perry is now an appellate judge and resigns the bench so he can defend his former secretary, Della Street, against a charge of murdering her slimy boss. The boss is a nasty millionaire (played by Patrick O'Neal) who tells his selfish kids he's cutting them out of his will before he predictably meets his maker. Della, of course, is innocent, and Perry rushes in to save the day. Perry's old pal, private investigator Paul Drake, is dead, but his son, Paul Drake Jr. (Katt), is carrying on the family tradition and helps Perry prove Della's innocence.

Shooting got under way in Toronto in late July 1985, and it was immediately apparent that Silverman's intuition was correct. Perry Mason's comeback was an event.

Dean Hargrove, who was up in Toronto on location, recalled the excitement that began building almost immediately after shooting began. "I picked up a copy of The Globe and Mail, their national paper, and I think it was like a two-page spread, or at least a big full-page, and two-thirds of the page was a picture of Raymond and Barbara, and then it went on to talk about *Perry Mason*," he said. "And in that moment, it occurred to me that this may really be something, because Toronto is a film town—it's not a town where a show has come there and everybody is going to write about it.

"And then I would hear, 'Well, *Time* magazine has called, and *Newsweek* and *People* have called,' and you just sort of get that feeling. But I really didn't expect it to have that kind of response. It was quite startling."

It was like old home week for Raymond and Barbara. They'd kept in touch over the years—Barbara even did an *Ironside* episode—but they hadn't seen each other in a while (William Katt described their relationship as being like that of two old college friends). "The first day we went into the courtroom set and sat down beside each other, and it just took twenty-five years out of our lives," Raymond said. "We were already twenty-five years younger and that's neat."

"It was *right*," Barbara said. "Absolutely. That's why I wanted to do it. On the opening day of shooting, we were in the courtroom. I was late getting on the set, and Ray was already there . . . He said, 'Morning,' walked to the front of the room, turned around, stopped, and we grinned at each other. We hadn't seen each other in this situation in twenty years. He said, 'I have never known so many years to evaporate before.'"

Perry Mason looked a bit different now than he had in 1966. There was Raymond's immense weight gain, of course, and now he complemented his large frame with a sleek silver-and-black beard that lent him a distinguished, avuncular presence—perfect for Perry's vaunted position as a judge ("Mason would *never* have retired," Raymond said).

With all the hype leading up to NBC's airing of *Perry Mason Returns*, it was as if the original show never left the scene. "The movie is goofily engrossing on its own; it's creaky, but it's friendly-creaky," enthused the *Washington Post* in a preview leading up to the premiere. "Fans of the original program will get added sentimental kicks from seeing Perry and Della together again. As for Burr . . . He isn't just an actor or a force anymore, he's a figure in the topography of mankind."

Perry Mason Returns aired on December 1, 1985, and by December 2, it was clear that NBC had a huge hit on its hands—and that Raymond had resuscitated his flagging career. The two-hour movie steamrolled its network competition and was the highest-rated program of the week, beating NBC's formidable *The Cosby Show* and snaring a whopping 27.2 rating and a 39 share—meaning that 39 percent of all television sets in use during those two hours were tuned to *Perry Mason Returns*. It was the highest-rated television movie of the year. Before the day was out, NBC chief Brandon Tartikoff ordered another *Perry Mason* movie into production.

Perry Mason Returns was sweet vindication for Silverman, proving that the onetime boy wonder still had the magic touch when it came to programming. Silverman wasn't a one-trick pony, either; he was also producing *Matlock*, which was a bona fide hit for CBS and had revived Andy Griffith's career.

"At that time, the airwaves were flooded with comedy programs. There were virtually no shows like *Perry Mason* on the air," Silverman said in explaining the success of *Perry Mason*

Returns. "It was a combination of putting it on at the right time, because it really represented counterprogramming to almost everything that was on the air, and the fact that people liked Perry Mason and they liked Raymond Burr. He was absolutely a television icon."

Raymond had a simpler explanation. "People remember the early days of television with a lot of affection, and *Perry Mason* is associated with those early memories," he said. "I think in these times people also want a reaffirmation of our system of justice."

It was a time for reunions. With Perry Mason now back as his on-screen alter ego, Raymond returned as Steve Martin in *Godzilla 1985*, a Japanese-produced big-screen update of 1954's *Gojira*. He'd always had a soft spot in his heart for the giant fire-breathing lizard, and much to the surprise of many, he jumped at the chance to appear thirty-five years later in this update. "I *like* Godzilla," he said. "I think Godzilla is a marvelous human creature. None of us paid enough attention to him," he said in all seriousness. "Godzilla came to be because we were using nuclear power badly. I'm sure Godzilla was trying to warn the world, although he was killing a lot of people doing it. Or *she* was."

Raymond got the call for *Godzilla 1985* two weeks before he was scheduled to start shooting *Perry Mason Returns.* Like his first experience with Godzilla, he was offered a boatload of money, again for just one day's work. "When they asked me to do it the second time I said, 'Certainly,' and everybody thought I was out of my mind. But it wasn't the large sum of money. I wasn't bad in the second *Godzilla.* I wasn't good. I was just nothing in it," he said. "We called him Mr. Martin in the second picture because Steve Martin the comedian came up in between times."

NBC's second Perry Mason movie, *The Case of the Notorious Nun,* aired in May 1986 and was even more popular than its predecessor, snaring a 42 audience share. Silverman talked of making three or four *Perry Mason* movies a year, and with the franchise taking off, Raymond and Robert decided to sell the house in North Hollywood, which fetched a cool $2.5 million (*Star Wars* producer George Lucas was a prospective buyer but passed). They pulled up stakes and moved to Dry Creek Valley in Healdsburg, a small, scenic town in northern California located in the heart of Sonoma County's wine-growing country.

Robert's father found the eight-acre spread, which Robert purchased in 1976, and Raymond now moved his collection of livestock, pets, and flowers up to the new homestead. He also envisioned bigger things for the property. "Raymond said, 'I think we should put in some grapes.' He'd always had this dream about having a winery because he loved to cook," Robert said. "That was his favorite thing of all, cooking for people. Of course, he couldn't cook for less than twenty people at a time, but he loved it."

Preparations for the eventual vineyard got under way shortly after the couple moved into their new home. They had some help in preparing the land for the vineyard from Dennis Kelli, who'd been Raymond's personal chauffeur for quite a while and spent lots of time with the actor, working on a retainer and also running errands when needed.

"When he first started ripping the ground up to put in their own root stock, I think a lot of the people up there were kind of laughing," Kelli said. "They were saying, 'What does this actor know about vineyards? Look at that, he's spending so much money,' because he did put an incredible amount of drainage in there . . . He planted grass and they said, 'Oh, that's overkill.'"

They weren't laughing over ten years after Raymond's death, when a terrible storm flooded the valley—while the vineyard remained untouched. "Robert said it was because of the precautions taken by Raymond," Kelli said.

Raymond was rejuvenated by his new *Perry Mason* success, and he now talked of other projects. He and Robert joined forces with British producer James Burke to announce a company called Royal Blue Limited, which they said would produce programming on a global scale. The company would encompass records, movies, television, publishing, and educational pursuits.

Among the projects planned for Royal Blue Limited was *Riverboat Circus*, a two-hour television movie, which was written by Raymond and would be filmed in Portugal. It told the story of a man who turns his back on the world to live his life aboard a riverboat. Raymond also went to great lengths in press interviews to talk up a miniseries, *The Last Privateer*, in which he would play Enos Collins, who was once the richest man in nineteenth-century North America and who lived to be ninety-seven years old after rubbing shoulders with Henry Wadsworth Longfellow and Abraham Lincoln. Neither project ever saw the light of day.

He signed another television endorsement deal, this time shilling for Canada's National Real Estate Service (NRS) in a series of thirty-second commercials. He also began planting the seeds for an *Ironside* reunion, figuring that if America was embracing Perry Mason, why not see if Robert T. Ironside had the same appeal ten years later?

"I talked with Universal about an *Ironside* project at the same time Fred Silverman contacted me about the Perry Mason movies," he said. "I'm definitely considering *Ironside*. Don Galloway is eager to get involved in the project. The key, of course, is a script. Good television detective stories are tough to come by, even if a noted hero is featured."

In the midst of all this activity, and in between *Perry Mason* movies, Raymond signed on to host eighty-five episodes of a new syndicated show called *Trial by Jury,* which dramatized courtroom proceedings through flashbacks. Like the *Perry Mason* movies, *Trial by Jury* was produced by Viacom and featured Raymond as a retired judge who guided viewers through trials by highlighting key testimony and summarizing evidence. At the end of each show, a "jury," consisting of real people (not actors), deliberated the case and arrived at a verdict.

Raymond's weight was still ballooning out of control, and he still used a cane to help him get around. Since he was a heavy smoker and he winded easily, he had trouble moving more than a few feet at a time and shot most of his wrap-around scenes for *Trial by Jury* sitting down. It was not a pleasant sight.

And still, while he had trouble catching his breath, he insisted on shooting his part of *Trial by Jury* in Denver's thin air in an old theater owned by a friend. The "jury" part of the show was filmed in Los Angeles.

The Mile-High City held a special place in Raymond's heart, since he'd grown extremely fond of its picturesque mountain scenery and its people while filming several *Perry Mason* movies there. He was also a part of the local cultural scene, helping to build support for a Denver public school for the arts and to raise money for the Denver Children's Hospital. In 1993, the University of Colorado awarded him the degree of Doctor of Human Letters for his contributions to television and the movies.

He also spoke out against a boycott organized around Amendment 2, an anti-gay-rights initiative passed by Colorado voters in 1992 that earned their state the sobriquet "the Hate State." Amendment 2 also earned the enmity of Hollywood celebrities, who shunned Colorado's ski slopes in silent defiance against the amendment. "You fight bad legislation by working with the system to change it. You don't boycott; you don't walk away," Raymond told the *Denver Post*. "You educate people. You get those who care involved and attempt to change things."

In January 1993, Raymond, Barbara Hale, and about sixty cast and crew members from several television productions shooting in Colorado took out an ad in *Variety*, urging their showbiz colleagues to disregard the boycott. "Some people in Colorado made a mistake, but to boycott is another mistake," the ad read in part. "Discrimination is wrong, legalized discrimination is worse."

Raymond's fondness for Denver was so strong that Viacom thought of building a studio there. The production company had pumped an estimated $12 million into the local economy since filming on the *Perry Mason* movies began. It spent $110,000 alone in building sets for the movies (including Perry's office) in the city's Lowenstein Theater, which it rented for $40,000. One of its other shows, the *Father Dowl-ing Mysteries,* starring Tom Bosley, was also filming in Denver at the time. A studio made sense.

More important, Denver was also far away from the Via-com suits, who weren't allowed onto the *Trial by Jury* set, on Raymond's orders.

"There was no sound, no good acoustics [in the theater], and it made it a pretty difficult production to shoot there," said *Trial by Jury* executive producer Mary James, who be-came a close friend to the actor. "But Raymond wanted to see Denver make money, so we shot there.

"The thing about Raymond was that he was such a huge star for so long and so consistently, that I think what hap-pened is that he had almost this King Tut thing going on where he was just so used to being treated like such a major celebrity . . . you think anyone who's been treated that way for so long, they don't know how to *be* anything else."

Mary spent a lot of time with Raymond, not only shoot-ing the show but accompanying him on press junkets at his insistence. "He had this whole bizarre notion that I was going to go on TV with him, which made no sense at all," she said. "He was just funny that way, you know? Like he would play with the executives."

He used his leverage to his advantage, pulling the old "too tired to work" routine more than once during the production of *Trial by Jury.* He knew that the Viacom executives were too cowed to do much about it, too leery of upsetting their gar-gantuan meal ticket to rock the boat. They kept their mouths shut when Raymond insisted on shooting some wraparounds in one of Denver's old government buildings, an undertaking requiring special lighting and other equipment that cost Viacom money over and above the show's budget. After all the fussing, Raymond then told Mary he couldn't shoot that day "because the script wasn't right," and he took the next three days off.

Raymond was scheduled to begin shooting another *Perry Mason* movie after wrapping the first season of *Trial by Jury* and after returning from a trip to Europe he was taking with Robert and Robert's parents. He invited Mary to join them, and she met them in Seville. Their itinerary included a drive over to the coast of Portugal and then up to the northern coast. But for Raymond it was all about the food. Lots of it.

"We would stop at restaurant after restaurant. I mean, you just couldn't believe how much food there was," Mary recalled. "We would go to all these castles and have these incredible meals, and Raymond would be back with the cooks, planning out what we were going to have. The whole route was based on the restaurants."

Television audiences, meanwhile, continued to gobble up the *Perry Mason* movies. Raymond was cranking out three to four movies each year, and the ratings justified continuing the franchise. But there were some changes along the way.

William Katt, who never seemed comfortable in his role as Paul Drake Jr., left in 1988 and was replaced by William R. Moses, who played Perry's junior partner, Ken Malansky. The spirit of William Talman lived on through Raymond's old friend actor Charles Macaulay, who played DA Markham—and *he* never won a case, either. Markham's name was also an inside joke recalling actor Monte Markham, who played Perry in CBS's short-lived *The New Perry Mason*.

And even now, over forty-five years since his first credited movie role in *San Quentin,* Raymond felt the need to repeat the lies about his fabricated personal life. During a 1990 interview in *Us* magazine, he mentioned being overseas, in the navy, "from '42 to the end of '43," when in fact he was acting at the Pasadena Playhouse. He was also asked directly, in that same interview, whether he'd been wounded by shrapnel during the war in which he never served.

"I'm not going to talk about my personal life," he answered tersely. "There are no big black secrets. I'm just not going to get involved with that."

Okay, he was asked, so why *don't* you talk about your personal life?

"They've offered me a million[-dollar] advance to write an autobiography," he said. "The first thing they want is a list of all the women I slept with, aside from the ones I married."

CHAPTER TWELVE

Twilight in the Vineyard

Raymond was seventy-four now, but he continued working at a pace that would have exhausted a man half his age. If the Burr genes were any indication of his life expectancy, he had plenty of time left to relax when he finally did decide to retire.

His grandmother had lived to the ripe old age of ninety-nine, and his father, feisty Bill Burr, lived for nearly another ten years in his beloved Canada before passing away in 1985. He was ninety-six and active up until the very end.

There was no practical reason for Raymond to slow down. And with several houses and very expensive tastes in food, art, and travel—and lots of bills to pay—he wasn't unhappy about the steady work. The *Perry Mason* franchise continued to hum along, and he worked about four weeks on each movie, relying on the TelePrompTer, as usual, to help him and no longer expected to carry the burden of an enormous workload.

The movies' numbers were down a bit, but they were still good enough to justify NBC's faith in ordering three to four more movies each year. And Raymond had the good timing to grow older in an era when senior citizens were flourishing on television. Suddenly, old was the new young. Sixty-five-year-old Andy Griffith's *Matlock* television series was still going strong. And Raymond's *Please Murder Me* costar Angela Lansbury, now in her late sixties, was well into her run on CBS's *Murder, She Wrote,* being discovered by a new generation of fans.

But trouble loomed on the horizon.

The first hint of bad news struck Raymond in early 1991, after he'd finished filming his newest *Perry Mason* movie, *The Case of the Glass Coffin,* in Denver. He'd been experiencing fierce pain in his gut, and he underwent a battery of tests at Cedars Sinai Hospital in Los Angeles, which showed a tumor in his colon. After immediate surgery he seemed fine, returning to work on his next *Perry Mason* movie after a short recovery period.

But it was revealed a few months later that doctors had removed a cancerous growth from his spine during the colon surgery and that Raymond was now undergoing exhaustive radiation treatments to fight the cancer. The tabloids were tipped off about Raymond's condition and were starting to sniff around, running screaming headlines that Raymond was dying.

Raymond went on the news-magazine show *Entertainment Tonight,* to quell the rumors that he was knocking on heaven's door. "I am not dying of cancer. I am in reasonably good health," he said, adding for good measure that he was about to leave for Denver to film three more *Perry Mason* movies. "I have plans to the year 2001—which may or may not come true," he added enigmatically.

One part of those plans was an *Ironside* reunion movie, which NBC officially announced in January 1992 as part of its schedule for the next season. Raymond also signed a new deal to return as a television pitchman for Canada's National Real Estate Service after a five-year hiatus from the company.

He received more bad news in December 1991. The cancer on his spine had now spread to his kidney, and his doctors recommended immediate surgery to have the kidney removed. Raymond refused. He was intent on filming the *Ironside* reunion movie and then on filming his next *Perry Mason* project, *The Case of the Killer Kiss*. "He said he had earmarked his earnings from the upcoming movies to his various charities and he didn't want to disappoint anyone," recalled his doctor, Selvyn Bleifer.

It took nineteen years to revive *Perry Mason* after its original run, and seventeen years had passed since *Ironside's* cancellation. But the entire cast—including Don Galloway, Don Mitchell, and Elizabeth Baur—was alive and well, and they all jumped at the chance to do the *Ironside* reunion movie, which would be filmed in Raymond's adopted city of Denver. Even Barbara Anderson, who'd left *Ironside* in a contract dispute after the third season, rejoined her former castmates for *The Return of Ironside*. Raymond was in severe pain and was fully aware he was playing with fire by delaying his cancer surgery. But he soldiered on, putting the surgery off until later and dying his hair and beard for the Robert T. Ironside role to distance himself physically from Perry Mason.

In the *Ironside* reunion movie, Robert T. Ironside is now retired and running a vineyard with his wife, Katherine (Dana Wynter). But he's thrust back into action after his old pal Ed Brown (Galloway), who's now working for the Denver police department, asks him to fill the chief's slot after his boss's sudden death. Ironside agrees, but only on a temporary basis—until Eve Whitfield's (Anderson) daughter is suspected of a double murder and Ironside vows to prove her innocence. He's aided, of course, by old cohorts Ed Brown, Mark Sanger (Mitchell), and Fran Belding (Baur).

Raymond told no one on the set about his illness and showed up every day for work, never letting on that he was in excruciating pain or that he was undergoing cancer treatments. "I didn't even know he was taking chemotherapy until I saw him shaking uncontrollably," Anderson said. After the movie wrapped, he did the usual round of promotional interviews, but he didn't mention his illness. Yet he hinted that something was amiss.

"I wasn't particularly pleasant to be around when we were working on this," he said regarding the *Ironside* movie. "But that gradually ebbed away when the whole production was finished."

He finally entered the hospital on February 1, 1993, to have the cancerous kidney removed, and he then spent several weeks in a nearby hotel as he underwent radiation treatments. But it was all for naught. In March, Dr. Selvyn Bleifer delivered the devastating news: the cancer had spread, and it was inoperable. There was no hope for recovery. "He never asked how much time he had left," Bleifer said. "He only spoke about how many things he still had unfinished."

True to his nature, Raymond shared the news with no one save for Robert and a few very close friends and threw himself into his work. He was determined to keep going until the bitter end. He flew to Paris and then to Spain with Viacom publicist George Faber, who knew about his death sentence, to help sell the *Perry Mason* movies overseas, which was never a difficult task (the show was enormously successful around the world). When he returned home, he began filming the next two *Perry Mason* movies, *The Case of the Tell-Tale Talk Show Host* and *The Case of the Killer Kiss*.

"I was back in Vancouver, and [Raymond] called and said, 'Can you come down?' recalled Dennis Kelli, his longtime chauffeur/friend. "And I went down there and he said, 'I've been diagnosed with cancer, and I don't know how long I've got.'"

The Return of Ironside premiered on NBC on May 4, 1993, to generally favorable reviews and decent numbers, snaring 19 percent of the viewing audience. "It's a fragmented case that takes a lot of gullibility, but it's extraordinary what Burr brings out of the characterization," *Variety* enthused.

The *New York Post*'s Adam Buckman hated the movie but loved Raymond. "*The Return of Ironside* presents viewers with a dilemma," he wrote. "It stinks, but it has Raymond Burr."

By July, Raymond was back in Denver, working on *The Case of the Killer Kiss*, but his condition was deteriorating. "Everybody knew he was in pretty bad shape, and they said, well, should we postpone it?" Faber said. "And Raymond said, 'Hell, no. We're going to do it. Just do it.' It broke your heart to see him, because you could tell he wasn't moving his usual way. He was sort of, not lethargic, but to the point of where he was a man who was not well."

He'd lost a lot of weight, the pain was excruciating, and he was no longer able to stand for any length of time. He shot the entire *Case of the Killer Kiss* from a wheelchair, standing only once on camera and willing himself to get through the scene. "I was devastated. It just grated on me badly," he told *TV Guide*. "In all my years of *Ironside,* I never sat in that wheelchair unless I was on camera."

He was stoic as always and wouldn't discuss his illness, not even with an old, dear friend like Barbara Hale. "We made a joke out of it," Hale said. "I had broken my hip and had to be in a wheelchair. He told me to come on over to his wheelchair and we'd make it a wheelchair for two."

"We were all worried about his health, so as soon as he finished [shooting] they would take him back to his room so he could sleep," recalled friend Charles Macaulay, who was once again playing DA Markham opposite Perry. "He was in terrible pain, and yet, to keep alert, he refused morphine, and he showed up on the set every day."

Producer Dean Hargrove was watching the dailies, and he noticed a huge change in Raymond's behavior on the set. "He would come in and he wouldn't speak to anyone, which was very unlike him, because he was very gracious always to the crew and guest stars," he said. "He would just sit down at the defense table and wait until he had to summon up the energy to perform.

"And you would literally see him make that transformation, and it was rather remarkable to see him do it," he said. "And then, when it was over with, you could see that he was spent. It was . . . what I thought to be a considerable act of physical courage and . . . it was remarkable and touching to see the way that he behaved and performed during that movie."

Director Christian Nyby, who was unaware of the extent of Raymond's illness, was surprised to hear a comment made by one of the cameramen after Raymond finished shooting his final scene: "I remember him saying to me, 'Well, that's the last time we're going to see him.'"

Immediately after shooting wrapped, Raymond left for Dry Creek Valley, heading home to spend his remaining time with Robert. Thirty-seven years earlier, he and Barbara Hale filmed the *Perry Mason* pilot. But their friendship went back further than that, to their days as kids on the RKO lot. Now it was time to say their good-byes.

"There were no words. No words," Barbara said. "He was being wheeled out to the car to be taken home, and we just looked at each other and I said, 'Have a good trip, honey.'"

His final few months were peaceful ones. He spent his days in his wheelchair, taking in the warm California sun on the patio and gazing out over the ripening vineyard. His gargantuan frame was shrunken a bit now, and his once-gregarious spirit turned inward toward reflection. He refused to take phone calls from friends, including Barbara; no one except his very inner circle, which included Charles Macaulay, was allowed to visit lest they see him in his frail condition. He was too proud for that. "He didn't want to see friends and receive flowers. That was too funereal," Macaulay said.

Dennis Kelli, who was unaware of Raymond's dire condition, stopped by Dry Creek Valley for a visit during those last summer months. "We just kind of sat around at the farm and they were talking about winding things down, and I'm thinking [it's] maybe to the point that he couldn't handle things," he said. "I didn't realize how sick he was. I didn't realize it was that bad. He just didn't want anybody to know."

By August, the cancer had spread, moving to his lungs and then to his brain. Yet he still refused the morphine, fighting every step of the way to keep his wits about him. If he wasn't alert, he wouldn't see the fall harvest, and wouldn't that be a shame?

TV Guide reporter Mary Murphy, in a beautifully written article detailing Raymond's final days, was able to ask him some questions via Robert and Charles Macaulay, who re-layed Raymond's answers back to her. Asked about his great-est regret in life, he singled out the one achievement that won him pop-culture immortality: Perry Mason. He could have remarried and had children, he said, could have led "a normal, everyday life" if not for the dreaded defense attorney. Asked if he had learned anything throughout his final illness, he answered: "Nothing. Except that death is ugly and messy and not one whit romantic." You could almost hear that once-booming baritone barking out his reply.

By the beginning of September, the Chardonnay grapes in the vineyard were ripened. Before too long, the vineyard would produce its first bottle of wine, turning Raymond's dream into a reality. He and Robert toasted the good news on the terrace with some vintage champagne.

He was slipping in and out of lucidity now and was hooked to a morphine drip to stanch the excruciating pain. He refused too much help from his doctor, Paul Marguglio, and from the nurses hired to care for him. That would be admitting defeat, and he wasn't prepared for that. Not yet. "He had been fight-ing like an army of men to keep from dying," Robert said.

As the end drew nearer, he spent most of his days lying in bed, staring at the ceiling or at the artwork adorning his bed-room walls. Then, as if struck by a thunderbolt, he suddenly sat up one day in early September and moved to the edge of his bed. "If I lie down, I'll die," he told Robert. Incredibly, he spent the next thirty hours sitting upright, refusing morphine.

He awoke on the morning of September 12, 1993, and immediately began questioning Robert about the Chardonnay grapes, about his beloved orchids, and even about the sheep on the ranch. But the unbearable pain returned shortly thereafter, and he was put back on the morphine. At around 5:00 p.m. he mercifully slipped into a coma; at 8:40 p.m. he slipped away, with Robert at his side.

He was seventy-six.

"It was, in the end, a sweet death," Robert said.

"He rarely lost a battle, but he knew that this was one he simply couldn't win," said Charles Macaulay. "It was a peaceful end after all the torment he endured."

CHAPTER THIRTEEN

Where There's a Will . . .

Raymond Burr's death was international news. Almost all of his obituaries repeated as fact his fabrications about the dead ex-wives, Annette Sutherland and Laura Andrina Morgan, his dead son Michael Evan Burr, and even his fictitious war record. But then again, what choice did they have? Raymond had repeated these stories so many times for nearly fifty years. Maybe after a while he even convinced himself that some of it was true.

The *New York Times* paid tribute to Burr with a long obituary that ran over two columns of type, the amount of space and verbiage usually reserved for A-list deaths. The obituary described Raymond as "a movie villain who became the ultimate defender" as Perry Mason—who was described as "gravelly-voiced and unrelentingly stern, with a habit of exhaling resonantly through his nostrils." In handling Raymond's romantic and personal life, the self-professed "Paper of Record" used the reference work *Current Biography* to state that "Mr. Burr was married three times . . . His only child, Michael Evan, by his first marriage, died of leukemia in 1953." It also repeated the nonsense about his spending time in China as a youth and about his service in the navy. There was no mention of Robert.

Raymond's obituary in the *Los Angeles Times* listed survivors as his sister Geraldine "and his longtime business associate and companion, actor Robert Benevides."

"I had always assumed that Raymond was gay, because he had a relationship with Robert Benevides for a very long time," said Dean Hargrove. "Whether or not he had relationships with women, I had no idea. I did know that I had trouble keeping track of whether he was married or not in these stories. Raymond had the ability to mythologize himself, to some extent, and some of his stories about his past . . . tended to grow as time went by."

Raymond carried his fabrications with him to the grave. His death certificate listed his marital status as "widowed" and his military service as "1943 to 1945." Robert was listed as "Friend."

As per his final wishes, Raymond was cremated. Five days later, Robert took Raymond's ashes, along with Minerva's ashes, up to Frasier Cemetery in New Westminster, where mother and son were buried alongside Bill Burr in the family plot.

A memorial service for Raymond was held on October 1, 1993, at the Pasadena Playhouse. Fifty years before, Raymond made his mark there; now, in death, his friends and colleagues gathered to remember his outsized personality. Old friend and costar Don Galloway emceed the service; Dean Hargrove, Raymond's doctor Selvyn Bleifer, longtime stand-in Lee Miller, and old family friend Bungy Hedley were among the speakers. The stage was cloaked in darkness, a lone spotlight illuminating an empty director's chair with "Raymond Burr" stenciled across its back. A bagpiper, wailing a lament, circled three times and walked away, the plaintive sound of his instrument receding in the distance. There wasn't a dry eye in the house.

NBC seized on the opportunity to use Raymond's death to its advantage (a warmhearted television tradition). It announced plans to air a prime-time special, *The Defense Rests: A Tribute to Raymond Burr*, which would be followed by a rerun of his penultimate *Perry Mason* movie, *The Case of the Tell-Tale Talk Show Host*. It followed that a week later by rerunning *The Return of Ironside*.

Raymond's final *Perry Mason* movie, *The Case of the Killer Kiss*, aired on November 29, 1993. Twenty-six million viewers tuned in to watch their hero get the bad guy for the last time. It was the week's fifth-most-watched prime-time show. Somewhere, Raymond was smiling. Even in death he was still the one everyone wanted to watch.

Raymond's death also left the unanswered question of whether NBC and Viacom would continue their profitable *Perry Mason* franchise without the man who fully embodied Erle Stanley Gardner's creation. "Certainly, the first thing is that no one's going to try to replace Raymond Burr," Hargrove said. "As far as we're concerned, that's unthinkable."

That held true . . . sort of. NBC soon put another *Perry Mason* movie into production, *The Case of the Wicked Wives*, in which it was explained that Perry was "away" in Washington, D.C., with attorney Anthony Caruso (Paul Sorvino) filling in. *Wicked Wives* aired on December 17, 1993, to the lowest ratings in the entire *Perry Mason* movie franchise. *The Case of the Lethal Lifestyle*, which aired the following May, didn't fare much better. In this one, Perry was "unavailable," and Hal Holbrook filled in as defense attorney William McKenzie.

With Raymond gone, the press slowly began to cast gentle doubts on many of his biographical claims. "There was a mysterious side to Ray," longtime double Lee Miller told *People* magazine. "Ray said he was married three times. I never met any of [his wives]. He never brought up that side of his life."

Raymond's longtime publicist John Strauss said his client "never mentioned any wives or a son" for the forty-plus years they did business together. More tellingly, he pointed out that Raymond worked nonstop in Hollywood during the year in which he claimed to be traveling the country with his dying son.

There were also the unconfirmed tabloid tales, wild stories about Raymond's private life spiced up with quotes from unidentified "friends" who described his closeted homosexual lifestyle in almost cartoonish terms.

There were claims that Raymond and Robert secretly "wed" in 1963 and that Raymond, according to a "friend of the couple's" quoted in *The Sunday Mail*, "enjoyed playing 'wife' to Robert. If you went to their house, Raymond would be wearing a frilly pink apron and doing the ironing. He fussed around like the woman of the house. Raymond always called Robert 'my husband.' He would knit sweaters for him in front of the fire."

At the time of his death, Raymond left an estate valued at over $30 million, even though Robert and Raymond's friends insisted that he'd given nearly all of his money away through charitable contributions and to friends in need. If that was the case, the estate's value rested in Raymond's many real estate holdings, including the spread in Dry Creek Valley.

His will, which he filed in San Jose, California, in March 1991, left everything to Robert—omitting all family members, including his only living sibling, his younger sister Geraldine, now living in Alaska (his brother, Edmond, had passed away several years before). "I give all my jewelry, clothing, books, works of art, household furnishings and furniture, automobiles and other items of a personal nature, together with any insurance on such property, to Robert Benevides," the will stipulated. Raymond made it clear in the will that he'd "intentionally omitted to provide for any of my heirs or other relatives living at the date of my death." Just what sin Geraldine had committed to be written out of the will remains anyone's guess. But she apparently didn't harbor any grudges, and she spoke lovingly of her big brother in a television biography of Raymond that aired in 2000.

As often happens with estates in which its millions are left to one person, Raymond's will was a lawsuit waiting to happen. In February 1994, two of Raymond's nieces and nephews, Minerva Burr and James Burr, contested the will in the Sonoma County courthouse. They claimed that Uncle Raymond was manipulated by Robert into bequeathing everything to him and cutting out the rest of the family. Robert had a terse response: "Anybody who thinks that anybody could have ever influenced Raymond Burr is crazy."

Niece Minerva Burr (named after Raymond's mother) claimed she was fighting for the money out of love for her uncle. "I really loved my Uncle Ray and I would never do anything to harm his memory," she said. "I am not being greedy. If I am successful I will share everything with my aunt, cousins and brothers."

The suit was thrown out eight months later.

Sadly, Raymond didn't live long enough to see his vineyard become a reality, but he would have been pleased by its growth and progress. Today, it's a thriving business still run by Robert, who honored his life partner by renaming it Raymond Burr Vineyards.

"It was never my dream, it was his dream," Robert said of the vineyards. "When he died in '93 we still hadn't released any of the wines. I finally decided it should be called Raymond Burr Vineyards. He didn't want it named after him, I know that. We had talked about that possibility and he didn't like that at all.

"But we're making great wines now. It's a memorial to him, to his idea, and I think it deserves to be named after him." A note on the vineyard's Web site describes the wine as Raymond's "living, breathing presence."

In 1998, five years after Raymond's death, the American Film Institute published its list of the one hundred greatest movies in American film history. Among the picks were two movies in which Raymond played key roles: *A Place in the Sun* and *Rear Window*.

In 2000, New Westminster's historic Columbia Theater was renamed the Raymond Burr Performing Arts Center in honor of its native son. Although he'd left New Westminster at the age of six, Raymond always held a special place in his heart for the city of his birth, returning there often through the years and helping to support its civic causes. Now his fellow Canadians remembered him with the ultimate compliment for an actor.

That same year, cable's A&E Network devoted an episode of its acclaimed *Biography* series to Raymond's life. *The Case of the TV Legend* included interviews with Robert, Don Galloway, Marilyn Hedley Gozzano (Bungy Hedley's sister), and Barbara Hale, among others. The familiar fabricated tales of Raymond's life were repeated in the hour-long retrospective, but now they were gently discounted. The documentary questioned Raymond's stories about the dead ex-wives, the dead son, and his war service by drawing a parallel to some of his more far-out movies, including *Godzilla:* "It appears that some details about his own personal life would prove to be just as wildly imaginative and fictitious."

And, like Raymond, it was all there for everyone to see—hiding in plain sight.

On Broadway

Crazy with the Heat
Opened January 14, 1941
Closed April 19, 1941
Produced by Kurt Kasznar,
Ed Sullivan
A musical revue
Book by Arthur Sheekman, Don
Herold, Mack Davis, Max Liebman,
Sam E. Werris; lyrics by Irvin
Graham; music by Irvin Graham
Cast: Grace Barrie, Bobby Busch,
Harriet Clark, Don Cummings,
Ted Gary, Luelle Gear, Hildegarde
Halliday, Willie Howard, Betty Kean,
Raymond Burr
Theater: 44th Street Theater

The Duke in Darkness
Opened January 24, 1944
Closed February 12, 1944
Produced by Alexander H. Cohen and
Joseph Kipness
Written by Patrick Hamilton
Cast: Edgar Stehli, Raymond Burr,
Louis Hector, Philip Merivale,
Horace Cooper
Theater: Playhouse Theater

In the Movies

Earl of Puddlestone (1940)—
uncredited
Directed by Gus Meins
Cast: James Gleason, Lucile Gleason,
Russell Gleason, Harry Davenport,
Lois Ranson
Studio: Republic Pictures

Without Reservations (1946)—
uncredited
Directed by Mervyn LeRoy
Cast: Claudette Colbert, John Wayne,
Don DeFore, Anne Triola, Phil Brown
Studio: RKO

San Quentin (1946)
Directed by Gordon Douglas
Cast: Lawrence Tierney, Barton
MacLane, Marian Carr, Harry
Shannon, Carol Forman, Raymond
Burr
Studio: RKO

Code of the West (1947)
Directed by William A. Berke
Cast: James Warren, Debra Alden,
Steve Brodie, John Laurenz,
Raymond Burr
Studio: RKO

Desperate (1947)
Directed by Anthony Mann
Cast: Steve Brodie, Audrey Long,
Raymond Burr, Douglas Fowley, Jason
Robards Sr.
Studio: RKO

Fighting Father Dunne
(1948)—uncredited
Directed by Ted Tetzlaff
Cast: Pat O'Brien, Darryl Hickman,
Charles Kemper, Una O'Connor,
Arthur Shields
Studio: RKO

I Love Trouble (1948)
Directed by S. Sylvan Simon
Cast: Franchot Tone, Janet Blair,

Janis Carter, Adele Jergens, Raymond
Burr
Studio: Columbia Pictures

Sleep, My Love (1948)
Directed by Douglas Sirk
Cast: Claudette Colbert, Robert
Cummings, Don Ameche, Rita
Johnson, George Coulouris, Raymond
Burr
Studio: United Artists

Raw Deal (1948)
Directed by Anthony Mann
Cast: Dennis O'Keefe, Claire Trevor,
Marsha Hunt, John Ireland, Raymond
Burr
Studio: Eagle-Lion Films

Pitfall (1948)
Directed by André De Toth
Cast: Dick Powell, Lizabeth Scott,
Jane Wyatt, Raymond Burr
Studio: Regal Films

Station West (1948)
Directed by Sidney Lanfield
Cast: Dick Powell, Jane Greer, Agnes
Moorehead, Steve Brodie, Raymond
Burr
Studio: RKO

Walk a Crooked Mile (1948)
Directed by Gordon Douglas
Cast: Louis Hayward, Dennis
O'Keefe, Louise Allbritton, Carl
Esmond, Onslow Stevens, Raymond
Burr
Studio: Columbia Pictures

Adventures of Don Juan (1948)
Directed by Vincent Sherman
Cast: Errol Flynn, Viveca Lindfors,
Robert Douglas, Alan Hale, Romney

Brent, Ann Rutherford, Raymond
Burr
Studio: Warner Bros.

Ruthless (1948)
Directed by Edgar G. Ulmer
Cast: Zachary Scott, Louis Hayward,
Diana Lynn, Sydney Greenstreet,
Lucille Bremer, Raymond Burr
Studio: Eagle-Lion Films

Criss Cross (1949)—uncredited
Directed by Robert Siodmak
Cast: Burt Lancaster, Yvonne
De Carlo, Dan Duryea, Stephen
McNally, Esy Morales
Studio: Universal International
Pictures

Bridge of Vengeance (1949)
Directed by Mitchell Leisen
Cast: Paulette Goddard, John Lund,
Macdonald Carey, Albert Dekker,
John Sutton, Raymond Burr
Studio: Paramount Pictures

Red Light (1949)
Directed by Roy Del Ruth
Cast: George Raft, Virginia Mayo,
Gene Lockhart, Raymond Burr,
Henry Morgan
Studio: United Artists

Abandoned (1949)
Directed by Joseph M. Newman
Cast: Dennis O'Keefe, Gale Storm,
Marjorie Rambeau, Raymond Burr,
Jeff Chandler
Studio: Universal International
Pictures

Black Magic (1949)
Directed by Gregory Ratoff
Cast: Orson Welles, Nancy Guild,

{222}

Akim Tamiroff, Frank Latimore,
Valentina Cortese, Raymond Burr
Studio: United Artists

Love Happy (1949)
Directed by David Miller
Cast: Harpo Marx, Chico Marx,
Groucho Marx, Ilona Massey, Vera-
Ellen, Raymond Burr
Studio: United Artists

Unmasked (1950)
Directed by George Blair
Cast: Robert Rockwell, Barbra Fuller,
Raymond Burr, Hillary Brooke, Paul
Harvey
Studio: Republic Pictures

Key to the City (1950)
Directed by George Sidney
Cast: Clark Gable, Loretta Young,
Frank Morgan, Marilyn Maxwell,
Raymond Burr
Studio: MGM

Borderline (1950)
Directed by William A. Seiter
Cast: Fred MacMurray, Claire Trevor,
Raymond Burr, José Torvay, Morris
Ankrum
Studio: Universal Pictures

A Place in the Sun (1951)
Directed by George Stevens
Cast: Montgomery Clift, Elizabeth
Taylor, Shelley Winters, Keefe
Brasselle, Raymond Burr
Studio: Paramount Pictures

His Kind of Woman (1951)
Directed by John Farrow
Cast: Robert Mitchum, Jane Russell,
Vincent Price, Tim Holt, Charles
McGraw, Marjorie Reynolds,

Raymond Burr
Studio: RKO

M (1951)
Directed by Joseph Losey
Cast: David Wayne, Howard Da Silva,
Martin Gabel, Luther Adler, Steve
Brodie, Raymond Burr, Norman Lloyd
Studio: Columbia Pictures

The Whip Hand (1951)
Directed by William Cameron Menzies
Cast: Carla Balenda, Elliott Reid,
Edgar Barrier, Raymond Burr, Otto
Waldis
Studio: RKO

The Magic Carpet (1951)
Directed by Lew Landers
Cast: Lucille Ball, John Agar, Patricia
Medina, George Tobias, Raymond
Burr, Gregory Gaye
Studio: Columbia Pictures

FBI Girl (1951)
Directed by William A. Berke
Cast: Cesar Romero, George Brent,
Audrey Totter, Tom Drake, Raymond
Burr
Studio: Lippert Pictures

New Mexico (1951)
Directed by Irving Allen
Cast: Lew Ayres, Marilyn Maxwell,
Robert Hutton, Andy Devine,
Raymond Burr, Jeff Corey
Studio: United Artists

Bride of the Gorilla (1951)
Directed by Curt Siodmak
Cast: Barbara Payton, Lon Chaney
Jr., Raymond Burr, Tom Conway, Paul
Cavanagh
Studio: Realart Pictures

Meet Danny Wilson (1952)
Directed by Joseph Pevney
Cast: Frank Sinatra, Shelley Winters,
Alex Nicol, Raymond Burr, Vaughn
Taylor
Studio: Universal International
Pictures

Mara Maru (1952)
Directed by Gordon Douglas
Cast: Errol Flynn, Ruth Roman,
Raymond Burr, Paul Picerni, Richard
Webb
Studio: Warner Bros.

Horizons West (1952)
Directed by Budd Boetticher
Cast: Robert Ryan, Julie Adams, Rock
Hudson, Judith Braun, Raymond
Burr, James Arness
Studio: Universal International
Pictures

A Star Shall Rise (1952)
Directed by John Brahm
Cast: Raymond Burr, Morris Ankrum,
Anthony Caruso, John Crawford,
Richard Hale
Studio: Congregation of the Holy Cross

The Bandits of Corsica (1953)
Directed by Ray Nazarro
Cast: Richard Greene, Paula
Raymond, Raymond Burr, Dona
Drake, Raymond Greenleaf, Lee Van
Cleef
Studio: United Artists

The Blue Gardenia (1953)
Directed by Fritz Lang
Cast: Anne Baxter, Richard Conte,
Ann Sothern, Raymond Burr, Jeff
Donnell, Richard Erdman
Studio: Warner Bros.

Serpent of the Nile (1953)
Directed by William Castle
Cast: Rhonda Fleming, William
Lundigan, Raymond Burr, Jean
Byron, Michael Ansara
Studio: Columbia Pictures

Tarzan and the She-Devil (1953)
Directed by Kurt Neumann
Cast: Lex Barker, Joyce Mackenzie,
Raymond Burr, Monique van Vooren,
Tom Conway
Studio: RKO

Fort Algiers (1953)
Directed by Lesley Selander
Cast: Yvonne De Carlo, Carlos
Thompson, Raymond Burr, Leif
Erickson, Anthony Caruso, John
Dehner
Studio: United Artists

Casanova's Big Night (1954)
Directed by Norman Z. McLeod
Cast: Bob Hope, Joan Fontaine,
Audrey Dalton, Basil Rathbone, Hugh
Marlowe, John Carradine, Raymond
Burr
Studio: Paramount Pictures

Rear Window (1954)
Directed by Alfred Hitchcock
Cast: Jimmy Stewart, Grace Kelly,
Thelma Ritter, Raymond Burr,
Wendell Corey
Studio: Paramount Pictures

Khyber Patrol (1954)
Directed by Seymour Friedman
Cast: Richard Egan, Dawn Addams,
Raymond Burr, Patric Knowles, Paul
Cavanagh
Studio: United Artists

Thunder Pass (1954)
Directed by Frank McDonald
Cast: Dane Clark, Dorothy Patrick,
Andy Devine, Raymond Burr, John
Carradine
Studio: Lippert Pictures

Violated (1954)
Directed by Kurt Neumann
Cast: Johanna Matz, Scott Brady,
Ingrid Stenn, Raymond Burr, Gisela
Fackeldey, Kurt Meisel
Studio: Corona Filmproduktion

Passion (1954)
Directed by Allan Dwan
Cast: Cornel Wilde, Yvonne De Carlo,
Raymond Burr, Lon Chaney Jr.,
Rodolfo Acosta
Studio: RKO

Gorilla at Large (1954)
Directed by Harmon Jones
Cast: Cameron Mitchell, Anne
Bancroft, Lee J. Cobb, Raymond
Burr, Lee Marvin
Studio: Twentieth Century-Fox

You're Never Too Young (1955)
Directed by Norman Taurog
Cast: Dean Martin, Jerry Lewis,
Diana Lynn, Nina Foch, Raymond
Burr
Studio: Paramount Pictures

A Man Alone (1955)
Directed by Ray Milland
Cast: Ray Milland, Mary Murphy,
Ward Bond, Raymond Burr, Lee Van
Cleef, Alan Hale Jr.
Studio: Republic Pictures

Count Three and Pray (1955)
Directed by George Sherman

Cast: Van Heflin, Joanne Woodward,
Philip Carey, Raymond Burr, Allison
Hayes
Studio: Columbia Pictures

Please Murder Me (1956)
Directed by Peter Godfrey
Cast: Angela Lansbury, Raymond
Burr, Dick Foran, John Dehner,
Denver Pyle
Studio: Distributors Corporation of
America

Godzilla, King of the Monsters
(1956)
Directed by Ishiro Honda
Cast: Akira Takarada, Momoko
Kôchi, Akihiko Hirata, Takashi
Shimura, Fuyuki Murakami,
Raymond Burr
Studio: Toho Film Co., Ltd.

Great Day in the Morning (1956)
Directed by Jacques Tourneur
Cast: Virginia Mayo, Robert Stack,
Ruth Roman, Alex Nicol, Raymond
Burr, Regis Toomey
Studio: RKO

Secret of Treasure Mountain
(1956)
Directed by Seymour Friedman
Cast: Valerie French, Raymond Burr,
William Prince, Lance Fuller, Susan
Cummings
Studio: Columbia Pictures

A Cry in the Night (1956)
Directed by Frank Tuttle
Cast: Natalie Wood, Raymond Burr,
Edmond O'Brien, Brian Donlevy,
Richard Anderson, Irene Hervey
Studio: Warner Bros.

Ride the High Iron (1956)
Directed by Don Weis
Cast: Don Taylor, Sally Forrest,
Raymond Burr, Lisa Golm, Otto
Waldis, Mae Clarke
Studio: Columbia Pictures

The Brass Legend (1956)
Directed by Gerd Oswald
Cast: Hugh O'Brian, Nancy Gates,
Raymond Burr, Reba Tassell, Donald
MacDonald
Studio: United Artists

Crime of Passion (1957)
Directed by Gerd Oswald
Cast: Barbara Stanwyck, Sterling
Hayden, Raymond Burr, Fay Wray,
Virginia Grey, Royal Dano
Studio: United Artists

Affair in Havana (1957)
Directed by László Benedek
Cast: John Cassavetes, Raymond Burr,
Sara Shane, Lilia Lazo, Sergio Pena
Studio: Allied Artists

Desire in the Dust (1960)
Directed by William F. Claxton
Cast: Raymond Burr, Martha Hyer,
Joan Bennett, Ken Scott, Brett Halsey,
Ed Binns, Jack Ging
Studio: Twentieth Century-Fox

P.J. (1968)
Directed by John Guillermin
Cast: George Peppard, Raymond
Burr, Gayle Hunnicutt, Brock Peters,
Wilfrid Hyde-White
Studio: Universal Pictures

Tomorrow Never Comes (1978)
Directed by Peter Collinson

Cast: Oliver Reed, Susan George,
Raymond Burr, John Ireland, Donald
Pleasence
Studio: Cinepix Film Properties

Out of the Blue (1980)
Directed by Dennis Hopper
Cast: Linda Manz, Dennis Hopper,
Sharon Farrell, Don Gordon,
Raymond Burr, Eric Allen
Studio: Robson Street

The Return (1980)
Directed by Greydon Clark
Cast: Jan-Michael Vincent, Cybill
Shepherd, Martin Landau, Raymond
Burr, Neville Brand

Airplane II: The Sequel (1982)
Directed by Ken Finkleman
Cast: Robert Hays, Julie Hagerty,
Lloyd Bridges, Chad Everett, Peter
Graves, William Shatner, Raymond
Burr
Studio: Paramount Pictures

Godzilla 1985 (1985)
Directed by Koji Hashimoto
Cast: Ken Tanaka, Yasuko
Sawaguchi, Yosuke Natsuki, Keiju
Kobayashi, Shin Takuma, Raymond
Burr
Studio: Toho Company

Showdown at Williams Creek
(1991)
Directed by Allan Kroeker
Cast: Tom Burlinson, Stephen E.
Miller, Michelle Thrush, Pascal
Bernier, Raymond Burr
Studio: British Columbia Film
Commission

ON THE RADIO (MAJOR SHOWS)

Pat Novak for Hire (1948–49, ABC)
Dragnet (1949–50, NBC)
Dr. Kildare (1950, Syndicated)
Mike Shayne (1950, ABC)
Fort Laramie (1956, CBS)

TELEVISION SERIES

Perry Mason
Network: CBS
Premiere: September 21, 1957
Finale: May 22, 1966
Cast: Raymond Burr, Barbara Hale,
William Talman, William Hopper,
Ray Collins, Wesley Lau, Richard
Anderson

Ironside
Network: NBC
Premiere: September 14, 1967
Finale: January 16, 1975
Cast: Raymond Burr, Don Galloway,
Elizabeth Baur, Don Mitchell,
Barbara Anderson

Kingston: Confidential
Network: NBC
Premiere: March 22, 1977
Finale: August 10, 1977
Cast: Raymond Burr, Art Hindle,
Pamela Hensley, Nancy Olson

Trial by Jury
Network: Syndicated
Aired: 1987
Cast: Raymond Burr, Alan Baltes,
Wendell J. Grayson, Kevin Hagen,
Bridget Hanley

AUTHOR INTERVIEWS

Richard Anderson

Mike Dann

Don DeLano

David Dortort

George Faber

Cosmo Genovese

Johnny Grant

Barbara Hale

Dean Hargrove

Bungy Hedley Hartshorn

Jeff Hayden

Arthur Hiller

Art Hindle

Doug Jackson

Mary James

Dennis Kelli

Angela Lansbury

Arthur Marks

Paul Mason

Eddie Muller

Paul Picerni

Libby Reynolds

Joel Rogosin

Shelley Schoneberg

Fred Silverman

Arnold Soloway

Gale Storm

James Ursini

Robert Wagner

Erroll Wintemute

NOTES

Chapter One

5   "I was the youngest salesman . . . " "Bill Burr Talks About His Famous Son." *The Delta Optimist*, March 21, 1979.

6   "My grandparents pulled out the rose garden . . ." Tom Shales, "A TV Heavyweight Returns to His Court as Perry Mason," *Washington Post*, May 23, 1986.

7   "The weather used to be a lot colder . . ." Erroll Wintemute, Interview with author, January 30, 2006.

7   "In the summers we enjoyed going down to the beach . . . " Erroll Wintemute, "The Case of the TV Legend." A&E *Biography* series, 2000.

7   "He never smiled much . . ." Laurie McLain, the Ona Hill Collection.

8   "When Raymond was a young boy . . . " "Bill Burr Talks About His Famous Son." *Delta Optimist*, March 21, 1979.

8   "And I decided I wanted to be an actor . . ." Roderick Townley, "Raymond Burr," *Us* magazine, March 19, 1990.

8   "The family was poor . . . " "Raymond Burr Remembered." *New Westminster Record*, November 12, 1997.

8   "When I got down there . . . " Laurie McClain, Ona Hill Collection.

9   "He just wasn't happy away from familiar surroundings . . . " Laurie McClain, Ona Hill Collection.

10   "I'm grateful for all the training . . ." Ona L. Hill, *Raymond Burr: A Film, Radio and Television Biography*, McFarland, 1994.

10   "When you're a little fat boy . . ." Tom Shales, "A TV Heavyweight Returns to His Court as Perry Mason," *Washington Post*, May 23, 1986.

11   "I would sneak very quietly . . ." Michael Leahy, "Those Perry Mason Days Were a Real Trial," *TV Guide*, May 14, 1988.

11   "It was so hard to put that uniform on . . ." Ona Hill Collection.

12   "While we were growing up . . ." Ona Hill Collection.

12   "He knew how to handle us . . . " Geraldine Burr, "The Case of the TV Legend," A&E *Biography* series, 2000.

12   "They were very, very close . . ." Geraldine Burr, "The Case of the TV Legend," A&E *Biography* series, 2000.

13   "Raymond suddenly became enamored . . ." Ona Hill Collection.

14   "All of us learned the meaning of hard work . . ." Ona L. Hill, *Raymond Burr: A Film, Radio and Television Biography*, McFarland, 1994.

Chapter Two

19   "Some of the material . . ." Ona L. Hill, *Raymond Burr: A Film, Radio and Television Biography*, McFarland, 1994.

20   "Although Ray is a very genial person . . . " Bobker Ben Ali, letter to Ona Hill, August 9, 1985.

21   "His devotion to the Playhouse . . ." Bobker Ben Ali, letter to Ona Hill, August 9, 1985.

22   "As serious theatre put away the thought . . ." Lewis Nichols, "The Art of Melodrama Comes a Cropper at the Playhouse and in *The Duke in Darkness*," *New York Times*, January 25, 1944.

22   "Raymond Burr, a newcomer to the New York stage . . ." John Chapman, *New York Daily News*, January 25, 1944.

22   "Stirring as the soldierly leader . . . " E. C. Sherburne, "The Duke in Darkness," *The Christian Science Monitor*, January 25, 1944.

23   "In London, he was featured in 'Tonight [sic] Must Fall' . . ." "Presenting Raymond Burr," *The Elitch Gardens Theater Program*, 1944.

25   "There is nothing very startling in the film . . ." Mae Tinee, "Ex-Convict's Story Told in Prison Movie," *Chicago Tribune*, January 30, 1947.

Chapter Three

27   "She was an excellent student . . ." Brett Bolton, "Raymond Burr's Ex-Wife Tells Her Story for the First Time," *TV Radio Mirror*, 1968.

28   "I met him at the Pasadena Playhouse . . ." Brett Bolton, "Raymond Burr's Ex-Wife Tells Her Story for the First Time," *TV Radio Mirror*, 1968.

28   "They asked if I would like to join . . ." Brett Bolton, "Raymond Burr's Ex-Wife Tells Her Story for the First Time," *TV Radio Mirror*, 1968.

28   "Ona Munson, the Belle Watling of G.W.T.W. . . . " Ed Sullivan, "Looking at Hollywood," *Chicago Tribune*, March 25, 1940.

29   "I had planned to wear . . ." Brett Bolton, "Raymond Burr's Ex-Wife Tells Her Story for the First Time," *TV Radio Mirror*, 1968.

29   "There was a small apartment on the basement floor . . ." Brett Bolton, "Raymond Burr's Ex-Wife Tells Her Story for the First Time," *TV Radio Mirror*, 1968.

30   "She had deep-set personal problems . . ." Richard Gehman, "The Case of the Oversize Actor," *TV Guide*, March 18, 1961.

30   "Our relationship was not a favorable one . . ." Brett Bolton, "Raymond Burr's Ex-Wife Tells Her Story for the First Time," *TV Radio Mirror*, 1968.

30   "She wasn't happy, I'm sure of that . . ." Brett Bolton, "Raymond Burr's Ex-Wife Tells Her Story for the First Time," *TV Radio Mirror*, 1968.

30   "As the heavy, literally and figuratively . . ." *New York Times*, August 20, 1948.

31   "When I saw Raymond Burr next . . ." Bobker Ben Ali, letter to Ona Hill, August 9, 1985.

34   "Raymond Burr, as Rick, the heavy . . ." Philip K. Scheuer, "*Raw Deal* Ingenious Action Film," *Los Angeles Times*, May 22, 1948.

34   "Raymond Burr and John Ireland contribute two . . ." Edward Barry, "Absorbing Tale Is Told in This Gangland Film," *Chicago Tribune,* August 24, 1948.

35   "How can one avoid calling him the archetypal heavy?" David Thompson, *The New Biographical Dictionary of Film, Fourth Edition,* Little, Brown/Knopf, 2002.

35   "Mr. Burr is appropriately cold and brutal . . ." *The Christian Science Monitor,* September 9, 1948.

36   "He tried to make you see the psychosis below the surface . . ." James Ursini, interview with author, May 2007.

36   "It was written for Harpo . . ." Tom Shales, "A TV Heavyweight Returns to His Court as Perry Mason," *Washington Post,* May 23, 1986.

37   "Raymond Burr is a standard, menacing villain . . ." *New York Times,* March 27, 1952.

40   "I went to Yucatan . . ." Pauline Townsend, "Paging Perry Mason," *TV Radio Mirror,* October 1957.

41   "No record of Raymond Burr . . ." Dan Ryan, "The Lies They Tell About Raymond Burr," *Inside TV,* November 1968.

41   "My first wife went down in the same plane . . ." Pauline Townsend, "Paging Perry Mason," *TV Radio Mirror,* October 1957.

42   "Ray had a pathetic nature about him . . ." Arthur Marks, interview with author, November 9, 2005.

43   "I was Ray's first wife . . ." Brett Bolton, "Raymond Burr's Ex-Wife Tells Her Story for the First Time," *TV Radio Mirror,* 1968.

43   "We didn't know it, let's put it that way . . ." Erroll Wintemute, interview with author, January 30, 2006.

45   "No, I never met him. Because there was no son . . ." Brett Bolton, "Raymond Burr's Ex-Wife Tells Her Story for the First Time," *TV Radio Mirror,* 1968.

Chapter Four

50   "Under Mr. Stevens' expert direction . . . " "The Screen: Dreiser Novel Makes Moving Film," *New York Times,* August 29, 1951.

51   "I've seen *A Place in the Sun* six times . . ." Tom Shales, "A TV Heavyweight Returns to His Court as Perry Mason," *Washington Post,* May 23, 1986.

51   "A wonderful combination of forcefulness . . ." George Stevens Jr., *A Place in the Sun,* Paramount DVD Collection, 2001.

51   "Ruth Roman and Raymond Burr struggle . . ." Mae Tinee, "Flynn Is Rugged Deep Sea Diver in This Movie," *Chicago Tribune,* May 8, 1952.

52   "I thought my eyes had gone bad . . . " Hedda Hopper, *Los Angeles Times,* November 30, 1951.

52   "He talked about his wife in England . . ." Paul Picerni, interview with author, December 8, 2005.

52   "When I took a look up from my cards . . . " Paul Picerni, *Steps to Stardom: My Story*, Bearmanor Media, 2007.

53   "But I loved Ray . . ." Paul Picerni, interview with author, December 8, 2005.

53   "Last but not least in the evening's entertainment . . . " "Raymond Burr Troupe Entertains at Hospital," 1954.

54   "Ray heard about some men . . ." Marilyn Hedley, "Our Christmas Near the North Pole," *Christian Science Monitor*, December 19, 1955.

54   "We expected to hear that warm, vibrant voice . . ." Marilyn Hedley, "Our Christmas Near the North Pole," *Christian Science Monitor*, December 19, 1955.

55   "That 1953 trip was pretty memorable . . ." Richard Dyer MacCann, "Actor Remembers GIs from Faraway Places," *Christian Science Monitor*, January 19, 1955.

55   "Roz Russell's kin . . ." Walter Winchell, "Man About Town," *Washington Post*, January 12, 1955.

55   "We once did *Charley's Aunt* in Korea . . ." Richard Dyer MacCann, "Actor Remembers GIs from Faraway Places," *Christian Science Monitor*, January 19, 1955.

56   "They get this real dumb character . . . " Robert Johnson, "TV's Make-Believe Lawyer," *Saturday Evening Post*, October 3, 1959.

56   "Into our bunker walked . . ." Robert Johnson, "TV's Make-Believe Lawyer," *Saturday Evening Post*, October 3, 1959.

56   "I can't describe the open-mouthed amazement . . ." Robert Johnson, "TV's Make-Believe Lawyer," *Saturday Evening Post*, October 3, 1959.

57   "I begged him when I became eighteen . . ." Bungy Hartshorn, interview with author, April 3, 2006.

58   "We have conducted extensive searches . . ." National Personnel Records Center, letter to author, September 15, 2006.

62   "For the first part of the picture . . ." Robert Johnson, "TV's Make-Believe Lawyer," *Saturday Evening Post*, October 3, 1959.

63   "Raymond Burr has been signed . . ." Hedda Hopper, "Looking at Hollywood," *Chicago Tribune*," November 24, 1953.

63   "Raymond Burr, hired by Alfred Hitchcock . . ." Hedda Hopper, "Looking at Hollywood," *Chicago Tribune*, January 9, 1954.

64   "Since enacting his role of the perpetrator . . ." Edwin Schallert, "Burr Joins Law," *Los Angeles Times*, August 27, 1954.

66   "There was a considerable amount of talk . . ." David Dortort, interview with author, April 19, 2006.

66   "That's why he was so good in it . . ." David Dortort, interview with author, April 19, 2006.

67   "As the pounds melted off . . ." Hedda Hopper, *The Whole Truth and Nothing But*, Doubleday, 1963.

67 "Burr was a very classy guy . . ." Suzanne Finstad, *Natasha: The Biography of Natalie Wood*, Harmony Books, 2001.

67 "I knew that they were good friends . . ." Robert Wagner, interview with author, January 30, 2006.

67 "He was just wild about her . . ." Richard Anderson, interview with author, March 10, 2006.

68 "It was the most devastating thing . . ." Suzanne Finstad, *Natasha: The Biography of Natalie Wood*, Harmony Books, 2001.

68 "She may have gone into a period where . . ." Suzanne Finstad. *Natasha: The Biography of Natalie Wood*, Harmony Books, 2001.

68 "Sulking . . . over the fact that the older man . . ." Suzanne Finstad, *Natasha: The Biography of Natalie Wood*, Harmony Books, 2001.

69 "It's beginning to look like a marriage for young Natalie Wood and Raymond Burr . . ." Suzanne Finstad. *Natasha: The Biography of Natalie Wood*, Harmony Books, 2001.

69 "To me he's exciting as an actor and as a person . . ." Suzanne Finstad, *Natasha: The Biography of Natalie Wood*, Harmony Books, 2001.

69 "Raymond Burr . . . makes no secret of the fact that he's carrying a torch . . ." Dorothy Kilgallen, "Will Eddie, Debbie Confirm Rumors?" *Washington Post*, December 2, 1957.

70 "I was very attracted to her . . ." Richard Gehman, "The Case of the Oversize Actor," *TV Guide*, March 18, 1961.

71 "An incredibly awful film . . ." Bosley Crowther, *New York Times*, April 28, 1956.

71 "Raymond Burr is as cold-hearted a villain . . ." Orval Hopkins, "Peggy Lee in Great Form: The Western's Good, Too," *Washington Post*, December 5, 1952.

71 "Ray was always identified as . . ." Arthur Marks, interview with author, November 9, 2005.

72 "Raymond Burr will play his first . . ." Thomas M. Pryor, "Studios Will Hum After Labor Day," *New York Times*, September 3, 1955.

72 "I had left MGM and was freelancing . . ." Angela Lansbury, interview with author, January 27, 2006.

73 "That was the beginning of me establishing myself . . ." Angela Lansbury, interview with author, January 27, 2006.

73 "He managed to maintain a . . ." Angela Lansbury, interview with author, January 27, 2006.

74 "In those days it was understood . . ." Angela Lansbury, interview with author, January 27, 2006.

74 "When I was doing heavies . . ." Kay Gardella, "Television's 'Perry Mason' Gets Weight off His Mind," *Washington Post*, December 22, 1957.

76 "He had a great big bedroom upstairs . . ." Bungy Hartshorn, interview with author, April 3, 2006.

76 "Ray has the oddest relationship with those people . . ." Richard Gehman, "The Case of the Oversize Actor," *TV Guide*, March 11, 1961.

77 "I always hoped . . ." Ona Hill Collection.

78 "I'm going to trade my old car in . . ." Ona Hill Collection.

Chapter Five

84 "Perry Mason has to be the equivalent . . ." Dorothy B. Hughes, *Erle Stanley Gardner: The Case of the Real Perry Mason*, Morrow, 1978.

86 "Apparently Fred MacMurray is the person . . ." Dorothy B. Hughes, *Erle Stanley Gardner: The Case of the Real Perry Mason*, Morrow, 1978.

86 "All right, we'll humor him . . ." Richard Gehman, "The Case of the Oversize Actor," *TV Guide*, March 4, 1961.

87 "Burr had the authority . . ." "Actor Burr's 'Authority' Perfect for Mason Role," *Sunday TV News Week*, March 16–22, 1957.

87 "She called and said . . . " Barbara Hale, interview with author, October 30, 2005.

88 "Bill Talman is really a wonder . . ." Dorothy B. Hughes, *Erle Stanley Gardner: The Case of the Real Perry Mason*, Morrow, 1978.

89 "I became an actor because . . ." Brian Kelleher and Diana Merrill, *The Perry Mason TV Show Book*, perrymasontvshowbook.com.

89 "We had a great time with it . . ." Arthur Marks, interview with author, November 9, 2005.

90 "The money aspect of it is often just a myth . . ." Marie Torre, "No 'Perrys' Feud': Both Too Amiable," October 1, 1958.

92 "We hope to have viewers so intrigued . . ." Fred Dickenson, "Bachelor on Beauty Binge," *Pictorial TView*, November 24, 1957.

92 "Question is, can Mason jar Como?" Hedda Hopper, Los Angeles *Times*, April 16, 1957.

92 "He loved food and he loved wine . . ." Arthur Marks, interview with author, November 9, 2005.

92 "She brought a big scale . . ." Barbara Hale, interview with author, October 30, 2005.

92 "If the pilot is any criterion . . ." Hedda Hopper, *Los Angeles Times*, September 3, 1957.

93 "I'm enthusiastic about Perry Mason . . ." Hal Humphrey, "New Perry Was a Heavy," 1957.

93 "If the series were opposing any program . . ." Lawrence Laurent, "Perry Mason Assaults Perry Como Popularity," *Washington Post*, September 21, 1957.

93 "This was a year or six months . . ." Barbara Hale, interview with author, October 30, 2005.

93 "In its translation to the TV medium . . ." Jack Gould, *New York Times*, September 23, 1957.

NOTES

94   "Mr. Burr [appears] to do his best acting . . ." Brian Kelleher and Diana
      Merrill, *The Perry Mason TV Show Book*, perrymasontvshowbook.com.

94   "Was deftly handled, never far-fetched . . ." Brian Kelleher and Diana
      Merrill, *The Perry Mason TV Show Book*, perrymasontvshowbook.com.

94   "The makeup of the show was very simple . . ." Arthur Marks, interview
      with author, November 9, 2005.

95   "Lawyer Mason counts on the D.A.'s being stupid enough . . ." "The
      Snoopers," *Time* magazine, May 28, 1958.

96   "You could tell because we got so much [feedback] . . ." Barbara Hale,
      interview with author, October 30, 2005.

97   "It was audience participation . . ." Barbara Hale, interview with author,
      October 30, 2005.

97   "There's no reason why Mason . . ." Brian Kelleher and Diana Merrill,
      The Perry Mason TV Show Book, perrymasontvshowbook.com.

Chapter Six

100   "I know he was genuine in liking . . ." Arthur Marks, interview with
      author, November 9, 2005.

100   "He had a great love for Barbara Stanwyck . . ." Barbara Hale, interview
      with author, October 30, 2005.

100   "I am an unmarried man . . ." Fred Dickenson, "Bachelor on Beauty
      Binge," *Pictorial TView*, November 24, 1957.

102   "A helluva good guy . . . " Arthur Marks, interview with author,
      November 9, 2005.

102   "Let's just say that the part isn't conducive . . ." Kay Gardella,
      "Television's 'Perry Mason' Gets Weight off His Mind," *New York Daily
      News*, December 22, 1957.

102   "Perry Mason has become a career for me . . ." Walter Ames,
      "Raymond Burr Can't Lose in Role of Perry Mason," *Los Angeles
      Times*, 1957.

103   "A nice fellow and very cordial all the time . . ." Arthur Marks, interview
      with author, November 9, 2005.

103   "Benevides started hanging around the set . . ." Arthur Marks, interview
      with author, November 9, 2005.

103   "But I know Ray liked [Benevides] . . ." Arthur Marks, interview with
      author, November 9, 2005.

104   "When the workers came to my house . . ." Arthur Hiller, interview with
      author, November 15, 2005.

106   "Frank Vitti, a boy that's with us tonight . . ." *A Star Is Born* DVD,
      Warner Bros. Home Video, 1999.

107   "It's true that I could like to be married . . ." Jerry Asher, "No Time for
      Marriage," *Screenland* magazine, March 1959.

109   "He made a lot of speeches . . ." Arthur Marks, interview with author,
      November 9, 2005.

109   "We saw children grow up . . ." Barbara Hale, interview with author, October 30, 2005.
109   "Sitting at the head of the huge table . . ." Richard Gehman, "The Case of the Oversize Actor," *TV Guide*, March 11, 1961.
110   "It went on for weeks . . ." Barbara Hale, interview with author, October 30, 2005.
111   "There were no secrets about the show . . ." Arthur Marks, interview with author, November 9, 2005.

Chapter Seven
113   "I worked with Ray through much of 1955 . . ." Dan Ryan, "The Lies They Tell About Raymond Burr," *Inside TV* magazine, November 1968.
114   "He said, 'I married that young lady . . ." Barbara Hale, interview with author, October 30, 2005.
115   "The TelePrompTer took the curse off hours . . ." Arthur Marks, interview with author, November 9, 2005.
115   "He always read his material on camera . . ." Rick McKay, "Rick McKay's Night on the Town with Fay Wray," *Scarlet Street*, 1998.
116   "At least a half-dozen characters . . . are so suspicious . . ." Brian Kelleher and Diana Merrill, *The Perry Mason TV Show Book*, perrymasontvshowbook.com.
117   "Perry Mason's program bears no semblance . . . " "Judge Hits Bar's Bid to Hear Perry Mason," *New York World-Telegram and Sun*, June 17, 1959.
117   "Basically, Perry Mason is a symbol of human morality . . ." Cynthia Lowry, *"Case of the Smart Lawyer—Why Perry Mason Wins,"* Associated Press, August 12, 1960.
118   "He raised a lot of weird stuff . . ." Andrew Mersmann, "Robert Benevides: Raymond Burr Vineyards," *Passport* magazine, October 2005.
118   "I've always been interested in art . . ." "Raymond Burr Finds Time for Many Other Interests," *Morning Telegraph*, July 13, 1962.
119   "It was very large and dignified . . ." Shelley Schoneberg, interview with author, March 6, 2006.
119   "He did not pretend to draw or paint . . ." Lori Pappajohn, "Raymond Burr Remembered," *New Westminster Record*, November 12, 1997.
119   "It was an open secret . . . that he was gay . . ." Bob Thomas, "Raymond Burr: The Case of the TV Legend," A&E *Biography* series, 2000.
120   "I was an actor . . ." Andrew Mersmann, "Robert Benevides: Raymond Burr Vineyards," *Passport* magazine, October 2005.
120   "Everyone reads it . . ." Humphrey Bogart, "Confidential magazine," www.wikipedia.org.
121   "My back was toward him at the [cash] register . . ." Libby Reynolds, interview with author, February 22, 2006.

122   "He wanted to know . . ." Libby Reynolds, interview with author, February 22, 2006.

122   "He drove me . . ." Libby Reynolds, interview with author, February 22, 2006.

122   "We introduced each other . . . " Libby Reynolds, interview with author, February 22, 2006.

123   "Sure enough the doorman . . ." Libby Reynolds, interview with author, February 22, 2006.

123   "I was helping him pack his bags . . ." Libby Reynolds, interview with author, February 22, 2006.

124   "The 'lawyer' who never lost a case . . ." "TV's Perry Mason Gets Fooled: The Case of the Miss Who Was a Mister-Y," *Confidential* magazine, April 1961.

124   "If I can put on a performance . . ." "TV's Perry Mason Gets Fooled: The Case of the Miss Who Was a Mister-Y," *Confidential* magazine, April 1961.

124   "Suddenly Libby broke away . . ." "TV's Perry Mason Gets Fooled: The Case of the Miss Who Was a Mister-Y," *Confidential* magazine, April 1961.

125   "It was a total fucking lie . . ." Libby Reynolds, interview with author, February 22, 2006.

125   "I knew about four or five people . . ." Libby Reynolds, interview with author, February 22, 2006.

126   "Unfortunately this actor is a noted . . ." Letter sent to Whitney North Seymour, Esq. FBI files, Raymond Burr, September 6, 1961.

127   "Bureau does not support this allegation . . ." H. L. Edwards, FBI files, Raymond Burr, November 14, 1961.

127   "He said that he had talked with Raymond Burr . . ." H. L. Edwards, FBI Files, Raymond Burr, November 21, 1961.

128   "The April, 1961, issue of *Confidential* magazine . . ." L. A. Jones, FBI files, Raymond Burr, February 22, 1962.

128   "The 1948 report . . ." L. A. Jones, FBI files, Raymond Burr, February 22, 1962.

129   "A perceptive performer . . . " Kay Gardella, "Little Things That Count to TV's 'Perry Mason,'" *New York Daily News*, May 8, 1962.

129   "I do things for the sake of . . ." Richard Gehman, "The Case of the Oversize Actor," *TV Guide*, March 4, 1961.

129   "Any person who makes a living . . ." Kay Gardella, "Little Things That Count to TV's 'Perry Mason,'" *New York Daily News*, May 8, 1962.

129   "We would take him down . . ." Arthur Marks, interview with author, November 9, 2005.

130   "We just dropped into a friend's house for a drink . . ." "Perry Mason's DA Jailed in Hollywood Party Raid," *Los Angeles Times*, March 14, 1960.

NOTES

130 "I don't think it will help his career . . ." "Perry Mason's DA Jailed in
       Hollywood Party Raid," *Los Angeles Times*, March 14, 1960.
131 "CBS took the stand . . ." Bob Thomas, "Perry Mason Rallies to
       Defense of His Courtroom Opponent," *New York Post*, April 10, 1960.
131 "The present situation involving William Talman . . ." Bob Thomas,
       "Perry Mason Rallies to Defense of His Courtroom Opponent," *New
       York Post*, April 10, 1960.
131 "It isn't against the law . . ." "Morals Charges Against Talman, Others
       Dropped," *Los Angeles Times*, June 18, 1960.
132 "Talman was a horse's ass . . ." Arthur Marks, interview with author,
       November 9, 2005.
133 "It was principally Ray . . ." Richard Gehman, "Raymond Burr: TV's
       Perry Mason," *Look* magazine, October 10, 1961.

Chapter Eight
136 "Burr gives another of his subtle performances . . ." Charles Stinson,
       "Old South Survives *Desire in the Dust*," *Los Angeles Times*, October
       28, 1960.
136 "Gazing into each other's eyes . . ." Louella Parsons, "Hollywood Is
       Talking About," *Washington Post*, July 10, 1960.
136 "Raymond Burr has had to engage . . ." Hedda Hopper, *Los Angeles
       Times*, May 23, 1961.
136 "The Final Caper for Perry Mason . . . " Morrie Ryskind, *Los Angeles
       Times*, May 19, 1961.
137 "Sometimes Ray got into a snit . . ." Arthur Marks, interview with
       author, November 9, 2005.
137 "Ray has stated flatly that . . ." "The Case of the Reluctant Perry
       Mason," *TV Guide*, June 3, 1961.
137 "If he's unhappy with us, I'm extremely sorry . . ." "The Case of the
       Reluctant Perry Mason," *TV Guide*, June 3, 1961.
138 "Gail Jackson had no use for CBS . . ." Arthur Marks, interview with
       author, November 9, 2005.
139 "I've never managed to solve . . ." Richard Gehman, "The Case of the
       Oversize Actor," *TV Guide*, March 4, 1961.
139 "I know more about Burger . . ." "The Case of the Handy Helpers," *TV
       Guide*, March 19, 1960.
140 "The doctor scrubbed . . ." Barbara Hale, interview with author,
       October 30, 2005.
140 "It was not supported by the public . . ." Hedda Hopper, *Los Angeles
       Times*, January 30, 1964.
141 "I have great plans for the future . . . " May Okon, "The Appeal of Perry
       Mason," *New York Daily News*, July 8, 1962.
141 "When we started [*Perry Mason*], my youngest baby . . ." Barbara Hale,
       interview with author, October 30, 2005.

NOTES

143   "I've always told myself . . . " Dwight Whitney, "Pleading His Own Case," *TV Guide*, July 24, 1965.

143   "It had some of the same things . . ." Dwight Whitney, "Pleading His Own Case," *TV Guide*, July 24, 1965.

144   "Money, that's why . . ." Sheila Graham, "2 Million Changes Burr's Mind," *Washington Times*, April 23, 1965.

144   "CBS figures we are worn out . . . " Val Adams, "TV Career Ending for Perry Mason," *New York Times*, November 18, 1965.

145   "They guaranteed the quality of the show . . ." Tom Shales, "A TV Heavyweight Returns to His Court as Perry Mason," *Washington Post*, May 23, 1986.

145   "[CBS chief] Bill Paley wanted to see the show in color . . ." Arthur Marks, interview with author, November 9, 2005.

145   "CBS felt that they had enough shows . . ." Arthur Marks, interview with author, November 9, 2005.

146   "Nothing about the end was nice . . ." Michael Leahy, "Those 'Perry Mason' Days Were a Real Trial," *TV Guide*, March 14, 1988.

Chapter Nine

148   "The first time I went . . . " *New York Post*, August 9, 1967.

148   "He was elated . . ." Arthur Marks, interview with author, November 9, 2005.

149   "Raymond did not want to go right into . . ." Paul Mason, interview with author, January 3, 2006.

150   "Raymond was looking for a place to get away . . ." Andrew Mersmann, "Robert Benevides, Raymond Burr Vineyards," *Passport* magazine, October 2005.

151   "As he was telling this to us . . . " Andrew Mersmann, "Robert Benevides, Raymond Burr Vineyards," *Passport* magazine, October 2005.

151   "I never really lived in Malibu . . . " C. Robert Jennings, "Burr for the Prosecution," *TV Guide*, September 16, 1967.

151   "We had a radio telephone . . ." Lori Pappajohn, "Raymond Burr Remembered," *New Westminster Record*, November 12, 1997.

152   "There's an entire village in the middle of the island . . ." Lawrence Laurent, "Burr Hit Again; Buys Fiji Isle," *Washington Post*, August 21, 1967.

152   "We import flour, salt and pepper . . ." Cecil Smith, "Raymond Burr: Ironside on the Road to Fiji," *Los Angeles Times*, February 8, 1970.

152   "When I first went to Fiji . . ." Cecil Smith, "Raymond Burr: Ironside on the Road to Fiji," *Los Angeles Times*, February 8, 1970.

152   "It's a hard place to get to, and I won't put an airstrip on it . . . " Barry Dillon, "Raymond 'Ironside' Burr Is Now Lord of Shark-Worshipping Island in South Pacific," February 6, 1979. Name of publication not available.

NOTES

152 "We had to fly from the main island . . ." Bungy Hartshorn, interview with author, April 3, 2006.

153 "His agent thought that he would never . . ." Lori Pappajohn, "Raymond Burr Remembered," *New Westminster Record*, November 12, 1997.

153 "There's more latitude for showing . . ." C. Robert Jennings, "Burr for the Prosecution," *TV Guide*, September 16, 1967.

154 "But [Universal chief] Sid Sheinberg wanted Raymond Burr . . " Paul Mason, interview with author, January 3, 2006.

155 "Although NBC called it a major motion picture . . ." Cynthia Lowry, "A New Character for Raymond Burr," *New York Post*, March 29, 1967.

156 "I was ready to blow someone's brains out . . ." Bob Williams, "After Two Hits, One Miss, Burr Readies One More," *New York Post*, December 5, 1977.

156 "I don't think it's ever happened in TV . . ." Bob Williams, "After Two Hits, One Miss, Burr Readies One More," *New York Post*, December 5, 1977.

157 "I certainly have an ego . . ." C. Robert Jennings, "Burr for the Prosecution," *TV Guide*, September 16, 1967.

157 "Raymond Burr scored in his portrayal . . ." Don Page, "*Ironside* Premieres on NBC Network," *Los Angeles Times*, September 15, 1967.

157 "A tepid whodunit of very modest interest . . ." Jack Gould, "NBC Offers *Ironside*, with Raymond Burr," *New York Times*, September 15, 1967.

157 "Surrendered any pretensions of suspense . . ." Bob Williams, "On the Air," *New York Post*, September 15, 1967.

157 "In *Ironside* I've switched from the defense to the prosecution . . ." C. Robert Jennings, "Burr for the Prosecution," *TV Guide*, September 16, 1967.

158 "I think it was about our sixth episode . . ." Paul Mason, interview with author, January 3, 2006.

158 "Raymond was enigmatic . . ." Joel Rogosin, interview with author, February 19, 2006.

160 "My only position on the war . . ." Jack Leahy, "An Arresting Actor," *New York Daily News*, August 24, 1969.

161 "If I want to hear about Vietnam . . ." C. Robert Jennings, "Burr for the Prosecution," *TV Guide*, September 16, 1967.

161 "The Bob Hope Show's fine . . ." C. Robert Jennings, "Burr for the Prosecution," *TV Guide*, September 16, 1967.

161 "The impressions he came up with . . ." Clay Gowran, "Burr's Vietnam Special in Questionable Taste," *Chicago Tribune*, October 6, 1967.

161 "Burr's presence certainly adds to the hour . . ." Hal Humphrey, "Actor Burr in the Vietnam Theater," *Los Angeles Times*, October 4, 1967.

163 "I think our younger generation has a lot going for them . . ." Kay Gardella, "Burr Is Dreaming of His Island," *New York Daily News*, June 29, 1969.

163   "Those handicapped must realize . . ." Laurie McClain, "An Inspiration to Millions," January 1972.

164   "The things I do as Chief Ironside . . ." Laurie McClain, "An Inspiration to Millions," January 1972.

164   "There is no way I would ever allow . . ." Laurie McClain, "An Inspiration to Millions," January 1972.

164   "The handicapped are one of the biggest . . ." Erica Lander, "Raymond Burr: Hollywood's Secret Unwed Father," *Photoplay.* Name of publication unavailable.

165   "I said to the NAACP guy . . ." Paul Mason, interview with author, January 3, 2006.

165   "Millions of people watch a black man . . ." Ona L. Hill, *Raymond Burr: A Film, Radio and Television Biography*, McFarland, 1994.

165   "Our show is about a winner . . ." Don Page, "Cy Chermak: Make It Plausible and Get Raymond Burr," *Los Angeles Times*, July 11, 1971.

166   "When they told me about it . . ." Jeff Hayden, interview with author, February 19, 2006.

167   "He claimed that was the case . . ." Joel Rogosin, interview with author, February 19, 2006.

167   "I'm getting closer to that time in my life . . ." Kay Gardella, "Burr Is Dreaming of His Island," *New York Daily News*, June 29, 1969.

167   "A feudal setup and Burr is lord of the manor . . ." Cindy Adams, "Ironside Is Also a Chief in Fiji," *TV Guide*, November 7, 1970.

169   "It's not so much the medical pronouncements . . ." Jane Ardmore, "Raymond Burr Rushed to Hospital!" *Photoplay*, August 1973.

172   "He looked at me and said . . ." Bill Kaufman, "Portrait of a Pope as a Man," *Newsday*, April 22, 1973.

172   "A bunch of us went to Fiji . . ." Joel Rogosin, interview with author, February 19, 2006.

173   "He is improving, but is under observation . . ." Jane Ardmore, "Raymond Burr Rushed to Hospital!" *Photoplay*, August 1973.

174   "They sedated him for three days . . ." Geraldine Burr, "Raymond Burr: The Case of the TV Legend," A&E *Biography* series, 2000.

174   "Not me. I like New Westminster . . ." Alan Jay, "South Pacific Isle Utopia to Raymond Burr," *New Westminster Columbian*, November 18, 1966.

175   "I hated that wheelchair . . . " Ian Woodward, "The Case of the Overweight Actor." Publication data unavailable.

Chapter Ten

177   "He had six to seven different refrigerators . . ." Don DeLano, interview with author, February 27, 2006.

179   "Burr is back with a winner . . ." Kevin Thomas, "Burr Back with 'The Power Play,'" *Los Angeles Times*, September 15, 1976.

179   "Raymond Burr looks and acts . . . " Katie Kelly, "Raymond Burr: Out of Wheelchair, into City Room," *New York Post*, March 23, 1977.

179   "*Kingston* has the look of an old, rather tired show . . ." Cecil Smith, "A Burr Under Angel's Saddle?" *Los Angeles Times*, March 23, 1977.

179   "A little too much for all but [Raymond's] most faithful fans . . ." John Carmody, "Not So Mild Mannered Reporter," *Washington Post*, March 23, 1977.

180   "I don't need to say anything else . . ." Art Hindle, interview with author, April 11, 2006.

180   "Burr was totally in control of that series . . ." Art Hindle, interview with author, April 11, 2006.

181   "He said, 'I feel so much better' . . ." Art Hindle, interview with author, April 11, 2006.

181   "I hated to lose that one . . ." Judson Hand, "Burr Sticks to His Orchids," *New York Daily News*, July 22, 1977.

181   "The worst experience I ever had . . ." Jay Maeder, "The Defense Never Rests," *New York Daily News*, May 25, 1986.

182   "I'll make personal appearances . . ." Judson Hand, "Burr Sticks to His Orchids," *New York Daily News*, July 22, 1977.

182   "He tried to find a school . . ." Don DeLano, interview with author, February 27, 2006.

184   "I don't overeat . . ." Tom Shales, "A TV Heavyweight Returns to His Court as Perry Mason," *Washington Post*, May 23, 1986.

184   "I have been asked a number of times . . ." Roderick Townley, "Raymond Burr," *Us* magazine, March 19, 1990.

Chapter Eleven

188   "I just thought it was a good idea . . ." Fred Silverman, interview with author, November 25, 2005.

189   "He said, 'Get Raymond Burr and you've got a deal . . ." Fred Silverman, interview with author, November 25, 2005.

189   "It took me twenty seconds to agree . . ." Kay Gardella, "He's in the Courtroom Again," *New York Daily News*, November 27, 1985.

189   "We turned the first draft of the script in to NBC . . ." Dean Hargrove, interview with author, February 7, 2006.

189   "Raymond was at an age . . ." Fred Silverman, interview with author, November 25, 2005.

190   "We wanted to simplify it a little bit . . ." Fred Silverman, interview with author, November 25, 2005.

190   "When they came to me . . ." Barbara Hale, interview with author, October 30, 2005.

190   "When we first got the project . . ." Barbara Hale, interview with author, October 30, 2005.

191 "I think she was a very important part of the mix . . ." Fred Silverman, interview with author, November 25, 2005.

191 "Bill didn't really want to do it . . ." Dean Hargrove, interview with author, February 7, 2006.

191 "I picked up a copy of *The Globe and Mail* . . ." Dean Hargrove, interview with author, February 7, 2006.

192 "The first day we went into the courtroom set . . ." "Perry Mason Back in Court," *New Westminster Sunday TV Times*, May 23–30, 1986.

192 "It was *right* . . ." Barbara Hale, interview with author, October 30, 2005.

193 "Mason would *never* have retired . . ." Jay Maeder, "The Defense Never Rests," *New York Daily News*, May 25, 1986.

193 "The movie is goofily engrossing on its own . . ." Tom Shales, "Perry Mason's Case of the Welcome Return," *Washington Post*, November 29, 1985.

193 "At that time, the airwaves were flooded . . ." Fred Silverman, interview with author, November 25, 2005.

194 "People remember the early days of television . . ." Stephen Farber, "Burr and Griffith Back in Familiar TV Roles," *New York Times*, April 12, 1986.

194 "I *like* Godzilla . . ." Jay Maeder, "The Defense Never Rests," *New York Daily News*, May 25, 1986.

194 "Godzilla came to be because . . ." Roderick Townley, "Raymond Burr," *Us* magazine, March 19, 1990.

194 "When they asked me to do it the second time . . ." Tom Shales, "A TV Heavyweight Returns to his Court as Perry Mason," *The Washington Post*, May 23, 1986.

195 "Raymond said, 'I think we should put in some grapes'. . ." Andrew Mersmann, "Robert Benevides," *Passport* magazine, October 2005.

195 "When he first started ripping the ground up . . ." Dennis Kelli, interview with author, January 9, 2006.

196 "Robert said it was because . . ." Dennis Kelli, interview with author, January 9, 2006.

197 "I talked with Universal about an *Ironside* project . . ." Dusty Saunders, "*Ironside* Returning?" *Scripps Howard News Service*, December 8, 1986.

198 "You fight bad legislation . . ." Dana Parsons, "You Don't Have to Hate Gays to Keep Loving Colorado," *Los Angeles Times*, January 20, 1993.

199 "There was no sound, no good acoustics . . ." Mary James, interview with author, February 2006.

199 "He had this whole bizarre notion . . ." Mary James, interview with author, February 2006.

200 "We would stop at restaurant after restaurant . . ." Mary James, interview with author, February 2006.

201 "I'm not going to talk about my personal life . . ." Roderick Townley, "Raymond Burr," *Us* Magazine, March 19, 1990.

NOTES

201 "They've offered me a million[-dollar] advance . . ." Roderick Townley, "Raymond Burr," *Us* Magazine, March 19, 1990.

Chapter Twelve

205 "He said he had earmarked his earnings . . ." "The Defense Rests," *People* magazine, September 27, 1993.

206 "I didn't even know . . ." "The Defense Rests," *People* magazine, September 27, 1993.

206 "I wasn't particularly pleasant to be around . . ." Jay Bobbin, "Raymond Burr Returns as 'Ironside,'" *Tribune Media Services*, May 2, 1993.

206 "He never asked how much time . . ." "The Defense Rests," *People* magazine, September 27, 1993.

207 "I was back in Vancouver . . ." Dennis Kelli, interview with author, January 9, 2006.

207 "It's a fragmented case . . ." Tony Scott, *Variety*, May 4, 1993.

207 "*The Return of Ironside* presents viewers . . ." Adam Buckman, "The Unwelcome Return of *Ironside*," *New York Post*, May 4, 1993.

207 "Everybody knew he was in pretty bad shape . . ." George Faber, interview with author, January 24, 2006.

208 "I was devastated . . ." Mary Murphy, "With Raymond Burr During His Final Battle," *TV Guide*, September 25, 1993.

208 "We made a joke out of it . . ." Barbara Hale, interview with author, October 30, 2005.

208 "We were all worried about his health . . ." Mary Murphy, "With Raymond Burr During His Final Battle," *TV Guide*, September 25, 1993.

208 "He would come in and he wouldn't speak . . ." Dean Hargrove, interview with author, February 7, 2006.

209 "I remember him saying to me . . ." Christian Nyby, "The Case of the TV Legend," A&E *Biography* series, 2000.

209 "There were no words . . ." Barbara Hale, interview with author, October 30, 2005.

209 "He didn't want to see friends and receive flowers . . ." "The Defense Rests," *People* magazine, September 27, 1993.

209 "We just kind of sat around at the farm . . ." Dennis Kelli, interview with author, January 9, 2006.

210 "Nothing. Except that death is ugly . . ." Mary Murphy, "With Raymond Burr During His Final Battle," *TV Guide*, September 25, 1993.

210 "He had been fighting like an army of men . . ." Mary Murphy, "With Raymond Burr During His Final Battle," *TV Guide*, September 25, 1993.

211 "If I lie down, I'll die . . ." Mary Murphy, "With Raymond Burr During His Final Battle," *TV Guide*, September 25, 1993.

211 "It was, in the end, a sweet death . . ." Mary Murphy, "With Raymond Burr During His Final Battle," *TV Guide*, September 25, 1993.

211 "He rarely lost a battle . . ." "The Defense Rests," *People* magazine, September 27, 1993.

Chapter Thirteen
213 "A movie villain who became the ultimate defender . . ." "Raymond Burr, Actor, 76, Dies; Played Perry Mason and Ironside," *New York Times*, September 14, 1993.
214 "And his longtime business associate and companion . . ." "Raymond Burr Dies," *Los Angeles Times*, September 13, 1993.
214 "I had always assumed that Raymond was gay . . ." Dean Hargrove, interview with author, February 7, 2006.
215 "Certainly, the first thing is that no one's going to try . . ." Rick Du Brow, "Finding New Actor for 'Mason' Role is 'Unthinkable,'" *Los Angeles Times*, November 29, 1993.
216 "There was a mysterious side to Ray . . ." "The Defense Rests," *People* magazine, September 27, 1993.
216 "Never mentioned any wives or a son . . ." "The Defense Rests," *People* magazine, September 27, 1993.
216 "Enjoyed playing 'wife' to Robert . . ." "TV's Perry Takes His Gay Secrets to the Grave," *Sunday Mail*, November 30, 2003.
217 "Anybody who thinks that anybody could have ever influenced . . ." Peter Sheridan, "Battle of the Burrs; Family Goes to Court over Perry Mason Star's Will," *London Daily Mail*, February 18, 1994.
217 "I really loved my Uncle Ray . . ." "Burr Battle on His Gay Will," *Scottish Daily Record & Mail*, October 25, 1994.
218 "It was never my dream . . ." Andrew Meersman, "Robert Benevides," *Passport* magazine, October 2005.
219 "It appears that some details . . ." "The Case of the TV Legend," A&E *Biography* series, 2000.

SELECTED BIBLIOGRAPHY

"Actor Burr's 'Authority' Perfect for Mason Role." *Sunday TV News Week*, March 16–22, 1957.

Adams, Cindy. "Ironside Is Also a Chief in Fiji." *TV Guide*, November 7, 1970.

Adams, Val. "TV Career Ending for Perry Mason." *New York Times*, November 18, 1965.

Ames, Walter. "Raymond Burr Can't Lose in Role of Perry Mason." *Los Angeles Times*, 1957.

Ardmore, Jane. "Raymond Burr Rushed to Hospital!" *Photoplay*, August 1973.

Asher, Jerry. "No Time for Marriage." *Screenland* magazine, March 1959.

Barry, Edward. "Absorbing Tale Is Told in This Gangland Film." *Chicago Tribune*, August 24, 1948.

Ben Ali, Bobker. Letter to Ona Hill, August 9, 1985.

"Bill Burr Talks About His Famous Son." *The Delta Optimist*, March 21, 1979.

Bobbin, Jay. "Raymond Burr Returns as 'Ironside.'" Tribune Media Services, May 2, 1993.

Bolton, Brett. "Raymond Burr's Ex-Wife Tells Her Story for the First Time." *TV Radio Mirror*, 1968.

Buckman, Adam. "The Unwelcome Return of *Ironside*." *New York Post*, May 4, 1993.

"Burr Battle on His Gay Will." *The Scottish Daily Record & Mail*, October 25, 1994.

Carmody, John. "Not So Mild Mannered Reporter." *Washington Post*, March 23, 1977.

"The Case of the Handy Helpers." *TV Guide*, March 19, 1960.

"The Case of the Reluctant Perry Mason." *TV Guide*, June 3, 1961.

"The Case of the TV Legend," A&E *Biography* series, 2000.

Chapman, John. *New York Daily News*, January 25, 1944.

Christian Science Monitor, September 9, 1948.

Crowther, Bosley. *New York Times*, April 28, 1956.

"The Defense Rests." *People* magazine, September 27, 1993.

Dickenson, Fred. "Bachelor on Beauty Binge." *Pictorial TView*, November 24, 1957.

Dillon, Barry. "Raymond 'Ironside' Burr Is Now Lord of Shark-Worshipping Island in South Pacific." February 6, 1979.

Du Brow, Rick. "Finding New Actor for 'Mason' Role Is 'Unthinkable.'" *Los Angeles Times*, November 29, 1993.

Farber, Stephen. "Burr and Griffith Back in Familiar TV Roles." *New York Times*, April 12, 1986.

FBI Files, Raymond Burr. September 6, 1961; November 14, 1961; November 21, 1961; February 22, 1962.

Finstad, Suzanne. *Natasha: The Biography of Natalie Wood*, Harmony Books, 2001.

Gardella, Kay. "Burr Is Dreaming of His Island." *New York Daily News*, June 29, 1969.

———. "He's in the Courtroom Again." *New York Daily News*, November 27, 1985.

———. "Little Things That Count to TV's 'Perry Mason.'" *New York Daily News*, May 8, 1962.

———. "Television's 'Perry Mason' Gets Weight off His Mind." *Washington Post*, December 22, 1957.

Gehman, Richard. "The Case of the Oversize Actor." *TV Guide*, March 4, 11, and 18, 1961.

———. "Raymond Burr: TV's Perry Mason." *Look* magazine, October 10, 1961.

Gould, Jack. "NBC Offers *Ironside*, with Raymond Burr." *New York Times*, September 15, 1967.

———. *New York Times*, September 23, 1957.

Gowran, Clay. "Burr's Vietnam Special in Questionable Taste." *Chicago Tribune*, October 6, 1967.

Graham, Sheila. "2 Million Changes Burr's Mind." *Washington Times*, April 23, 1965.

Hand, Judson. "Burr Sticks to His Orchids." *New York Daily News*, July 22, 1977.

Hedley, Marilyn. "Our Christmas Near the North Pole." *The Christian Science Monitor*, December 19, 1955.

Hill, Ona L. Papers. Billy Rose Theater Collection, New York Public Library.

Hill, Ona L. *Raymond Burr: A Film, Radio and Television Biography*, McFarland, 1994.

Hopkins, Orval. "Peggy Lee in Great Form: The Western's Good, Too." *Washington Post*, December 5, 1952.

Hopper, Hedda. "Looking at Hollywood." *Chicago Tribune,* November 24, 1953; January 9, 1954.

———. *Los Angeles Times*, November 30, 1951; April 16, 1957; September 3, 1957; May 23, 1961; January 30, 1964

———. *The Whole Truth and Nothing But*, Doubleday, 1963.

Hughes, Dorothy B. *Erle Stanley Gardner: The Case of the Real Perry Mason*, Morrow, 1978.

Humphrey, Hal. "Actor Burr in the Vietnam Theater." *Los Angeles Times*, October 4, 1967.

Jay, Alan. "South Pacific Isle Utopia to Raymond Burr." *New Westminster Columbian*, November 18, 1966.

Jennings, C. Robert. "Burr for the Prosecution." *TV Guide*, September 16, 1967.

Johnson, Robert. "TV's Make-Believe Lawyer." *The Saturday Evening Post*, October 3, 1959.

"Judge Hits Bar's Bid to Hear Perry Mason." *New York World-Telegram and Sun*, June 17, 1959.

Kaufman, Bill. "Portrait of a Pope as a Man." *Newsday*, April 22, 1973.

Kelleher, Brian, and Diana Merrill. *The Perry Mason TV Show Book*, www.perrymasontvshowbook.com.

Kelly, Katie. "Raymond Burr: Out of Wheelchair, into City Room." *New York Post*, March 23, 1977.

Kilgallen, Dorothy. "Will Eddie, Debbie Confirm Rumors?" *Washington Post*, December 2, 1957.

Lander, Erica. "Raymond Burr: Hollywood's Secret Unwed Father." *Photoplay*. Publication date unavailable.

Laurent, Lawrence. "Burr Hit Again; Buys Fiji Isle." *Washington Post*, August 21, 1967.

———. "Perry Mason Assaults Perry Como Popularity." *Washington Post*, September 21, 1957.

Leahy, Jack. "An Arresting Actor." *New York Daily News*, August 24, 1969.

Leahy, Michael. "Those Perry Mason Days Were a Real Trial." *TV Guide*, May 14, 1988.

Leitch, Thomas. *Perry Mason: TV Milestones Series*, Wayne State University Press, 2005.

Lowry, Cynthia. *"Case of the Smart Lawyer—Why Perry Mason Wins."* Associated Press, August 12, 1960.

———. "A New Character for Raymond Burr." *New York Post*, March 29, 1967.

MacCann, Richard Dyer. "Actor Remembers GIs from Faraway Places." *Christian Science Monitor*, January 19, 1955.

Maeder, Jay. "The Defense Never Rests." *New York Daily News*, May 25, 1986.

McClain, Laurie. "An Inspiration to Millions." Name of publication unavailable, January 1972.

McKay, Rick. "Rick McKay's Night on the Town with Fay Wray." *Scarlet Street*, 1998.

Mersmann, Andrew. "Robert Benevides: Raymond Burr Vineyards." *Passport* magazine, October 2005.

"Morals Charges Against Talman, Others Dropped." *Los Angeles Times*, June 18, 1960.

Murphy, Mary. "With Raymond Burr During His Final Battle." *TV Guide*, September 25, 1993.

National Personnel Records Center. Letter to author, September 15, 2006.

New York Post, August 9, 1967.

New York Times, March 27, 1952.

Nichols, Lewis. "The Art of Melodrama Comes a Cropper at the Playhouse in *The Duke in Darkness*." *New York Times*, January 25, 1944.

Okon, May. "The Appeal of Perry Mason." *New York Daily News*, July 8, 1962.

Page, Don. "Cy Chermak: Make It Plausible and Get Raymond Burr." *Los Angeles Times*, July 11, 1971.

———. "*Ironside* Premieres on NBC Network." *Los Angeles Times*, September 15, 1967.

Pappajohn, Lori. "Raymond Burr Remembered." *New Westminster Record*, November 12, 1997.

Parsons, Dana. "You Don't Have to Hate Gays to Keep Loving Colorado." *Los Angeles Times*, January 20, 1993.

Parsons, Louella. "Hollywood Is Talking About." *Washington Post*, July 10, 1960.

"Perry Mason Back in Court." *New Westminster Sunday TV Times*, May 23 to May 30, 1986.

"Perry Mason's DA Jailed in Hollywood Party Raid." *Los Angeles Times*, March 14, 1960.

A Place in the Sun, Paramount DVD Collection, 2001.

"Presenting Raymond Burr." *The Elitch Gardens Theater Program*, 1944.

Pryor, Thomas M. "Studios Will Hum After Labor Day." *New York Times*, September 3, 1955.

"Raymond Burr, Actor, 76, Dies; Played Perry Mason and Ironside." *New York Times*, September 14, 1993.

"Raymond Burr Dies." *Los Angeles Times*, September 13, 1993.

"Raymond Burr Finds Time for Many Other Interests." *The Morning Telegraph*, July 13, 1962.

Ryan, Dan. "The Lies They Tell About Raymond Burr." *Inside TV*, November 1968.

Ryskind, Morrie. "The Final Caper for Perry Mason." *Los Angeles Times*, May 19, 1961.

Saunders, Dusty. "*Ironside* Returning?" Scripps Howard News Service, December 8, 1986.

Schallert, Edwin. "Burr Joins Law." *Los Angeles Times*, August 27, 1954.

Scheuer, Philip K. "*Raw Deal* Ingenious Action Film." *Los Angeles Times*, May 22, 1948.

Scott, Tony. *Variety*, May 4, 1993.

"The Screen: Dreiser Novel Makes Moving Film." *New York Times*, August 29, 1951.

Shales, Tom. "Perry Mason's Case of the Welcome Return." *Washington Post*, November 29, 1985.

———. "A TV Heavyweight Returns to His Court as Perry Mason." *Washington Post*, May 23, 1986.

Sherburne, E. C. "The Duke in Darkness." *The Christian Science Monitor*, January 25, 1944.

Sheridan, Peter. "Battle of the Burrs: Family Goes to Court over Perry Mason Star's Will." *The London Daily Mail*, February 18, 1994.

Smith, Cecil. "A Burr Under Angel's Saddle?" *Los Angeles Times*, March 23, 1977.

———. "Raymond Burr: Ironside on the Road to Fiji." *Los Angeles Times*, February 8, 1970.

SELECTED BIBLIOGRAPHY

"The Snoopers." *Time* magazine, May 28, 1958.

A Star Is Born, DVD, Warner Bros. Home Video, 1999.

Stinson, Charles. "Old South Survives *Desire in the Dust.*" Los Angeles *Times,* October 28, 1960.

Sullivan, Ed. "Looking at Hollywood." *Chicago Tribune,* March 25, 1940. *New York Times,* August 20, 1948.

Thomas, Bob. "Perry Mason Rallies to Defense of His Courtroom Opponent." *New York Post,* April 10, 1960.

Thomas, Kevin. "Burr Back with 'The Power Play.'" *Los Angeles Times,* September 15, 1976.

Thompson, David. *The New Biographical Dictionary of Film, Fourth Edition,* Little, Brown/Knopf, 2002.

Tinee, Mae. "Ex-Convict's Story Told in Prison Movie." *Chicago Tribune,* January 30, 1947.

———. "Flynn Is Rugged Deep Sea Diver in This Movie." *Chicago Tribune,* May 8, 1952.

Torre, Marie. "No 'Perrys' Feud': Both Too Amiable." *New York Daily News,* October 1, 1958.

Townley, Roderick. "Raymond Burr." *US* magazine, March 19, 1990.

Townsend, Pauline. "Paging Perry Mason." *TV Radio Mirror,* October, 1957.

"TV's Perry Mason Gets Fooled: The Case of the Miss Who Was a Mister-Y." *Confidential* magazine, April 1961.

"TV's Perry Takes His Gay Secrets to the Grave." *Sunday Mail,* November 30, 2003.

Whitney, Dwight. "Pleading His Own Case." *TV Guide,* July 24, 1965.

Williams, Bob. "After Two Hits, One Miss, Burr Readies One More." *New York Post,* December 5, 1977.

———. "On the Air." *New York Post,* September 15, 1967.

Winchell, Walter. "Man About Town." *Washington Post,* January 12, 1955.

Woodward, Ian. "The Case of the Overweight Actor."

INDEX

estate, Benevides inheriting, 217–18
eyesight, 166–67

fabrications, biographical, 17, 23,
    39–45, 99
  degrees in, psychology/English
    literature, 41
  marriage, 41–42, 99, 113–14
  "nephew" in, Vitti as, 106, 118
  in obituaries, 216
  Perry Mason and, 97
  son in, 44
  war service, 57–58, 152
family. *See also* fabrications,
    biographical; siblings
  will contested by, 217–18
father, 4–5, 77–78, 203
  death of, 203
FBI, 126–28
FBI Girl, 223
The Fever Tree. See Affair in Havana
Fighting Father Dunne, 24–25
Fiji. *See* Naitauba
filming
  Ironside pilot, 154–55
  Perry Mason, 90, 100, 101, 102
film noir, 35
finance, 58–59, 75
Finstad, Suzanne, 67
fire. *See* Great New Westminster Fire
    of 1898
Firing, Talman, 130–33
Fisher, George, 105
flirting, Munson alleged, 28–29, 43
flowers, 14, 75, 117–18, 177
  business of, 181–82
Flynn, Errol, 51
food, love of, 200
Fort Algiers, 35, 224
Fort Laramie, 75, 79, 85, 227
foster children, 141–42, 147
Freedom Foundation, 109
friendship(s), 19, 54
  Hedley, 76

inner circle of, 209
Wood, 64–70, 88, 99, 100

Gable, Clark, 38–39
gallbladder, 175
Galloway, Don, 219
Garbo, Greta, 29
Gardner, Erle Stanley, 81–84, 85,
    146, 215. *See also Perry Mason*
  "The Case of the Twice Told
    Twist," 145
  The Case of the Velvet Claws, 81
Garland, Judy, 105
Gauguin, 30
Gershwin, Ira, 19
GI, homosexual reference to, 180–81
Gillette, Chester, murder trial of, 47
Gleason, Jackie, 91, 149
The Globe and Mail, 191–92
Godzilla, 226
Godzilla: King of the Monsters,
    70–71, 219, 225
  revival of, 194–95
Gojira, 70
Gold, Sid, 103
Gone with the Wind, 28–29
Gorilla at Large, 225
gossip columnists, 92–93, 105, 136.
    See also Hopper, Hedda
Gould, Jack, 157
Graham, Sheila, 69
grandfather, 2–5
Granny Get Your Gun, 83
Grant, Cary, 95
Great Day in the Morning, 225
Great Depression, 12
Great New Westminster Fire of 1898, 4
Griffith, Andy, 193, 203–4
Gunsmoke, 85

Hale, Barbara, 87, 100, 190–91, 192
Hamilton Burger (character), 82, 86,
    117
  Talman scandal/firing and, 130–33

CPSIA information can be obtained
at www.ICGtesting.com
Printed in the USA
BVHW041100060119
537129BV00024B/759/P

9 781423 473718